Leaving No Child Behind?

Options for Kids in Failing Schools

Edited by

Frederick M. Hess and

Chester E. Finn, Jr.

palgrave
macmillan

First published 2004 by
PALGRAVE MACMILLAN™
175 Fifth Avenue, New York, N.Y. 10010 and
Houndmills, Basingstoke, Hampshire, England RG21 6XS
Companies and representatives throughout the world

PALGRAVE MACMILLAN is the global academic imprint of the Palgrave Macmillan division of St. Martin's Press, LLC and of Palgrave Macmillan Ltd. Macmillan® is a registered trademark in the United States, United Kingdom and other countries. Palgrave is a registered trademark in the European Union and other countries.

ISBN 1–4039–6588–9 hardback

Library of Congress Cataloging-in-Publication Data
    Leaving no child behind?: options for kids in failing schools / edited by Frederick M. Hess and Chester E. Finn, Jr.
        p. cm.
    Includes bibliographical references and index.
    ISBN 1–4039–6588–9
      1. School choice—United States. 2. United States. No Child Left Behind Act of 2001. 3. Educational accountability—Law and legislation—United States. 4. Educational equalization—United States. I. Hess, Frederick M. II. Finn, Chester E., 1944–

LB1027.9.L43 2004
379.1'11—dc22   2004046722

A catalogue record for this book is available from the British Library.

Design by Newgen Imaging Systems (P) Ltd., Chennai, India

First edition: September 2004
10 9 8 7 6 5 4 3 2 1

Printed in the United States of America.

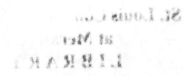

Contents

CHAPTER 7

CHAPTER 8

CHAPTER 9

CHAPTER 10

CHAPTER 11

CHAPTER 12

CHAPTER 13

Acknowledgments

This volume emerges from a conference held at the American Enterprise Institute on January 15–16, 2004, under the auspices of the institute and the Thomas B. Fordham Foundation, a meeting co-chaired by the editors. At that conference, the chapters were presented, commented upon, criticized, discussed, and sometimes praised. The project, comprising the conference, this volume, and other related activities, was supported by several generous sponsors, including the Annie E. Casey Foundation, the Koret Foundation, and the Walton Family Foundation.

We thank the chapter authors. And we would particularly like to thank the discussants at the conference, who shared valuable insights and experiences while deepening the thinking and strengthening the analysis of both authors and editors. The discussants were: Mitchell Chester, assistant superintendent of policy and accountability, Ohio Department of Education; Jeff Cohen, president, Catapult Learning; Michael Cohen, president, Achieve; Jane Cunningham, chairman of the education committee, Missouri House of Representatives; Keisha Hegamin, president and CEO, Philadelphia Chapter of the Black Alliance for Educational Options; Tom Houlihan, executive director, Council of Chief State School Officers; Lisa Graham Keegan, CEO, Education Leaders Council; John Liechty, associate superintendent, Los Angeles Unified School District; Gail Littlejohn, president, Dayton Public School Board; Nina Shokraii Rees, deputy undersecretary, Office of Innovation and Improvement, U.S. Department of Education; John Stevens, executive director, Texas Business and Education Coalition; and Joe Williams, education reporter, *New York Daily News*.

Finally, we would like to offer our profound thanks to Emily Kluver, Andrew Kelly, and Derek Minshew for their invaluable assistance in coordinating the research and producing this volume. In addition, we are grateful to David Pervin, our editor at Palgrave Macmillan.

1

Introduction

Frederick M. Hess and Chester E. Finn, Jr.

Education has been near the top of the national domestic agenda since the 1980s. In that time, the federal government has passed innumerable small pieces of legislation, twice reauthorized the Elementary and Secondary Education Act, dabbled with national standards and tests, and supported a mixed bag of innovations such as charter schools and the National Board for Professional Teaching Standards. Despite substantial effort, much creativity, plenty of politics, and many billions of dollars, however, none of this activity has amounted to much, with Washington continuing to foot only about 7 percent of the nation's K-12 education bill and most of the real action taking place in states and districts.

Separate and apart from events alongside the Potomac, most states during the 1990s were swept up in multiple school-improvement strategies. The most notable of these were the push for standards- and test-based accountability and the effort to expand families' educational options. By century's end, a number of states, including Florida, Massachusetts, Texas, and Colorado, had passed ambitious school accountability plans whereby schools (and, sometimes, students) were held responsible for their performance on state assessments.

Meanwhile, charter schools and other diverse forms of public school choice grew exponentially, with states like Arizona, Florida, Colorado, Michigan, and Texas in the lead. By early 2004, nearly three thousand charter schools were serving more than 650,000 children across the United States. As Richard Colvin points out in chapter 2, the use of public school choice in the United States rose dramatically during the 1990s. The most recent data from National Center for Education Statistics show that in 1993, 4.7 million children attended a public school they had chosen. By 1999, that figure was 6.85 million.

Despite these and all other state-level reforms, national test scores remained low—and alarmingly flat—even as dropout rates remained high. International education comparisons yielded periodic evidence that other countries were outstripping the United States in academic achievement and, more recently, number of years of schooling. And education remained among the foremost concerns of American citizens. Owing to this confluence of circumstances, both candidates during the 2000 presidential campaign promised aggressive national action on education if elected. GOP candidate George W. Bush, then governor of Texas, promoted the Lone Star State's strong accountability program as a national model.

Upon taking office, Bush immediately sent Congress a blueprint for far-reaching legislation that featured strong accountability and school choice elements and drew heavily upon the Texas model. After nearly a year of negotiations, the White House and congressional leaders hammered out a bipartisan compromise—now known to all as the No Child Left Behind (NCLB) act—that enjoyed the strong support not only of most Republicans but also of such prominent Democrats as Massachusetts senator Edward M. Kennedy and California representative George Miller, the ranking members of Congress's two education committees. Winning that breadth of support, however, entailed making many changes to the original Bush reform plan.

In particular, the White House yielded on its initial support for such controversial choice-based reforms as school vouchers and instead agreed to more limited options for children in low-performing schools. In working out these and innumerable other compromises and additions, the NCLB legislation grew exceedingly complex. The challenge would be for the federal government, working with and through states and local school districts, to make this complex contraption move smartly down the road to educational excellence.

NCLB represented a significant departure from past practice. For the first time, the federal government required that academic performance lead to concrete consequences for schools—and that children in inadequate schools have the opportunity to seek assistance or move elsewhere. What the law's bipartisan boosters rarely noted, however, was that, although the statute was intended to give families in low-performing schools new options, school districts and states retained most of the control over those options.

From the time No Child Left Behind was signed by President Bush in January 2002, it was clear that its intricate provisions deserved extensive monitoring and evaluation. There would be an obvious need to evaluate the performance of students, schools, and states and to identify and elucidate "best practices." Besides such summative research, however, there would be an acute need for the work-in-progress studies that analysts term "formative assessments"—research designed to illumine and explain how the legislation was actually translating into policy and practice across the nation and how it might be improved.

Two years after NCLB became law, it's too early to assess how its various provisions have affected pupil achievement. But it's not too soon to ask whether these provisions are being conscientiously and constructively implemented or whether the key programs authorized by this statute are being established and used in a manner consistent with legislative intent. If things are off to a promising start, it makes sense to give the relevant provisions time to work and states and districts the opportunity to carry on, albeit with suitable oversight and evaluation. If things are going badly, however, federal policymakers should consider making appropriate midcourse corrections. Such steps, taken while states and districts are still crafting their own policies and practices, could alleviate far more painful efforts later to undo problematic practices after they've become ingrained and routinized.

In considering the challenges posed by NCLB, one must recognize that this sprawling law is vastly more ambitious than its predecessor, the original Elementary and Secondary Education Act first enacted in 1965. Despite Lyndon Johnson's grand assertions that ESEA would boost the achievement of disadvantaged youngsters and thus help to end poverty in America, in fact that legislation focused on moving money around: sending targeted federal support to school districts. Its implementation challenge centered on calculating the amounts that districts were entitled to, actually disbursing the new money, and ensuring that it was spent in permissible ways. Though this required complex calculations and new enforcement machinery, the original program nestled reasonably well into existing arrangements for governing and administering America's public schools. By contrast, NCLB's goals, mechanisms, and remedies require any number of unfamiliar, even unnatural, acts on the part of states, districts, and schools. Hence we ought not merely assume that early complications will work themselves out in due course.

Formative analyses must be undertaken with humility. Even sound new policies and programs ordinarily require time to come to fruition before they can fairly be judged. It's possible to pull up the seedling prematurely to see whether its roots are growing. On the other hand, delay too long in appraising the workings of a complex, new, high-stakes federal law, and much can go awry. Waiting to understand the nuances and realities of implementation can also permit resistance to harden, perverse incentives to become entrenched, and poorly conceived practices to rigidify. In the case of the policies examined in this volume, we opted to take the chance that an early appraisal might make it possible to spot problems, highlight sensible strategies, and address design flaws while practices are still in formation. (One must wonder whether such an effort, launched right after the passage of ESEA in 1965, could have helped policymakers to address its problems sooner and more easily.)

At NCLB's heart is the requirement that states annually test all public school students in grades 3–8 in reading and math and that every state measure whether its public schools (and school systems) are making "adequate yearly progress" (AYP) toward universal pupil proficiency in core subjects. In order to make AYP, schools must have a sufficient percentage of students performing acceptably and making the requisite gains from year to year.

Crucially, schools must show gains not only for their overall student body but also for pupil subgroups delineated by grade level, ethnicity, gender, socioeconomic status, English proficiency, and special needs. If schools do not make the progress mandated by the state, various sanctions and interventions are supposed to follow, all of them intended to rectify the problem and set the school on a path toward rising achievement. Our concern here is with two of the most controversial and high-profile sanctions that NCLB visits upon schools that fail to meet its performance expectations: the requirement that eligible students in such schools be provided with the option of moving to a better public school or the opportunity to receive free tutoring, which the act refers to as "supplemental educational services."

NCLB-Style Public Choice and Supplemental Services

These twin provisions are intended both to provide better education options to students stuck in faltering schools and to create incentives for those schools to improve. Under NCLB, if a school fails to make AYP for two consecutive years, and it's a school that receives Title I dollars, its students must be offered "public school choice." Under that provision, the district is obliged to provide each child with options of alternative public (and charter) schools that are making satisfactory progress. If a child's (Title I) school fails to make AYP for a third consecutive year, the district is to provide him/her with the opportunity to enroll in supplemental educational services—essentially about 30 hours of free after-school tutoring. Such tutoring can be provided by a variety of suppliers, including private vendors of education services or the school system itself, and is to be paid for with a portion of the school's federal Title I dollars (money meant to promote learning for disadvantaged kids).

Congress intended that these provisions would do two things: afford better education options to students stuck in faltering schools while also creating incentives (via competitive pressure) for those schools to improve. If schools fail to improve in the fourth year, they are subjected to a school improvement plan, and schools that fail to improve in a fifth year are to be restructured. In this volume, however, we focus only upon these two choice provisions. Another part of NCLB mandates that children attending "persistently dangerous" schools be eligible for school choice. But it's up to states to define what "persistently dangerous" means, and to date they have identified remarkably few such schools. Since this provision has accordingly been little used, and since its implementation must address the same challenges that confront public choice in schools that fail to make adequately yearly progress, we devote no special attention to the dangerous schools provision.

On paper, the legislation is very ambitious. NCLB says that districts where all public schools fail to make "adequate yearly progress" must try, "to the extent practicable," to establish agreements with other schools and districts to ensure that students have the option to select better schools, even across district borders. Subject to a legislative cap on total required expenditures, districts must also furnish transportation to pupils who exercise their option to attend another school.

Supplemental educational services are additional sources of academic instruction designed to boost the achievement of students in schools that have failed to make AYP for at least three years. Such services may include tutoring and other after-school services and may be offered by public and private providers. All providers must be approved by the state, but they can include district public schools, charter schools, local education agencies, educational service agencies, faith-based organizations, and for-profit as well as non-profit private entities. States are instructed to maintain a list of approved providers from which parents may choose (though school districts are responsible for entering into contracts with them). States are also ordered to promote maximum participation by providers to ensure that parents have as many options as possible, and are charged with evaluating providers and monitoring the quality of their services.

The local school system must annually inform parents of eligible children about the availability of public choice options and supplemental services and must provide information on approved tutorial providers operating within that district. Upon request, the school district is also supposed to help parents determine which provider would best fit their children's needs. When parents have made their selection, the local education agency is supposed to contract with that provider to deliver the services the family desires. In practice, what has happened is that districts usually contract with certain approved providers, then instruct interested parents to choose from that list. This is just one example of the ways in which the law is being implemented in a manner somewhat different from what its authors envisioned.

Because public choice and supplemental services are central to the NCLB strategy, it's important to appreciate the dual goals of those who crafted them: to nudge faltering schools to improve while also assisting children to make stronger academic progress than they would make if left to struggle in an ineffectual teaching/learning environment.

NCLB's choice provisions should not, therefore, be considered primarily in the context of the nation's ongoing and often fractious "school choice" debate but, rather, on their practical effect. How effective are they at helping students to master essential academic content, particularly in reading and math? Are they spurring troubled schools to improve and providing them with tools like tutoring that serve their students more effectively?

Because it's early in the implementation cycle, we cannot definitively answer these two big questions. The appropriate question for *today* regarding NCLB is whether its component parts, as presently constituted, have a reasonable *chance* of succeeding, given time and practice, or whether they assume some things that are extremely unlikely to happen. If the latter, then the law requires rethinking and reshaping, not just patience and practice.

Nobody should be surprised that such ambitious and untested provisions in a sweeping federal law would run into all manner of diverse local realities, some of which mesh nicely with them but others of which tend to frustrate them; or that it will take fine-tuning and revision to get them working right. There are many moving parts here, and much that can go wrong. The legislation rests upon a tangled set of expectations regarding the behavior of families, schools, districts, private providers, and states. How these elements actually mesh is crucial to the fate of this effort.

To examine the workings of those provisions during NCLB's first two years of implementation, we invited talented scholars and veteran analysts to probe what was actually happening and seek to understand what might be learned from America's early experience with NCLB-style public school choice and supplemental services. They have now done precisely that. And it turns out that there is much to be learned.

Overview of the Book

Given the law's complexity, we thought it important that the researchers consider its developments at several levels. Hence this volume begins with two essays offering background on the design of NCLB's two choice-based provisions and supplying relevant context. Richard Colvin, director of the Hechinger Institute on Education and the Media at Teachers College, Columbia University, considers the nation's extensive prior experience with public school choices of many kinds, and highlights the lessons for NCLB. Colvin begins by explaining the public school choice provision of NCLB and its lineage, then turns to providing a rich and instructive sketch of the nation's many forms of school choice and discusses the rapid growth of options and their utilization in recent years. He explains how concerns like capacity, transportation, and political resistance have restricted the availability of public school choice and what states and districts can do to meet these challenges.

In the companion piece focused on supplemental services, Siobhan Gorman of the *National Journal* examines the brand-new (and peculiarly designed) supplemental service provision and how the market of service providers is taking shape. Gorman provides a quick primer on the parentage of the supplemental services provision, the statute's design, and the measures required to make the program work. She then examines the challenge posed by the law's unusual reliance on an emerging market of supplemental service providers. In so doing, she provides the most thorough and detailed account yet of the providers that are entering the market, how they view the opportunities, and what obstacles impede their efforts.

We then turn to the state level. Using data from an extensive survey of state education department officials, Villanova University professor Robert Maranto and education researcher April Gresham Maranto examine whether states are implementing the choice-related provisions of NCLB. In general, they find a less than rosy picture. Even grading on a curve, most states earn D's and F's. It appears that most state departments have focused on NCLB's challenging standards and accountability provisions, and are just beginning to implement parental choice. The authors speculate that this may change over time, if states receive sufficient pressure from the U.S. Department of Education, and from journalists and activists. Indeed in some cases this has already occurred.

Jane Hannaway, director of the Education Policy Center at the Urban Institute, and Kendra Bischoff, a research assistant at the Urban Institute, explore the response of Florida to the NCLB choice provisions. Because Florida has a highly developed test-based accountability system as well as a number of state policies that promote school choice, we might expect Florida to provide a "best-case scenario" for the choice provisions. Instead, we find the picture of school performance based on the state system in sharp conflict with the picture of school performance under NCLB. We also find a situation in which school choice is simply unworkable. In addition to drawing a state-level picture, the chapter presents the responses of two disparate school districts—urban Miami–Dade County and rural Jefferson County.

Alex Medler, an independent education consultant and former official in the Clinton administration Department of Education, considers the case of Colorado, finding real challenges confronting rural schools and a mixed record at both state and district levels. Colorado's small rural districts have limited opportunities for offering student transfers and attract fewer tutoring providers than large urban districts. Existing policies and politics naturally affect how districts act. Though identifying schools that require intervention on a timely basis is difficult throughout the state, districts with existing public school choice programs can generally implement NCLB's interventions if they so choose. Districts without existing choice programs, or whose leaders oppose choice, can find ways to obstruct NCLB.

David Plank, co-director of the Education Policy Center at Michigan State University and a professor in the College of Education, and Christopher Dunbar, assistant professor of Educational Administration at Michigan State University, find that supplemental services and public choice have gotten off to a rocky start in Michigan. The clear signals that NCLB is expected to send to schools about how they are performing have been muddied by a variety of factors, including lowered academic standards for student "proficiency," delays in the release of test scores, and the simultaneous implementation of a state accountability system that overlaps and to some extent competes with NCLB. School districts have done relatively little to implement the school choice and supplemental services provisions of NCLB, and the Michigan Department of Education lacks the capacity to ensure compliance. These may be start-up issues that will be resolved over time, but in the authors' view they reflect fundamental problems that call the long-term effectiveness of the law into question.

Finally, William Howell, assistant professor of government at Harvard University, details the results of a survey of a thousand public school parents in the ten largest Massachusetts school districts. He finds that although parents claim to be familiar with NCLB, the vast majority of those who qualify for the act's choice and supplemental services do not even know that their child's school is on the state's list of schools deemed in need of improvement. Still, parents with children in such schools are especially interested in pursuing alternative schooling options, though this interest tends to be directed toward options that NCLB does not afford—specifically, private schools. Among his policy recommendations, Howell suggests that non-district agencies be charged with disseminating information about NCLB and that parents in underperforming public schools have the option of sending their child to any public school within the district, not just those that have met adequate yearly progress.

In the volume's final section, we turn to the experiences of individual districts. Michael Casserly, executive director of the Council of the Great City Schools, summarizes the results of a survey of the nation's largest city school districts and their implementation of the choice and supplemental services provisions of NCLB. Results from the 50 responding cities indicate that both programs are taking shape but that participation rates are low. The paper spells out some of the issues that local school districts are grappling with. Casserly's paper is the first empirical study looking at how student transfers and supplemental services are being put into place in the country's major urban school systems.

Julian Betts, professor of economics at the University of California—San Diego, and Anne Danenberg, research associate at the Public Policy Institute of California, consider the case of San Diego and find low but fast-rising participation in NCLB's school choice program and widespread participation in supplemental services. Betts and Dannenberg detail serious challenges, perhaps the most important being that California does not release its list of schools "needing improvement" until late August, leaving the San Diego Unified School District only a few weeks to contact families eligible for busing and to design bus routes and process applications. The authors also find a potentially serious unintended consequence—that the movement of low-scoring students under NCLB choice may throw receiving schools into improvement or "failing" status, and they recommend that NCLB implement a more longitudinal approach to measuring school quality that is immune to changes in the composition of the student body.

Harvard's William Howell reappears with an examination of the choice-implementation experience of Worcester, Massachusetts, a small city that is fiercely resisting these provisions of NCLB. Though thousands of children in the district qualify to transfer out of their school and to receive supplemental services, Howell found that only one child took advantage of the act to switch to a higher-performing public school, and one other child received tutoring from a private provider. Reasons for these low take-up rates, Howell suggests, trace back to high student mobility rates, intradistrict choice plans currently in place, low parental knowledge about the act, district procedures that discourage parents from pursuing the act's new education options, and obstacles that prevent private providers from directly contacting students who qualify for their services.

Finally, in the sprawling suburban district of Montgomery County, Maryland, Douglas Reed, associate professor of government at Georgetown

University, explores the questions of which schools are losing which students to NCLB choice and where those students are going. The story of NCLB choice and supplemental services implementation in Montgomery County has been one of reluctant but emerging compliance. Reed finds that although only a small percentage of students eligible for NCLB school choice are utilizing the option, a more significant number are seeking out supplemental services despite delays in establishing those programs. The choice mechanism also appears, in its first two years of implementation, to have been disproportionately exercised by white and non-poor students, with Hispanic students, in particular, preferring to stay at their neighborhood schools.

In the concluding chapter, we provide some summary thoughts and offer recommendations that draw upon what we learned from this research and the authors' analyses as well as our own observations of these and other provisions of NCLB. The bottom line: innumerable challenges confront NCLB-style public choice and supplemental services, but policymakers can yet act to address these in straightforward and sensible ways.

2

Public School Choice: An Overview

Richard Lee Colvin

Giving parents choices in the schools their children attend is one of the pillars of the No Child Left Behind Act, the eleven-hundred-page doorstop legislation that is remaking the relationships and responsibilities of the federal government, the states, school districts, and individual schools. President Bush proposed that law as one of his first official acts in office and a year later, in early 2001, he signed legislation that had gained broad, bipartisan support. Under the 1994 law, states were expected to establish standards for what students are to learn and to measure the performance of schools and school districts against those standards. If schools did not make adequate progress toward a goal set by the state, first districts and then states were to intervene to help those that repeatedly fell short. Consequences of some sort—reconstitution with new leaders, perhaps—lay over the horizon for schools that failed most egregiously and persistently. But that was just one of the possible remedies on the a la carte menu from which states could choose. Another of the possible responses to repeated failure was that school districts could allow students attending a low-performing school to transfer to other public schools. Though a small but uncounted number of districts held transfers out as a theoretical possibility, no students got the opportunity to do so under the preexisting law.

The No Child Left Behind law is explicit about using school choice as a lever for pushing school reform and improvement as well as for creating better educational opportunities for individual students. If a school receiving federal Title I money for disadvantaged children fails for two straight years to make sufficient progress toward the eventual goal of raising all children to academic proficiency, then it must allow students to enroll in a higher-performing school elsewhere in the district and must spend some of its federal aid for disadvantaged students to enable this movement.

The notion behind offering public school choice is to give students and their parents an alternative to the instruction in their assigned classroom and school. If the test scores of all students—regardless of race or native language or income level or disability—are not high enough, then all of the students, including those who scored well, are to be given options beyond the school walls. The fate of the student is delinked, as it were, from the quality of the school or its teachers. The students and their parents get to shop around. They are no longer trapped by attendance boundaries or limited to the help available from the teachers in a single school.

Although the states retain the right to say how much progress schools have to make each year, every school must boost every child to proficiency in math, reading, and science by the year 2014. In addition, schools were to have tested 95 percent of their students (and 95 percent of every subgroup of students) and have met certain other goals, such as graduation rate, attendance, and the rate at which students whose native language is not English attain fluency. (The 95 percent tested rule was eased a bit in early 2004.) Although those targets apply to all schools, only those that receive federal money on behalf of poor, minority, and non–English speaking students are subject to the law's choice provisions. Students also are supposed to be allowed to transfer out of schools identified as "persistently dangerous." But states have gotten around that by defining "persistently dangerous" in such a way that virtually no schools are so labeled. Still, it is widely expected that the number of schools to be subject to the law's school choice provisions will rise dramatically unless the law is altered.

The right to choose one's school, in and of itself, is neither new nor, in many communities, even controversial. What is new, however, is that under NCLB, the academic performance of students is what triggers the opportunity to transfer to a new, higher-performing school or the opportunity to get extra help outside of class. Nationally, providing parents and students with options has many purposes—to maintain middle-class support for public schools, to boost racial integration, to satisfy court orders, to ease overcrowding, to provide a specialized education, to expand opportunities. Under NCLB, the right to leave one's school for another becomes an entitlement for children in failing schools.

As the legislation neared passage in late 2001, the Republican staff of the U.S. House Committee on Education and the Workforce highlighted the school choice provisions of the law. The tests of English and math that the NCLB act requires of students in grades 3 through 8 and at least once in high school are supposed to arm parents with information about the performance of the schools. (Another test, in science, is to be added for students in at least one grade in elementary, middle, and high schools beginning with the 2007–2008 school year.) Parents can then use that information to decide whether to vote with their feet and transfer or at least seek outside help. The law "represents a significant breakthrough on the road to equal educational opportunity in America," a report from the committee proclaimed.[1] The law would free "children trapped in chronically failing schools" to transfer to successful schools nearby.

But it was almost immediately clear the choice provisions of the law would not be self-implementing. School districts would still have a great amount of latitude to set up rules and procedures and notification schedules and the like. Parents would not have a choice of sending their children to any school they wished, even in their home district. Rather, they would be given a selection of schools that met the criteria. In many cases, the choices offered under NCLB would be more restricted than those available under preexisting choice programs. Thus, the school choice provisions of NCLB represent both sweeping and fundamental change in the mechanism of school reform and a minor adjustment to far more expansive school choice programs, some of which had been in place for decades.

The idea of giving parents alternatives to the neighborhood school has been around since the 1960s, when so-called alternative schools began springing up around the country. These days just about every major city has one or more schooling options—including magnet schools, open-enrollment plans that allow transfers to schools beyond a student's neighborhood, open enrollment within particular zones as a means of promoting integration and other types of programs. A handful of cities, including Hartford, St. Louis, and Rochester, New York, also allow students to transfer from city schools to those in suburbs, and vice versa. So it's important to keep in mind that the school choice provisions of NCLB come on top of and in some cases override preexisting programs allowing parents to choose a school. It should also be noted that, just as with existing programs, the right to choose as envisioned by NCLB is limited by a number of factors. The key factors have proven to be:

- Capacity. The most successful schools in many urban districts—most often magnet schools, charter schools, or selective schools that require students to pass a test to get in—have insufficient space. Magnet schools nationally, according to one recent estimate, have more than 150,000 children on waiting lists. But either because they lack the resources or the human capital or the will, school districts have failed to create new schools modeled after popular and highly successful existing schools. NCLB provides neither the directive nor the incentive for them do so.

- Transportation. Many public school programs allowing parents to choose a school provide some form of subsidized or free transportation, usually based on parents' income. NCLB improves that situation. But the amount that school districts have to spend on transportation and on tutoring is capped at 20 percent of the money they receive through Title I, which represents the largest of the federal programs for disadvantaged students. That means that, should large numbers of students take advantage of their right to transfer, not all may be able to do so unless they can provide their own transportation. So far, however, that does not appear to be a problem.
- Political resistance. Many school districts have accepted the concept of giving parents options only reluctantly. This should come as no surprise. Most often, the right to choose one's school has come at the insistence of school district outsiders—the courts, state politicians, or activists. Rarely, if ever, have school districts taken the initiative to offer students more options or to pressure schools to improve.
- Lack of parental engagement. Years of policy studies have shown that it is often very difficult to get parents of needy children to participate. School districts must invest energy and resources in making sure that all parents know their options. But, even then, well-off parents are more likely to exercise their options. NCLB does not give school districts incentives to aggressively recruit parents to participate. As papers in this volume demonstrate, school districts vary in the degree to which they are encouraging parents to do so.
- Geography. Some districts, such as those in Los Angeles, in Florida, and in rural areas of the West, are so far-flung that transfers are impractical; many other districts consist of a single school.
- Procedures and logistics. Factors as seemingly banal as the date by which parents have to sign up to transfer, whether they have to visit the school they want to transfer to, and whether they have to meet with a school official in order to register their desire to transfer have been shown to affect participation rates in existing school choice programs. Similar factors will affect the use of NCLB's choice provisions.

Growth of School Choice

Yet, even with all of these limitations—limitations of resources, of political will, of creativity—the number of students attending schools they had chosen in this country was rising dramatically even prior to NCLB. Today, roughly 90 percent of American students attend public schools, a figure that's varied only slightly for many years. But the stability of that number obscures a major shift in enrollment. The most recent data from the National Center for Education Statistics show, between 1993 and 1999, a 46 percent increase in the percentage of students attending a public school that they—rather than the school district where they reside—chose. In 1993, 4.7 million children attended a public school of their own choosing.[2] Six years later that figure was 6.85 million. This represents a change from 11 percent of all students attending a chosen public school to 14.5 percent. The trend has accelerated faster among poor and African American students than among middle-class and white students. Although the exercise of choice is more prevalent in urban areas, it also is growing in rural America—expanding from less than 7 percent of students to well over 10 percent of students.

Another set of statistics underscores the spread of this phenomenon as well as the weakening of educators' previously adamant opposition. The percentage of public school districts that allow students who live elsewhere to enroll has risen from about 26 percent in 1993 to about 46 percent in 1999. In the western United States, that percentage is a startling 73 percent. Similarly, the percentage of school districts that allow students to choose among the schools in their home district, rather than allowing them to attend only the school down the street, has risen from about 14 to 25 percent during the same period.[3]

One such option involves "charter schools," a publicly funded school that is supposed to be free to operate outside the realm of many bureaucratic strictures. Charter schools emerged in the late 1980s in Minnesota and spread quickly. The charter school movement's growth has begun to level off, but about twenty-eight hundred charter schools now enroll more than seven hundred thousand students in 36 states, with the greatest concentrations in Arizona, California, and Michigan.[4]

In addition to charters, the incidence of interdistrict choice, which enables students to transfer to a school in another district, and intradistrict choice, which allows students to transfer to other schools within their home district, appear to be on the rise. Nine states, for example, require school districts to create interdistrict transfer policies that allow students from one district to attend school in another. But those policies often allow districts to limit who can participate. In another 26 states, such transfer policies are voluntary.[5] In many such states, few school districts accept transfer students. Ohio, for example, is one of the states that has a voluntary interdistrict transfer law, and no suburban school districts surrounding its major cities are willing to participate. In 17 states, school districts were already required to set up a system of intradistrict choice to allow students to attend schools not in their own neighborhood, prior to NCLB. In nine other states, such policies are voluntary.[6]

In addition, school districts operate magnet schools, which have a particular specialty, such as art or technology, so-called controlled choice plans aimed at maintaining economic or racial integration while allowing freedom of movement, specialized academies and schools-within-schools. Dual enrollment programs—which allow students to take community college classes for high school credit, sometimes at the college and sometimes right in their own high school—are spreading rapidly, and participation is multiplying, tripling in Virginia in one year, for example.[7] The Internet is opening up a whole other venue for choice, via virtual schools that are offered by public school districts or states and cyber charter schools that convene some or all of their classes on line and cater to the tastes and needs of home-schoolers. A few districts and states have voucher programs that provide public funding to cover private school tuition. Corporate tax credits are helping underwrite private school scholarships in a handful of states.

Publicly funded voucher programs for private school tuition now operate in Milwaukee, Cleveland, and Florida. In Florida, a reported twelve thousand students receive McKay Scholarships, which allow disabled students to opt out of public schools, and more than fourteen thousand students receive scholarships paid for by tax-exempt donations, which means the money is being diverted from state coffers.[8] Since the passage of NCLB, the U.S. Supreme Court declared that the voucher program in Cleveland, which pays for students' private school tuition, mostly at religious schools, was constitutional. The state of Colorado also has passed a voucher program for students attending low-performing schools. And in January of 2004 Congress approved a voucher program that will allow up to seventeen hundred students in the District of Columbia to attend private schools. In addition, the Bush administration has asked for $50 million to fund additional local voucher initiatives. All of those programs have generated enormous amounts of attention, but they have greater symbolic than actual impact since, together, they serve only about thirty-six thousand students.

In addition, an estimated sixty thousand students are attending private schools across the country with help from privately financed "scholarships" that typically cover about half the cost of tuition. Children First America, one of two national umbrella organizations involved in such efforts, reports that more than a hundred programs in 39 states are currently operating and that more than $500 million has been contributed to offset tuition for one hundred thousand students over the past decade.[9]

But even though school choice has grown, resistance to further expansion remains. Michigan, in many ways, is representative of those opposing forces.

In 1993, Gov. John Engler declared before a joint session of the Michigan Legislature that "public education is a monopoly, and monopolies don't work."[10] Shortly thereafter, with Engler's support, Michigan became the fourth state in the nation to embrace charter schools, a hybrid type of public school that operates outside the direct supervision of traditional school districts. Three years later, Michigan freed students to cross invisible jurisdictional lines to attend public schools outside the communities where they reside.

More than seventy thousand Michigan students now attend 184 charter schools, a quarter of them in Detroit.[11] Three-quarters of those charters are authorized by universities, and most are operated by for-profit education management organizations.[12] In addition, nearly thirty-five thousand students now attend school in a district that's different from the one where they reside, a figure that's grown an average of 45 percent each year since the program was launched.[13] Thousands more high school students take free college classes that rack up both high school and college credits through a third program. And more than seven thousand "seats" are occupied electronically in the free Michigan Virtual High School, which supplies classes to more than six hundred schools.[14] Those who enroll online also are taking classes in traditional public and private high schools or alternative schools and are studying independently at home.

The monopoly's grip on education, it appears, has been considerably weakened, in some parts of the state more than in others. But it's hardly a wide-open, unregulated market. Michigan still does not subsidize private school tuition. Voters in the fall of 2000 overwhelmingly defeated an attempt to do just that for children enrolled in poorly performing public schools. Although about 70 percent of the state's school districts now accept students who want to transfer in, some do so only selectively.[15] Because the population is more widely dispersed, students in rural parts of the state have fewer options than do those in more heavily populated areas in the south and southeast. The number of charter schools that can be created by universities is capped, and school districts have shown no interest in authorizing competitors. The Detroit teachers union has defeated several efforts to raise that number and even thwarted a philanthropist's desire to underwrite the construction of 15 badly needed high schools in the city, rather than give in. And charter schools operated by for-profit entities discourage students needing special education services from applying, meaning that those students have fewer viable choices than do non-disabled students. High school students also have fewer options because they are more expensive to educate, and few charter schools serve them.

Yet, public education also seems to be stretching newfound competitive muscles. The product line is more varied, more attention is being paid to serving the needs of the customer, and there seems to be more concern about quality. One reason for this is that, under the state's system of school finance, state aid goes with the student wherever he or she chooses to enroll. The Lansing Public School District, for example, has opened magnet schools, a type of school that focuses on a particular topic to draw students from across a district or region, and full-day kindergartens, both aimed at persuading students to stay in Lansing schools rather than hauling their backpacks, and the state money that accompanies them, elsewhere.[16]

The schools in Detroit, in slow-motion collapse for decades, have been hurt the most by competition, losing more than 10 percent of their students and more than $160 million a year to other school districts and to charter schools.[17] That exodus has accelerated a decline in enrollment brought about by the depopulation of the city and left behind the neediest students, who are the most expensive to serve, because many charter schools resist accepting those who are disabled or far behind in their studies.[18] But even in its financially straitened condition, the Detroit Public School District is working hard on reform in order to compete with charter schools and nearby suburban districts. Under the leadership of a strong CEO, the district has invested in a new reading curriculum, aligned its professional development to that curriculum, begun closely monitoring student progress, replaced 80 principals, tied principals' contracts to achieving school achievement goals, and focused on the lowest-achieving schools. An outside evaluation said test scores are rising and "the reform of public education in Detroit is in full swing" as a result of "a new determination to raise achievement and a clearer sense of direction and purpose."[19]

In many ways, the growth of as well as the limitations on parents' schooling options in Michigan are emblematic of what's occurring across the country. As a May 2003 report on schooling options in Massachusetts concluded, "the education system can be increasingly described as a mixed delivery model—with public, private and quasi-public providers—as is the case with the health care and early childhood sectors."[20] In *Choosing Schools*, Mark Schneider, Paul Teske, and Melissa Marschall say that choice is consistent with American beliefs and values and reflects the faith Americans and their leaders place in markets; the U.S. Supreme Court has declared giving parents more options in schooling to be lawful, even if such programs involve private, religious schools receiving public funds. Bringing options to education also seeks to leverage what we know about good schools, which is that parents buy into the school's mission and make an effort to become involved.[21]

Giving parents options also is popular—a 2003 poll sponsored by the Education Policy Center at Michigan State University found that 67 percent of African Americans in the Detroit area, where charter schools already enroll more than twenty thousand students, favor charter schools as an alternative to the municipal school district.[22] Nationally, a solid majority of Americans support the idea that parents ought to be able to choose a school for their children, at least in the abstract.[23] More than half say their options should include any public school, not just those in their neighborhood. And 86 percent say that children ought to be able to transfer out of schools that are failing.[24]

But it's fair to say that many questions remain about whether the emerging mix of schools and options is serving the interests of all students. How, for example, can communities and states ensure that students of all races and income levels have access to a range of good schools? How can they create a wide variety of schools? How can they make sure parents—particularly those who are poor or who don't speak English—have access to good information about the choices available to them? How can they make transportation available for those who need it to attend the school that best fits their needs? How can communities make sure that those who choose to attend the school down the street are not harmed by the choices of others?

The school choice provisions of NCLB add to this momentum. But as many of the chapters in this volume point out, the implementation of that law will not be easy, and it may not lead to a dramatic expansion in the growth of available options—certainly nothing of the magnitude as had been hoped—for several years. Still, more options rather than fewer options surely lies ahead. So the more important questions have to do not with whether parents should or should not be allowed to choose the schools their children attend but rather with how to make sure that freedom works in the interest of all students as well as for the interest of the larger public. Existing choice programs may offer some clues as to how to achieve these aims.

Residential Choice

The most widespread type of enrollment option is, obviously, that which is exercised when parents buy or rent a home based on their perception of the quality of the schools. It is hardly an accident that real estate agents in Los Angeles and New Jersey and many other states bring along on house-hunting trips with potential buyers a laminated copy of the local newspaper's annual listing of test scores. Nor is it mere civic-mindedness that causes real estate agents to call newspapers every spring as the real estate market heats up, asking when a new batch of test scores will come out. Homes in neighborhoods where the local school's test scores are higher are sold for more money. The search for "the best" is intense, and those who are able to spend the money to get the best don't want to share it with those who aren't able to do so.

Intradistrict Choice

New York City

Although obtaining national numbers for how many students actually avail themselves of this type of choice is problematic, intradistrict choice is likely the second most common form of choice. One recent estimate says that the various types of intradistrict choice might involve four to five million students.[25] Another estimate suggests that figure could be eight million students in twelve hundred school districts.[26]

It is also the form of school choice most analogous to that envisioned by NCLB. The evidence is strong that parents who are more sophisticated, engaged, affluent, and aggressive are most likely to take advantage of such systems. Some districts, such as New York, have set up elaborate procedures to try to make sure that students from across the academic spectrum have a choice of schools. But the policies often are undermined by informal arrangements between parents and principals. In a promising development, New York is following in the footsteps of a few districts around the country and requiring all eighth-graders to choose a high school to attend, even if it is the one in their neighborhood. That should level the playing field.

New York City has long had an expansive system of schooling options, going back to the 1970s. In 1974, New York City's Community School District No. 4, which serves much of East Harlem, began converting its junior high schools into alternative schools and by 1982 had abandoned attendance zones altogether. Every sixth-grader had to choose from schools with themes such as biomedicine, communications, performing arts, and so on. Schools that proved popular thrived, though they were kept small; those that failed to attract students were eliminated from the menu.[27]

That's just one system of choice that operates in the 1.1 million-student system. As in large cities such as Los Angeles, Chicago, Boston, and many others, several types of school choice operate simultaneously. The right to choose from a menu of public schools is so well ingrained that, in certain circles of parents with school-age children, it is a central topic of conversation. Schools Chancellor Joel I. Klein often says that if that were to change, and all students were to be randomly assigned to public schools that they were required to attend, parents in the nation's largest city would become instant

revolutionaries. Or given the fact that the city's private schools are oversub-
scribed, thousands of parents would immediately begin looking to move to
the suburbs.

Parents also are allowed to search for middle schools, with the added
element that many schools consider students' test scores in making admissions decisions. But that does not guarantee sufficient variety to accommodate all preferences. A mother on the Upper West Side who is searching for
a middle school for her son said her neighborhood boasts three highly
regarded schools that have managed to retain significant numbers of middle-
class students. But all three, she said, seek out highly gifted students who do
well in rigorous, structured, academic settings. Her son, she said, is more into
music and art than academic subjects, so she's dissatisfied with the choices available to her. "It's so grim, it's like the Soviet Union," she said in an interview.[28]

In 2002, about sixty-six thousand New York City students out of eight
hundred thousand in grades K-8 attended a school other than the one in
their immediate neighborhood, indicating that far fewer students were exercising choice than would have been the case had there been sufficient interest on the part of the parents or space in desirable schools.[29] The process gets
more complicated and nerve wracking at the high school level. On paper,
again, the district's 236 high schools offer a seemingly endless array of
specializations.

The elite, selective schools—Stuyvesant, Bronx Science, and Brooklyn
Technical, plus three additional highly demanding schools that opened in
recent years on the campuses of community colleges—take students based on
their performance on an entrance exam. The competition is intense.
Nineteen of every 20 who applied to Stuyvesant in 2002 were turned away.[30]
La Guardia High School for the arts requires an audition or portfolio of work
and accepted only one of every 44 applicants in 2002.

For students entering high school in the fall of 2004, the rest of the high
schools in New York will use what the system says is a "matching" model that
is similar to how medical schools choose students. Students not seeking
admission to the elite schools will list up to 12 choices. But the schools are free
to set different rules for admission, and only 120 of them take students from
all five boroughs.[31] A set of schools and programs known as Education
Options are required to accept students from across the achievement spectrum, to ensure that middling students and low-scoring students get a shot at
attending the most desirable high schools. A lottery is used to dole out seats
when demand exceeds supply. But a complicating factor is that the Education
Options schools are required to admit students who score in the top 2 percent
on a seventh-grade English test to their first-choice school. At the most

popular schools, those high-scoring students can claim all of the seats set aside for students who are achieving above grade level. In a quirk of well-intended policy, that means students who score on grade level, rather than above, actually have a far better statistical chance of getting into their first-choice school.

In the past, that process has meant that many students failed to get admitted to any of the schools they wanted to attend and were assigned to attend their neighborhood school. According to the *New York Times*, in 2002, thirteen thousand ninth-graders were not admitted to any of the schools to which they had applied.[32] That drove many parents in desperate search of private alternatives. The new system is designed to make sure all students get one of their choices. That shift has caused some grumbling from parents who, in the past, would have been able to lobby principals or guidance counselors to free up a slot in highly desirable schools. The policy also does nothing to create more attractive high schools to ease the competition for seats in the most desirable schools.

Klein, the schools chancellor, acknowledged the fundamental problem. "I have a chronic shortage of good high schools," he told the *New York Times*.[33] "I am trying to maximize what's good for 80,000 kids in the system. That's my obligation."

Klein wants to create two hundred new, innovative schools and has attracted tens of millions of dollars in private funds to aid that effort. Microsoft chairman Bill Gates last year donated $51.2 million to private groups that will create at least 67 of those schools. (Nationally, the Bill and Melinda Gates Foundation has donated $590 million to create sixteen hundred small schools in cities including Los Angeles, Milwaukee, Seattle, San Diego, and Chicago.)[34] The groups that will create the schools include an organization called New Visions for Public Schools, which already has created 40 schools in the city, the College Board, the Institute for Student Achievement, and the Asia Society. In addition, Klein and Mayor Michael R. Bloomberg also are championing the creation of 50 charter schools and in the fall of 2003 announced they had raised $40 million in donations, half the money necessary to reach that goal.[35]

In making the announcement both Bloomberg and Klein, who lead the nation's largest school district, sounded like staunch advocates of creating more options in schooling. "Charter schools foster innovation and attract vital new resources to our school system," Bloomberg said.

"Today's announcement is a testament to our belief that there is more than one way to deliver high quality public education," Klein added.[36]

By contrast, about two hundred and twenty thousand New York students were eligible to transfer from low-performing schools during the first year of implementation of the No Child Left Behind Act. But only fifteen hundred actually did so. In the second year, eight thousand students transferred under the provisions of NCLB. Existing choice appears to dwarf prospective choice.

Boulder Valley, Colorado

Colorado requires school districts to set up intradistrict choice programs. The 495-square-mile Boulder Valley School District has offered its students a choice of schools, on a space-available basis, since 1961. In the mid-1990s, a group of parents in the twenty-eight-thousand–student district became concerned about a perceived lack of academic rigor and began pressing for more options. By the end of the 1990s, the number of specialized options available had grown from 5 to 16, including some that specifically focused on academics, a clear response to the demands of parents.[37]

Now, not only can students still enroll in any school, they also can choose a "focus" school featuring a particular theme, a neighborhood focus school that has a theme but gives priority to neighborhood residents, a so-called strand school that's something of a hybrid, and charter schools. One in five students in the district now chooses to attend a school not in his or her immediate neighborhood.

A systematic review of the program by University of Colorado at Boulder professors Kenneth R. Howe and Margaret A. Eisenhart found that most district residents believe the program is inequitable. Factors cited include inadequate information, a lack of transportation, tight application deadlines, and special admissions requirements. The survey also found that many believe that open enrollment has increased disparities in district schools, brought about increased segregation of minority students, and allowed some schools to prosper at the expense of others. The report said that the annual reporting of test scores for each campus caused parents to seek to leave schools with relatively low test scores for ones with higher scores.

In Boulder Valley, the authors contend, open enrollment had increased economic and racial stratification at the schools and set up a "zero-sum game" in which some campuses gained, but only at the expense of others.[38]

The authors recommended that the district make a greater effort to provide parents with information, pay for transportation, increase funding for schools with large numbers of disadvantaged students, and take other actions to ensure that all students have an equal chance to get a decent education in a school that they chose. On the other hand, the competition set up by the open-enrollment program seems to have made the district responsive to the demands of parents who wanted more rigorous academics. The labels of "in need of improvement" that NCLB applies to schools and NCLB's emphasis on test scores could also have both positive and negative consequences.

Boston, Massachusetts

Boston has had a troubled history with desegregation and has embraced choice as an alternative to busing. Boston now gives parents of elementary school students about 30 schools to choose from, using a lottery when demand exceeds the seats available and providing transportation for those who live beyond walking distance. Transportation costs the 139-school district $58 million per year, which in a time of budget cutting is causing some second thoughts. All of the district's non-selective high schools take students from anywhere in the city.[39]

To help parents choose schools, the district has set up resource centers in each of the three large attendance zones. Those centers are costly, but Boston and other districts have found that the investment is necessary to provide parents with the information they need to make good choices.[40] As previously noted, NCLB does not require school districts to reach out in this way to parents.

Potential Harm

Schools that are not popular can be harmed by such arrangements. That phenomenon has been noted in Chicago, where 150,000 out of 433,000 students attend schools they have chosen rather than been assigned to. Undesirable neighborhood schools have lost large numbers of students with decent test scores and motivated parents, who have moved to more successful schools elsewhere. In 2001 an analysis by Catalyst Chicago noted that the 12 "least popular" high schools in the city lost between 62 percent and 77 percent of the students within their attendance boundaries to other schools. And of the students that opted to go elsewhere, 40 percent of them had test scores high enough to qualify them to attend selective schools in the district. As the higher performing students left, the demand for honors and Advanced Placement classes dried up at the schools left behind; this made the "last resort" schools even more unattractive. Not surprisingly, every one of the 12 least popular schools was facing consequences for having consistently low test scores.[41] To halt that downward spiral, some of the schools have replaced their principals, launched new programs aimed at attracting high-performing students, refurbished buildings, and aggressively recruited neighborhood students. Some schools appear to be rebounding. This, of course, is the salutary effect that pro-choice advocates hope to see from competition. But it's unclear whether these reform efforts will succeed.

Controlled Choice

Across the river from Boston, the Cambridge, Massachusetts, school district has one of the nation's oldest controlled choice programs. Such programs are on the rise as court-ordered busing programs are phased out and as race-based choice programs are challenged in court as discriminatory. All such plans offer parents some options but limit them in order to serve the broader district goal of integrating schools by race or by income. In Cambridge, the goal is to integrate schools economically. To do that, all students in the seven-thousand-student district are required to apply to the schools they'd like to attend.

The goal of the program is a 44 percent–55 percent mix, with students who are poor in the minority. But half of the district's elementary schools did not achieve that desired mix for 2002–2003. At the most popular school, chief operating officer Jim Maloney said, four out of five applications were from more well-off students. "In the end, you've got to have good schools and a wide range of programs to choose from," Maloney said. "If parents feel that only some of your programs are good, and they don't get into one of those schools, then they're not happy. It's a built-in competition among principals for enrollment."[42]

Magnets

Magnet schools first appeared on the education scene in the early 1970s in Cincinnati and Milwaukee. These schools focus on a particular aspect of the curriculum, such as art or music, or a particular profession, such as law or medicine. In 1975, a federal court recognized that such schools could serve as an alternative to mandatory busing as a mechanism to achieve integration. Federal subsidies contributed to the rapid growth of magnet schools, and by the mid-1990s it was estimated that more than 1.2 million students were attending more than twenty-four hundred magnet schools nationally.

The bulk of those schools are in urban areas, and they are particularly popular in the South, upper Midwestern states such as Illinois and Minnesota, and in California and Nevada.[43] At least a third of the students in Los Angeles, Cincinnati, and Buffalo, New York, attend magnet schools.

Such schools are supposed to reduce segregation, maintain middle-class support and lead to higher student achievement. But some worry that low-income students are underrepresented in such schools, that the selective admissions policies of some magnet schools deny access to students who have not done well academically, and that the higher cost of magnet school programs may draw resources away from non-magnet schools.

Still, a variety of studies suggest that magnet schools tend to succeed in meeting the goals set for them and that the supply of magnet schools has not kept up with the demand. In the mid-1990s, 90 percent of 173 districts that participated in a national survey reported that they had waiting lists for their magnet schools.[44] The academic achievement record of students in magnet schools is generally thought to be positive, but the test scores are difficult to disentangle from the demographic differences between magnet school students and those in comprehensive schools. Researchers also suggest that the apparent achievement gains may be explained by magnet schools' spending, which often is several hundred dollars more per pupil than in traditional schools.[45]

A recent analysis of student achievement in the magnet school programs in Prince George's County, Maryland, however, concluded that students who attended them were learning about the same as were students in comprehensive, non-thematic schools. "Some of the programs made a difference and some of the programs don't make a difference," Leroy Tompkins, the systems chief accountability officer, told the *Washington Post*.[46]

Charter Schools

Charter schools emerged in Minnesota in the early 1990s and now, more than a decade later, are beginning to have a significant effect on enrollment in a number of school districts.

The 139-school Boston school district projects that its enrollment will decline in the fall of 2004, in part because of the increasing number of children enrolling in charter schools. The district said it has lost forty-three hundred students to charter schools; throughout Massachusetts, more than nineteen thousand students are enrolled in charters. Boston expects even more of its students to enroll in charters because additional schools are scheduled to open.[47] The district calculates that it has had to forgo $40 million in revenue because of the drop in enrollment.

Similarly, Minneapolis, which saw the first charter school open in 1992, has lost about forty-two hundred students to charter schools. Fueling the growth in the number of charter schools are grants from the Gates Foundation and Walton Family Foundation to non-profit agencies to expand the charter movement.[48]

The Miami–Dade County Public Schools also are experiencing strong competition from charter schools and the Florida voucher and tax-supported scholarship programs, which combined enroll about ten thousand students. To fight back, the district is phasing in a greatly expanded menu of school options, which will be financed by a $14.6 million federal grant. The district will create more magnet schools, which will be located closer to more students' homes. Among the alternatives could be additional schools located in businesses where parents work.

"I'm a fervent believer in public education being the backbone of our way of life," said Merrett R. Stierheim, the district's former superintendent told *Education Week.* "I'm also pragmatic enough to realize that the issue of choice and competition is here to stay. Why not give that choice to our parents and students within our public school system?"[49]

But even as charter schools have spread, it's been difficult to get a handle on their performance. Charter schools in Michigan, for example, when matched to similar non-charter schools, rack up smaller achievement gains and greater losses, according to an evaluation by the Evaluation Center at Western Michigan University in Kalamazoo.[50] Test scores in California show that low-income students in California do better in traditional schools than they do in charter schools.[51] Grover J. "Russ" Whitehurst, who as head of the federal Institute of Education Sciences is charged with transforming education into an research-based pursuit, has said there's little solid evidence that charters are more effective than traditional schools.[52]

On the other hand, a recent study by Jay P. Greene found that charter schools in Colorado can claim strongly positive results. Studies of charter schools in Arizona and Connecticut have found positive effects as well. The 32 Knowledge Is Power Program (KIPP) schools around the country, the Accelerated School in Central Los Angeles, View Park Accelerated Charter in the Crenshaw area of Los Angeles and University Prep Academy in Detroit are all among a growing body of highly effective schools that charter school laws made possible. All of those schools have attracted strong leaders who have set ambitious goals and have attracted outside supporters willing to help them achieve those goals. NCLB, however, does not expand the number of charter schools.

Interdistrict Choice

A variety of programs around the country offer students the opportunity to go to school in a district different from the one where they live. Most such programs are voluntary, and many districts choose not to take part. But nine states actually require districts to allow students to enroll in schools outside their boundaries. The percentage of students using such programs tends to be around 1 percent to 3 percent of the students in the state; in Nebraska, however, that figure is 6.5 percent.[53]

Analyses in Georgia, Massachusetts, Minnesota, and Wisconsin have found that white students participate in interdistrict choice programs at a significantly higher rate than do minority students, leading to concerns that such programs are exacerbating racial segregation. In Massachusetts, for example, about 90 percent of the students who enroll in schools outside their home district are white, compared to 75 percent of the students in the state as a whole. One reason for this is that none of the suburban school districts surrounding Boston and other cities is willing to participate. This is a common occurrence in states that have voluntary programs, such as the one in Massachusetts.[54]

Minnesota's interdistrict choice program was phased in beginning in 1987, making it the nation's oldest. Last year, more than thirty thousand students attended school in districts other than the one where they reside even though transportation is not provided. Beginning in 2000, low-income children in Minneapolis became eligible for free transportation to suburban schools and priority placement in desirable magnet schools.

Virtual Schools

A product of the Internet, so-called virtual schools or cyber schools are spreading nationally. More than 15 states now operate such schools, in which students can enroll part time or just take classes. The most recent estimate is that 88 virtual schools are operating in the United States. In 2002, those schools enrolled about 180,000 students, but that number was expected to explode to more than 1 million by the 2004–2005 school year.[55]

Some of these schools are operated by school districts or a consortium of districts, which allow students to take individual classes. Others are operated as charter schools. A study from Luis Huerta and Fernanda Gonzalez at Teachers College estimates that sixty-eight thousand students are enrolled in what the authors call "non–classroom-based" charter schools, which receive an estimated $442 million in state aid.[56]

States are wrestling with how to monitor these schools to make sure that the instruction that's being purchased with state money is being delivered; they're also struggling to figure out the actual costs of such schools; because they don't have to provide classrooms, their costs are far lower than in regular schools. Such environments test the definition of schools, because students who take all of their instruction through such schools need never leave home.

Home Schooling

A final category of choice that is gaining in acceptance is home schooling. Once considered to be a fringe activity engaged in solely by conservative Christians and counterculture types, home schooling is now officially sanctioned by every state and an infrastructure of organizations, businesses, and Internet sites has sprung up to cater to those families who are pursuing that path. Estimates as to the number of students being home-schooled range from 850,000 by the National Center for Education Statistics to 2.1 million by advocates.

Choice Lessons

What's clear is that school choice is now one of the defining characteristics of the American public education landscape. What's less clear is how much the NCLB adds to the mix. In Minnesota, 30 percent of public school students already choose their public schools. In Milwaukee, one in four students attends either private schools, charter schools, or suburban schools at public expense. In Kansas City, a third of the students are in magnet schools. In Long Beach, California, 52 percent of the students are enrolled in magnet schools.

After more than three decades of experience, it's apparent that choice alone is not a powerful enough remedy for the problems of American education. Otherwise, we'd see large gains in academic achievement in such places as Dayton, Ohio. Dayton boasts of a thriving education market. Parents can choose from 19 charter schools with offerings ranging from fundamental skills to career-oriented themes such as entrepreneurship or health care.[57] The area has large systems of Catholic schools and Christian schools, and nearly a thousand students attend those schools with the help of privately financed vouchers. The school district itself also offers variety: every elementary school embodies one of seven themes, including the Montessori approach, arts, science, and computer technology, and parents can choose to send their children to any of the district's six high schools.

The competition has pushed the school district to get its political and financial house in order. A reform-minded majority was elected to the school board. The percentage of parents who think that the public schools in Dayton are getting better is on the rise.[58] And voters have approved recent bond issues to repair decrepit buildings. Giving parents schooling options has not destroyed education, as many public school loyalists fear it will.

Yet an educational renaissance is hardly in sight. Only 59 percent of the students in Dayton attend traditional public schools, which may or may not be a good thing, depending on one's perspective. Only one in four parents in the Dayton school district say, given the choice, they would send their children to a high school run by the school district.[59] Yet, the alternatives available, at least in the public sector, are not clearly superior. Although charter schools' test scores are rising, they remain lower on average than the subpar scores of the school district itself.[60] And since running a high school is more expensive and more difficult, there is a dearth of charter schools designed to serve older students, even though there appears to be a demand.

Until NCLB, however, school choice was only linked theoretically to school reform and improving public education. Now, that relationship is explicit. Schools that repeatedly fall short of state-set targets could find themselves losing students and revenues. So, if NCLB plays out as intended, that should create pressure on schools and districts to mobilize the resources to improve. But that will occur only if educators see a clear relationship between what happens to them and what happens to their students and only if they believe that the NCLB accountability targets are reasonable and achievable.

That pressure to improve will emerge, however, only if parents choose to exercise the choices available to them under NCLB. That is not a given. Though magnet schools and charter schools may have waiting lists, it's not clear whether those waiting lists are real or not. In other words, if a slot opens up, it's not clear that a parent would be willing to move from the school her child is attending to the charter school or magnet school. It's even less certain that parents will want to move their children to schools that are only marginally better and that may be relatively far away—the types of choices available under NCLB. Interdistrict transfer programs in many places are undersubscribed, and poor students, those NCLB is aimed at helping, are less likely to take advantage of school choice. The same thing could well happen with NCLB choice, unless school districts, or some other agency, intervene and provide parents with the motivation and the information to help them do so.

It's also true that many states and districts have been unresponsive to the demand for more choice. And NCLB's rules don't necessarily change that. In New Jersey, for example, the state has an "interdistrict" enrollment program, but only 15 districts are allowed to participate. In June of 2003, the statewide "Office of Interdistrict Public School Choice" reported: "We hear daily from parents who want to participate in public school choice but who are frequently disappointed to learn that this opportunity is not available to them." The state department of education recommended that the pilot program be expanded statewide. But there's little enthusiasm among educators for doing so.[61]

If school districts were businesses, of course, they'd seek to satisfy such consumer demands. That is happening in some places such as New York City and Chicago, where it is recognized that having more viable choices not only serves the interests of the consumer but the district as well. But that represents a major shift in thinking for the public schools.

In Chicago, for example, the district spends $100 million annually to transport a third of its students out of their neighborhoods to the schools that they've chosen to attend, in the process bypassing underutilized neighborhood schools. By contrast, nineteen thousand Chicago students were eligible to transfer to new schools under NCLB rules, and space was found for only a thousand of them.[62]

So the Chicago Public Schools' hard-charging young CEO, Arne Duncan, is working to make those neighborhood schools more attractive. One of his most innovative ideas has been to open fee-based preschools in 20 elementary schools. Parents pay $6,500 a year for their children to attend, and the programs have long waiting lists. About 80 percent of the children enrolled in those programs remain at the neighborhood school for kindergarten, Duncan said.

"Every school has to be a school of choice, and to do that we have to have dramatically higher quality schools that are good enough to attract the middle class," Duncan said during a presentation to the Hechinger Institute on Education and the Media at Teachers College, Columbia University. "This is a personal battle. I want to send my children to my neighborhood public school."

But most school districts have failed to respond in that way, which demonstrates that they have yet to adopt an entrepreneurial, customer-focused philosophy. In particular, they have failed to create new and innovative schools. The process of creating new schools so as to give students more choices is hardly easy. It's fraught with difficulties and costs. In St. Louis, for example, the magnet schools routinely turn away thousands of students who want to enroll. But those schools spend, on average, about 30 percent more per pupil than do the traditional schools, and the district, which has long been criticized for massive overspending on administration, has been unwilling to free up the additional money to create those schools. NCLB is unlikely to add sufficient pressure to cause the district to suddenly become competitive and entrepreneurial.

The federal government has attempted to fill in the funding gap by offering money to districts to create magnet schools. This year, for example, $110 million was available for that purpose. School districts also could tap into a $385 million fund for innovative approaches to schooling that is part of NCLB.[63]

In addition to money, however, federal incentives could motivate school districts to create new schools. It's true that schools that fail to make adequate progress year after year can be forced to, essentially, start all over again, and that may be incentive enough. But it would be useful if NCLB framed the creation of new schools positively, as a way to serve children directly.

Another cost associated with school choice is transportation. Such costs vary, of course, depending on the size of the school district, the density, the availability of public transit, and so on. But if school choice is to be available on an equal basis to students of all circumstances—those who have family cars as well as those who don't, those whose parents are available to drive them as well as those who are not—then low-income students will need transportation. This doesn't necessarily have to be provided by the school district. Cities could step in to provide municipal bus or train service. Or the federal government could finance community agencies to help parents take advantage of the choice provisions of NCLB. NCLB includes money for transporting students who want to transfer out of low-performing schools. But that money may not be enough. And school districts may not want to spend it. It could well be that to make the choice provisions of NCLB work, the states or the federal government will have to create outside agencies to make the school districts more responsive.

Another element of a good school choice program that can be expensive is information. Examinations of school choice indicate that efforts to set up websites or mail out flyers to keep parents informed have not been sufficient for leveling the playing field between affluent, well-educated parents and those who are less well-off and less sophisticated. This problem is not insurmountable. Again, the states or the federal government could invest, as it is doing, in community agencies that will help get out the word. School districts have little incentive to get more students to take advantage of school choice. But communities do.

Analysts at the Education Policy Center at Michigan State University have written that, overall, school choice in the state is a "work in progress" and that they could find "little evidence of systemic improvement so far." Instead, they said, local factors and statewide rules are combining to produce "a variable yet patterned set of effects" in different parts of the state.[64]

School choice can be done fairly and in a way that is consistent with the highest American values and its academic aspirations. But the details matter, and we don't yet know enough to design policies that properly balance the rights and interests of individuals with the interests of the public. In particular, it seems that there's been little research into what happens when various types of options—charters, magnets, privately funded vouchers, interdistrict choice, intradistrict choice, dual enrollment with colleges, and virtual schools—all exist in the same district.

NCLB should hasten all of these trends, because it explicitly links the academic performance of students to consequences for the school. It may take a while, for all the reasons that are noted in this chapter and in this book. But that may eventually lead school districts to get serious about either fixing the failing schools or offering viable alternatives. That would be a significant culture shift within public education. And should that occur, students will benefit—those who do choose to transfer, as well as those who do not.

Notes

1. Committee on Education and the Workforce, U.S. House of Representatives, press release on H.R. 1, Dec. 13, 2001.
2. National Household Education Surveys, *Trends in the Use of School Choice 1993 to 1999* (Washington D.C.: U.S. Department of Education, National Center for Education Statistics, May 2003).
3. Ibid.
4. Krista Kafer, "School Choice, 2003, What's Happening in the States" (Washington, D.C.: Heritage Foundation Press, 2004).
5. Jennifer Dounay, Education Commission of the States, untitled presentation, Hechinger Institute on Education and the Media, Los Angeles, California, May 2003.
6. Ibid.
7. Vanessa Smith Morest and Melinda Mechur Karp, "Merging College and High School: The Institutional Realities of Implementing PK-16 Reform" (New York: Community College Research Center, Teachers College, Columbia University), draft, April 2003.
8. Kimberly Miller, "Scholarship Voucher System Unchecked," *Palm Beach Post,* July 13, 2003, and ongoing coverage; Jay P. Greene and Greg Forster, "Vouchers Do Help the Disabled," *Palm Beach Post,* December 11, 2003.
9. Available at www.childrenfirst.org.

10. Matthew J. Brouillette and Matthew Ladner, "The Impact of Limited School Choice on Public School Districts, 2000" (Midland, Mich.: Mackinac Center for Public Policy, 2000). Available at www.mackinac.org.

11. Christopher Reimann and Tara Donahue, "Declining Support for Charter Schools: Results from the 2003 State of the State Survey" (East Lansing, Mich.: Education Policy Center, Michigan State University, 2003).

12. David Arsen, David N. Plank, and Gary Sykes, "A Work in Progress," *Education Next,* winter 2001.

13. Kafer, "School Choice, 2003."

14. James McCurtis, Jr., "Virtual High School Makes the Grade," *Lansing State Journal,* November 22, 2003.

15. David N. Plank and Christopher Dunbar, Jr. "Leaving No Child Behind? False Start in Michigan." Paper presented at conference "Leaving No Child Behind? Options for Kids in Failing Schools," American Enterprise Institute, January 15–16, 2004, Washington, D.C.

16. Arsen et al., "A Work in Progress."

17. Ibid.

18. Ibid.

19. Council of Great City Schools, *Better Schools for a Stronger Detroit* (Washington, D.C.: May 2003).

20. Kathryn McDermott, Susan Bowles, and Andrew Churchill, *Mapping School Choice in Massachusetts, Data and Findings,* 2003 (Boston: Center for Education Research and Policy at MassINC, 2003).

21. Mark Schneider, Paul Teske, and Melissa Marschall, *Choosing Schools* (Princeton, N.J.: Princeton University Press, 2000).

22. Reimann and Donahue, "Declining Support."

23. Public Agenda, *On Thin Ice* (New York: Public Agenda, 1999).

24. Public Agenda, *Where Are We Now: 12 Things You Need to Know About Education and Public Opinion* (New York: Public Agenda, 2003).

25. Jeffrey R. Henig and Stephen D. Sugarman, "The Nature and Extent of School Choice," in *School Choice and Social Controversy: Politics, Policy, and Law,* ed. Stephen D. Sugarman and Frank R. Kemerer (Washington, D.C.: Brookings Institution Press, 1999).

26. Ibid.

27. Amy Stuart Wells, *Time to Choose: America at the Crossroads of School Choice Policy* (New York: Hill and Wang, 1993), pp. 53–57.

28. Interview with Leslie Berger, May 2003.

29. Abby Goodnough, "Policy Eases the Way out of Bad Schools," *New York Times,* December 9, 2002.

30. Leslie Berger, "School Maze," *New York Times,* December 1, 2002, City Weekly, Section 14, p. 1.

31. David M. Herszenhorn, "Revised Admission for High Schools," *New York Times,* October 3, 2003.

32. Ibid.
33. Ibid.
34. Available at www.gatesfoundation.org.
35. New York City Board of Education press release on charters (September 2003).
36. Ibid.
37. Kenneth R. Howe and Margaret A. Eisenhart, "A Study of Boulder Valley School District's Open Enrollment System" (Boulder, Colo.: Boulder Valley School District, October 2000).
38. Ibid.
39. Reporting by Alexander Russo, interviews with Boston officials, fall 2003.
40. Ibid.
41. Elizabeth Duffrin, "Half of High Schoolers Bypass Their Local Schools," *Chicago Catalyst,* December 2001.
42. Reporting by Alexander Russo, interviews with Boston officials, fall 2003.
43. Dounay, Education Commission.
44. Bruce Fuller et. al., *School Choice: Abundant Hopes, Scarce Evidence of Results* (Berkeley, Calif.: Policy Analysis for California Education, 1999).
45. William L. Taylor and Corinne M. Yu, "Difficult Choices: Do Magnet Schools Serve Children in Need?" (Washington, D.C.: Citizens' Commission on Civil Rights, spring 1997).
46. Nancy Trejos, "Magnets' Test Score Advantage Minimal," *Washington Post,* December 11, 2003.
47. Anand Vaishnav, "Enrollment in City's Public Schools Projected to Drop Next Year," *Boston Globe,* January 1, 2004.
48. John Welsh, "Charter Schools Mark a Record," *St. Paul Pioneer Press,* December 29, 2003.
49. Catherine Gewertz, "Miami-Dade Will Launch Choice Plan," *Education Week,* November 6, 2002.
50. Gary Miron and Christopher Nelson, "What's Public about Charter Schools," *Education Week,* May 15, 2002.
51. David R. Rogosa, "Student Progress in California Charter Schools" (Stanford, Calif.: CRESST). Available at http://www-stat.stanford.edu/~rag/api/charter9902.pdf.
52. Grover J. "Russ" Whitehurst, presentation, Hechinger Institute on Education and the Media (New York City, November 2003).
53. Dounay, Education Commission.
54. McDermott et al., *Mapping School Choice.*
55. Julie Z. Aronson and Mike J. Timms, "Net Choices, Net Gains: Supplementing High School Curriculum with Online Courses" (San Francisco: WestEd, December 2003).
56. Luis Huerta and Fernanda Gonzalez, "Cyber and Home School Charter Schools Increase Public Home Schooling Options Despite Limited Accountability and State Oversight" (New York: National Center for the Study of Privatization in Education, 2004).

57. Scott Elliott, "Shopping for Your Child's School: More Choices Put Parents in Study Hall," *Dayton Daily News,* August 19, 2002, and "Charter Schools' First Checkup Pivotal Point," *Dayton Daily News*, July 29, 2002.

58. Thomas B. Fordham Foundation, *Having Their Say, The Views of Dayton-Area Parents on Education,* 2003 (Washington, D.C.: Thomas B. Fordham Foundation, 2003).

59. Ibid.

60. Elliott, "Charter Schools' First Checkup."

61. New Jersey Department of Education, *Interdistrict Public School Choice, June* 2003 (Trenton, N.J.: Office of Interdistrict Public School Choice, New Jersey Department of Education, 2003).

62. Arne Duncan, untitled presentation, Hechinger Institute on Education and the Media, New York City, November 2003.

63. Available at www.ed.gov.

64. David Arsen, David N. Plank, and Gary Sykes, *The Rules Matter* (East Lansing, Mich.: Education Policy Center, Michigan State University, 2001).

3

The Invisible Hand of NCLB

Siobhan Gorman

In the summer of 2002, Martha Fritchley was leafing through the Yellow Pages in search of tutoring companies. It had been about six months since the No Child Left Behind education reform bill had become law, and one of the bill's provisions required repeatedly failing schools to offer their students outside tutoring. An assistant superintendent for the Hall County School System in Georgia, Fritchley needed to enlist companies to tutor children in a handful of failing schools in her district. She wanted to find an in-home tutoring company and bumped into a company called Club Z.

Fritchley called Scott Morchower, who owned a local Club Z franchise. Morchower hadn't heard of the new federal law or its tutoring provision, but he met with Fritchley and was immediately hooked on the idea. Morchower called several nearby districts to offer up his services. In Forsyth County, Club Z became the sole tutor for the county's 75 struggling students in the 2002–2003 academic year. Some of those students jumped as many as three grade levels. And while Hall County had few takers for the federal tutoring program that year, 14 enrolled with Club Z the following year.

Under the No Child Left Behind Act, these tutoring services, known as "supplemental educational services" in edu-speak, are paid for by school districts with part of the education money they receive from the U.S. Department of Education. Georgia was among the early states to implement this program. Most states truly got on board in the 2003–2004 academic year.

This nascent marketplace has all the components of a high school melodrama—there's the popular crowd, the bullies, the overachievers, the do-gooders, and the geeks. (The leading roles are played, in order, by: large, corporate tutoring providers; school districts; smaller national providers; local, largely non-profit, organizations; and online tutors.) But without a chaperone in this new, free-market niche in public education, it's been a schoolyard free-for-all—with muddled results. This chapter offers an initial assessment of the new marketplace that is emerging in response to the federally funded tutoring program.

"The results we came out with were awesome," says Morchower, whose national parent Club Z is among the small, national overachievers. So awesome, in fact, he apparently worked himself out of a job—at least in Forsyth County. All Forsyth County Schools leapt right off the failing schools list, so their students were no longer eligible for tutoring services.[1] In the 2002–2003 school year, students in the supplemental services program made up 20 percent of his business, and with the success of his students that year, Morchower figured they would account for 40 percent the next year. No so. As of fall 2003, students in the program again made up 20 percent. With an unpredictable volume of clients, how does Morchower factor children from the federal program into his business plan? "I wish I knew," he says. "That's the $10 million question."

By some estimates, it's the $2 billion question. That's how much money some tutoring providers say could be up for grabs in this new federally funded marketplace. Yet, providers estimate only 2 to 3 percent of eligible students elected to participate in the first year of the program.

The supplemental services program is perhaps the federal government's largest free-market experiment in education. So far, more than a thousand tutoring providers have signed on to the program. But market uncertainty, combined with enormous variance in school districts' administration of the new federal law, produced some extremely rocky terrain for these tutoring providers. Though most providers maintain an optimistic if-you-build-it-they-will-come mind-set, the unevenness of parent participation and program implementation is causing significant anxiety among providers.

In the Beginning

Just days after his inauguration, President Bush sent Congress his proposal to reauthorize the Elementary and Secondary Education Act, which he called No Child Left Behind. The reauthorization was long overdue because a politically polarized Congress failed to produce a bill during the 2000 election year. To cut past partisanship, Bush convened a meeting, shortly after submitting his plan, with four key members of Congress—two Republicans and two Democrats, including Democratic stalwart Sen. Edward M. Kennedy of Massachusetts—for a meet-and-greet photo op at a public school in Washington, D.C. Though

Bush's No Child Left Behind bill ultimately proved bipartisan, it was the product of many ideological compromises. Now that the bill is in its implementation phase, it's become painfully clear that those compromises made elements of the bill, such as the supplemental services program, overly complicated, confusing, and perhaps unworkable.

Based largely on Bush's education reform proposal on the campaign trail, the No Child Left Behind bill required testing in reading and math for children in grades 3 through 8. Schools with test scores showing that students couldn't make adequate performance from year to year would be labeled "failing," or more gently, "in need of improvement." In their first year under that label, schools would receive an infusion of cash to help them make improvements. But schools that failed for two years in a row would have to allow their children to transfer to higher-performing public schools. And students in schools that failed three years straight would be eligible for an "exit voucher" worth about $1,500 toward a private school education.

But Bush made it clear from the outset that he was far more interested in having a proposal he could call bipartisan to burnish his "uniter-not-a-divider" credentials than he was in having a proposal that included a controversial voucher program. Even Bush's centrist Democrat allies had sent early signals that vouchers were a no-go. Then, in an early meeting with two senior White House aides, Sen. Kennedy tossed out the possibility that he might support a program that allowed the would-be "exit voucher" money to go instead toward tutoring. And the tutoring could be called the more politically palatable "supplemental services."

Once they recovered from the shock of Kennedy's offer, White House aides huddled with Republican senators to craft the provision. The White House's hope was that the tutoring voucher would be a sufficient sanction for failing schools because school districts had to pay for that tutoring out of the federal money they'd otherwise use in house. Bush also hoped the outside tutoring would give students in struggling schools an educational opportunity beyond what they'd otherwise be able to afford, which might also make small inroads for the school choice movement.

It took several attempts to construct a measure that Kennedy's team would accept. Anything that allowed parents to receive money directly from the federal government for tutoring was out because Democrats felt it looked too much like a voucher. Eventually, lawmakers modeled the provision after the Reading Excellence Act, which put several layers of government between Washington and parents. Typical of the kinds of compromises struck in Congress, it didn't make for a terribly user-friendly program. As one Senate Republican aide involved in the negotiations said, "Most education proposals start off from a very practical standpoint, and when they go through the bipartisan sausage maker, they become impractical because each side gets its two cents." Supplemental services was no exception.

Under the supplemental services program, states first approve a group of tutoring providers based on state criteria. Then districts draw up their own contracts with a subset of those providers. (Districts, themselves, can also be providers unless the whole district is on the "in need of improvement" list.) The contract spells out what services will be available, such as how many hours of tutoring they will provide for the district's set offering price. Districts then notify parents of their options. Parents must then enroll with the provider of their choosing. Meanwhile, tutoring providers try to be in the right place at the right time to take advantage of new business opportunities.

The bill's funding requirements give school districts considerable leeway in deciding how much to spend on tutoring, which ranges anywhere from $700 to $2,000 per child. The funding requirements for supplemental services in the new law have left districts and providers confused about how much they must spend on each child.

- First, the new law requires each district to spend at least 5 percent of the money it receives from a section known as "Part A" of the federal Title I program designated for educating poor children. This works out to anywhere between $37 million in a large city like New York to a few thousand dollars in small districts.
- Second, the bill requires districts to set aside 20 percent of that pot of Title I money for all "school choice" costs, which includes money for transporting children who transfer to another public school. School districts decide how much money they spend on tutoring, so long as it falls somewhere within this 5 to 20 percent range.
- Third, whatever money goes unspent through lack of demand, districts keep. And districts see the requirement to spend money on outside tutoring as a punishment.

When states took their first pass at implementing the program in the 2002–2003 academic year, a host of problems came to light. States established very short deadlines for providers to get their seal of approval. School districts applied in droves to be providers, which set up a potential conflict of interest because district officials were also responsible for administering the supplemental services program as a whole. Providers found it impossible to predict how many students they might have. And parents largely ignored the program.

As the 2003–2004 year's program revved up with nearly full participation from the states, only a few of the previous year's problems were addressed. For the most part, states have smoothed out their approval process, and there are some early indications that some more children may be taking advantage of the program. Still, most of the implementation problems await solutions.

The New Marketplace: A Snapshot

Before the No Child Left Behind Act, the marketplace for tutoring services was dominated by private tutoring businesses, which largely served well-off suburban children whose parents wanted them to get a leg up on their peers. This market, known as the retail tutoring market, was about $2 billion strong, according to Educate Inc., a national tutoring company better known by its previous name, Sylvan Learning Systems. In the retail tutoring marketplace, half of the tutoring providers were small local companies and individuals offering tutoring services, and the other half was made up of regional or national providers. In addition to the retail tutoring market, there was also a small, informal effort to promote public-private partnerships in tutoring, but it wasn't a well-defined marketplace. Educate Inc. tried to take advantage of both markets by splitting its operations into two companies. Sylvan Learning Centers offers tutoring from its own storefronts. Catapult Learning (formerly Sylvan Education Solutions) partners with schools for on-site tutoring.

The No Child Left Behind Act created a marketplace for publicly funded tutoring, but it's been difficult for providers or the government to get a handle on its scope because the program is new and has so many moving parts. At this point, federally funded tutoring represents a small and scattered marketplace with significant growth potential. In the early days of this program, there's been an explosion of tutoring providers—numbering more than a thousand nationally. The biggest players are large tutoring companies and school districts. Still, what we do understand about the market is far outpaced by what we do not.

Much of this interest is driven by the potential for big money. The total market could be as large as $2.4 billion and serve as many as 1.5 million children, according to Catapult. But other providers, such as Edison Schools, offer a more conservative estimate of $500 million.[2] Regardless, in the 2002–2003 school year, only an estimated thirty thousand to forty thousand children took advantage of the free tutoring, according to Catapult.[3] While

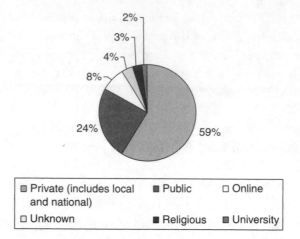

Figure 3.1. Kinds of Providers, October 2003

(*Source*: The U.S. Department of Education.)

2002–2003 represented only a partial implementation of the program, many providers worry that the 2003–2004 numbers won't shape up much differently because, by and large, parents still don't know about the program.

On the providers' side, at my last count in October and November 2003, there were close to 1,030 different tutoring providers approved to operate in the country. More than 60 national tutoring companies are approved in multiple states, and a tally of the number of providers approved in each state produces a national total of more than 1,450. The Education Department, which has been tracking the total providers in each state, found as of October 2003 that more than 70 percent of those providers were private and that 24 percent were part of the public school system (see figure 3.1).

The Department has also found enormous variance in the kinds of providers available among the states. Public schools represent anywhere from zero to 80 percent of the providers. Online providers could be anywhere from zero to 47 percent of available options. Religiously affiliated providers range from zero to 13 percent of the total providers, and universities represent between zero and 20 percent. There is also significant variation in the number of providers approved among the states. In my count at the outset of the 2003–2004 school year, they ranged from nearly 150 in Georgia to zero in Florida and appear to have only a mild correlation with the state's overall school-age population, which is largest in California, followed by Texas, New York, and Florida.

A caveat: Supplemental services statistics should be taken only as an estimate. All statistics on this program leave out at least four states—Florida, Maine, Nebraska, and Wyoming—which had yet to approve providers or had yet to compile their lists as for this writing in fall 2003. The total number of providers fluctuates because the state lists of approved providers change constantly, and not all states are diligent about updating their lists. Plus, for providers, making the state-approved list is only the first step. Just because a provider is approved in a state doesn't mean it has significant, or any, market penetration in that state.

Additionally, this numbers crunching revealed much about what we don't yet know. As of fall 2003, some surprisingly basic information fell into the "what we don't know" category. Here are a few samples:

- There are no firm numbers on the total number of children eligible for supplemental services. As of fall 2003, neither the Education Department nor providers had a real sense of how many children were likely to enroll in the coming year.
- As for cost, there's been no calculation of how much the federal government spent last year on supplemental services, nor is there a sense of how much it will spend this year.
- No one is counting new private providers—those who started up solely because of the supplemental services program.
- There is no national tally of the proportion of children who enroll in district programs versus other kinds of programs. Policymakers need one to help untangle important questions around districts that wear two hats—as an administrator of supplemental services and a tutoring provider.

Any good market analysis should tackle market share, but such an analysis isn't possible yet because there's no listing, nationally, of how many students are actually being served by a given provider or type of provider. Right now, the only way anyone can guess at market share is by counting the number of states in which a provider has been approved, which offers only the vaguest sense of market share.

It's understandable that there are many unanswered questions about this marketplace because the policy and practice are both very new. In discussions with researchers at institutions like the American Institutes for Research (AIR) and WestEd, non-profit research groups evaluating supplemental services for the Department of Education, it appears that most research on supplemental services is currently focused on case studies of districts to begin to work through questions of the best way to implement the new law.[4] Implementation studies are important, but so are examinations of the marketplace, which will shed considerable light on the strengths and weaknesses of this new policy.

Five Types of Providers

As this new marketplace evolves, five major provider cliques are emerging:
(1) large for-profit corporations; (2) school districts; (3) small for-profit firms;
(4) non-profit community-based organizations; and (5) online companies. At
this point, large corporate providers and school districts seem to be ruling the
marketplace. And their shares are likely to increase as the program matures
because both types of providers have the greatest ability to scale up and scale
back with market demands.

The Popular Crowd

Jeffrey Cohen was following the supplemental services program long before
it became law. As president of Catapult Learning, Cohen saw potential for
expansion under a federal tutoring program because it mirrored what he'd
been doing for 15 years—partnering with low-income schools to bolster their
lessons. "We see the supplemental services legislation as an affirmation of
what we've been doing," he says.

With their brand recognition, snazzy ads, and glossy brochures, large
corporate providers are the popular kids. Only a handful of players are in this
category (see figure 3.2). Still, this elite group appears to have the greatest
potential to garner a large market share because the companies in this category are approved in 20 to 30 states. Large corporate firms like Catapult have
been providing elementary and secondary tutoring to paying clients, so these
companies are well positioned to scale up their business.

With supplemental services, Cohen has had to tweak his business model:
though Cohen deals solely with schools in his regular business, under

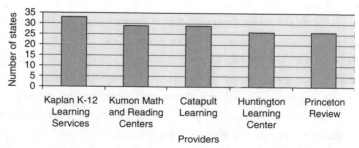

Figure 3.2. Top providers

(*Source*: American Institutes for Research and Original Reporting.)

supplemental services he must get approved by the state, contract with a district, and then sell his product directly to parents. He tries to work with the school district to allow Catapult to offer its tutoring at schools or nearby. Cohen says the supplemental services program offers him two opportunities: (1) to reach many more children, whose schools would not otherwise pay for Catapult's services, and (2) to build relationships with school districts, which could lead to further business outside the supplemental services program.

At the outset of the 2003–2004 school year, Catapult was approved in 29 states and projected it would serve between fifteen thousand and thirty thousand supplemental services students that year. In 2002–2003, Catapult served six thousand students, whom it charged anywhere between $40 and $80 an hour. In the coming years, Cohen says, supplemental services students could double his overall enrollment of seventy thousand students. "The first year, the program certainly wasn't profitable," he says. But he sees at least a 10 percent profit margin in its future.

Catapult's is not the only business model among large corporate providers. Princeton Review, approved in 26 states, has taken a school-based tack in which it negotiates with districts in the hopes of becoming a district's or school's sole provider. "We're looking to partner with districts that are actively interested in supplemental services," says Rob Cohen (who is of no relation to Jeffrey Cohen), executive vice president of the company's K-12 division. "I don't look at this as a retail business, like putting up billboards on the highways. I'm looking for districts to call us up." One Education Department official has said, however, that contracting with just one provider violates the new education law.

Still, Rob Cohen's hope is that he can avoid some of the headaches of working with school districts that are dragging their feet in implementing the program by simply not working with them. In the 2003–2004 school year, Princeton Review anticipates anywhere between twenty-five hundred and ten thousand supplemental services students. And Rob Cohen is projecting 50 percent growth in the next few years.

A third strategy among big tutoring companies that is popular with retail tutoring companies that operate from a storefront like Huntington Learning Centers is to just open the program they currently offer to supplemental services students. Transportation to these tutoring centers, which are often located in suburban strip malls, is up to the parents. In the 2002–2003 academic year, Huntington served five hundred supplemental services children, and Russ Miller, Huntington's vice president for new business development, estimated an enrollment of more than two thousand in 2003–2004. But the biggest challenge facing companies like Huntington, says Miller, is getting students to come. Huntington is evaluating two new options for reaching supplemental services students. One would establish centers in urban areas. The other would partner with schools to make the school the site of a Huntington learning center.

One player in this category has surprised the competition with the slowness of its entrance into this new marketplace: Edison Schools. Edison is a national school management company, and many large firms expected it to be a big player out of the gates. In the fall of 2003 it was approved only in nine states—about a third the number of its big corporate competitors. Having spent a year on research and development, Edison waited until late spring to market itself as a tutoring provider.

But while Edison served only a couple hundred students in 2002–2003, it served six thousand the following fall of 2003. Edison owes much of its 2003–2004 growth to setting up shop in New York City. At this point Edison Vice President Joel Rose, like his comrades, attributes his company's sluggish start to low parental participation and the unpredictability of getting selected by those parents that do participate. "Are we going to get half the school's population? Ten percent of the population?" he says. "It depends on who's got basketball practice and what other programs are going on at the school."

The Bullies

John Liechty knows a market when he sees one. At the beginning of the 2003–2004 school year, 186,000 of the nearly 750,000 students in the Los Angeles Unified School District were eligible for supplemental services. As the associate superintendent for extended day programs, Liechty sees tutoring as his district's "lifeblood," and he'd like the keep the money designated for it in the district. He also sees the program as a chance to tap new ideas from private companies and incorporate those ideas into the classroom. So he applied to the state to be a supplemental services provider and designed a Saturday school program that would contract out the actual tutoring to private providers.

With their ability to be a provider and control the districtwide funding for all supplemental services, districts have an enormous amount of control over the tutoring options available. That level of control offers up the opportunity for districts to bully other providers, and they're wielding that power in obvious and subtle ways. Though each district's reach is limited in scope, school districts as a group are becoming major players in this new provider marketplace. Of the more than one thousand providers nationwide, about one third are public schools. Some districts, like Los Angeles, use their provider status to contract with private providers. Others, like Toledo Public Schools, have opted to develop their own programs.

In Los Angeles, the district tutored about half of the thirteen thousand students who signed up for the supplemental services program in fall 2003. The district's main role is to provide administrative support and transportation services—and classrooms. Liechty is responsible for running the district's tutoring program and for administering the supplemental service program, which includes 26 different providers (of which Los Angeles Unified is only one) that have established contracts with the district.

Each of the district's six tutoring centers is run by a different company, like Kaplan. (Though in Los Angeles, no company is both subcontracting with the district and establishing itself as a separate provider in the area.) "Each one of those centers becomes almost a lab," Liechty says. "I'm looking for everybody and anybody to partner with." Liechty says this arrangement allows him to exercise more quality control and bargain down the price. Liechty hopes to double his enrollment in the next several years to around twenty-five thousand. He also needs to figure out how to turn a profit. So far, he's operating with net losses, which he said were somewhere between $40,000 and $400,000.

Smaller school districts may be on an even steeper learning curve. When Toledo Public Schools saw it might lose a lot of federal money, it decided to adapt its summer school program into an after-school course for supplemental services students. The program, says Georgianne Czerniak, a literacy support teacher with the Toledo Public Schools' Reading Academy, offers "an opportunity for the district to offer the service with trained teachers and to keep the money in the district." The summer school program posted great results: more than half the students gained grade-level proficiency after six weeks of classes 10 hours a week. But the tutoring program is only three hours a week for six weeks because that's all they can currently do with the $1,500 per student they receive. Calculating readers will note this works out to $83 an hour. Czerniak is struggling to find a business model that works.

In fall 2003, the plan was to offer primary and intermediate reading sessions for groups of 10 students at a few locations around the district. But only 23 students signed up for the Reading Academy. (Only 133 of the 1,544 eligible students districtwide enrolled in a supplemental services program.) She then discovered that all the parents wanted the tutoring sessions to be held at the schools their children regularly attended, so she scattered her program throughout the district with three or four children to a tutor. Another unanticipated cost was paying for an on-site administrator, as negotiated by the administrator's union.

Czerniak says her best chance to keep her program alive is to boost enrollment. She'd like it to reach 150 students in the next couple of years, so she hopes to enlist her fellow teachers in her effort. "We'd like it to be a money-making venture for us, too," Czerniak says. "I don't know what kind of profit we're going to make. We may even lose money this time around."

The Overachievers

Mark Lucas was skeptical about the opportunities he would find in the new federal tutoring program. As the CEO and founder of Club Z's national operation, he wasn't sure the federal money would every reach the pockets of for-profit providers. But when some Club Z franchises like Scott Morchower's were awarded contracts, Lucas' royalties increased tenfold, and that got his attention.

Meet the overachievers, the entrepreneurs, the class presidents. Club Z is one of a number of smaller, national corporate players that are less established but have an opportunity to tap into an important market niche: parents who want the reliability of a national company but the feel of a local tutor. It's difficult to gauge the market share this group holds, but it's small—probably no more than 1 percent of the thousand or so providers. Still, it has a potential to claim a fair share of the marketplace.

Launched in 1995, Club Z's claim to fame is that it offers in-home tutoring. Across the country, Club Z's regular program serves fifty thousand students a year. And after Lucas saw the surge in royalty checks, he decided the whole company should get involved, and he applied for state approval. As of fall 2003, Club Z was approved in 21 states. So far, Lucas says, Club Z is serving five thousand supplemental services children.

"One of the reasons we're so popular is we go to the home," Lucas says. How can he do it? Club Z trains a bevy of local tutors and then calls on them as needed and pays them only for the hours they work. Overhead costs are minimal, and Lucas says they are able to attract better tutors because they pay their teachers half of their $35 hourly rate. He says that pay compares favorably to his larger competitors, which pay their tutors around $9 an hour. And Club Z isn't much more expensive than, say, Princeton Review, which charges around $25 an hour. So Club Z offers parents fewer hours of tutoring, but it's one-on-one—and at home.

Lucas anticipates serving around ten thousand students within the next two years through supplemental services. "Our business model allows us to take advantage of programs like this because we're mobile," he says. The model has caught the eye of researchers like Larraine Roberts, a senior research associate at WestEd. "It's a unique approach," she said. "They're like the McDonald's of tutoring centers, and they bring the hamburgers right to the house."

The Do-Gooders

The supplemental services program has been a boon for Pastor Darius Pridgen at True Bethel Baptist Church in Buffalo, N.Y. A former school board member, Pridgen started a math tutoring program at his church four years ago to help students pass New York's math graduation requirement. But with a $4,000 budget and an all-volunteer tutoring force, the program was "mediocre," Pridgen says. Pridgen only recently learned about the supplemental services program. "Now the picture has changed dramatically," Pridgen says. Partnering with a housing project next door, which houses many children who attend a nearby failing school, the True Bethel program doubled in size, from 50 to 100 children, within a just few months.

Motivated largely by a desire to help children, the do-gooders earnestly work to improve local access to tutoring. Organizations in this group take the form of local non-profits, small businesses, and religious organizations. They probably represent the largest proportion of the thousand-plus providers— maybe 50–60 percent—because they're the cleanup crew. When the national companies decide a given area isn't profitable, local organizations are the only non-public school option parents have. A great number of community-based groups—such as YMCAs (at least nine), Boys and Girls Clubs (at least 14), and even churches—have added on or expanded tutoring operations because of the federal tutoring money. Still because these organizations are so diffuse and each individual organization serves relatively few, this group is unlikely to collectively influence the marketplace.

At True Bethel, Pridgen has switched from volunteer to hired tutors, and a certified teacher is on site during the three-day-a-week after-school program. He says paid staff are far more accountable. A member of the congregation, a math teacher, offered to get together with a few colleagues and write up the curriculum. And Pridgen has expanded the program to include children as young as sixth grade. While the previous program was available only for members of the congregation, this one is open to everyone, and the church provides limited transportation with its own bus.

But expansion presented a new quandary for Pridgen: what to do about struggling neighborhood students whose schools aren't eligible for supplemental services? He couldn't turn them away. "It's a little like robbing Peter to pay Paul," he says. But it's easier with a $100,000 budget, $80,000 of which comes from the supplemental services money.

The Geeks

In spring of 2002, Massachusetts's education department rang Burck Smith. His start-up company, SMARTHINKING, offered live, online, one-on-one tutoring 24 hours a day to college students. Would SMARTHINKING be able to offer a similar service for the state's struggling tenth-graders who needed to pass the state test? Smith, who had founded SMARTHINKING in 1999, thought he'd give it a shot. "We'd always thought we'd move into the highschool tutoring market," he said. "The overlap between high school and college tutoring is really dramatic." The company worked with two thousand high school sophomores and juniors and worked out problems along the way. So when the supplemental services program came along, Smith knew he had to get in the game.

The geeks are doggedly trying to make virtual tutoring as good as the real thing. Representing probably less than 1 percent of the thousand-plus unique providers nationally and 13 percent of the 1,450 approved providers in each state, online providers are still an unknown quantity. But they could fill an important niche in serving students who don't want to or can't get to a site-based provider. Major providers like Catapult are exploring ways to establish an online tutoring services. Online providers still have a long way to go to prove they are as effective as an in-person tutoring experience, but Smith sees the supplemental services program as a way to gain access to the public student market and to prove itself.

By fall 2003, SMARTHINKING was approved in 15 states. In the 2002–2003 school year, it served two hundred children. In the 2003–2004 academic year, Smith said he hoped to reach eight hundred students. Smith is facing the same low-participation problems that his competitors are, but one unique problem he and other online providers face is attendance. Smith learned from his program in Massachusetts that students tend to attend more when supervised. So he's pursuing that option where possible. His staff also follows up repeatedly with parents who sign their children up with SMARTHINKING, which can be a challenge with parents working odd hours.

Still, Smith says his online business model is one that is perfect for the supplemental services program. Though other companies need a critical mass of students to ensure profitability, Smith's doesn't. Plus, he has no fixed costs associated with delivering his program, beyond what he's already spent to develop the software and the cost of hiring additional tutors. SMAR-THINKING has quality advantages, too, Smith says. With a decentralized business model, he can get higher quality employees. More than 80 percent of his tutors have master's or doctorate degrees. He provides both English- and Spanish-speaking tutors. And it's no trouble to bring his services to scale if there's a surge in interest. In a few years, he says, he hopes to be serving ten thousand supplemental services students.

Location, Location, Location

In determining where to locate, all national providers have one guiding principle: profitability. And in this black box–like supplemental services marketplace, gauging a district's profitability is difficult. "There are a lot of moving pieces here that drive how profitable a particular district might be," says Edison's Rose. One major difference between supplemental services and most other federal education programs is that this program leaves it up to the invisible hand of the free market to determine what kinds of tutoring services are available where. There are no guarantees that providers will be evenly dispersed throughout the country. In fact, prudent business planning would ensure they won't be.

When it comes to deciding where to set up shop, some of the criteria are obvious: consumer base and revenue. But several other criteria are more specific to supplemental services: ease of working with a given district, the company's existing operation sites, and informal personal networks.

For providers, the first step is to get approved by the state. In the 2002–2003 academic year, the process was largely haphazard because states set deadlines for their applications in very short, seemingly arbitrary windows of time. Among providers, it was a standing joke that New York gave providers a half-hour window to apply. Applications also varied. While Wisconsin's took three hours to complete, Louisiana's took a week. But that hasn't stopped large providers. Like most large, national providers, Princeton Review "took the approach to basically apply everywhere," says Stephen Kutno, who until recently ran Princeton Review's K-12 division and is now with Scholastic Inc. So if a district emerges as a good business opportunity, the company is poised to jump on it.

State requirements for approval also vary widely. According to the Supplemental Educational Services Quality Center at AIR, 22 states have set out criteria against which to judge provider quality in "scoring rubrics." Colorado, which is seen as a model, developed almost two dozen separate measures by which an applicant's quality is judged, including the program's record of effectiveness and its plan to monitor future performance. Georgia is the only state that has made distinctions between "emerging" and "standard," which allowed Georgia to approve many more providers by lowering the quality standards for emerging providers. Yet, officials in Colorado say they were told by the federal government that provisional approval isn't allowed.

Basic Criteria: Volume and Revenue

Once approved in a state, a provider has a license to operate, but it must still write up a contract with each district. In targeting the districts in which they want to locate, providers look primarily at potential business volume and pricing. To gauge volume, providers first look for districts that will offer the highest concentration of eligible children, and urban districts have the most to offer there. But because the ultimate decision lies with parents, even establishing a contract with a district doesn't guarantee a steady clientele. If a provider can't attract enough students, it pulls out. "There is a threshold," says Catapult's Jeffery Cohen, who adds that the threshold varies depending on the location and the cost of doing business there.

The revenue analysis is more complicated. Each district's offering price for annual spending on tutoring for each child will vary because the program is funded as a percentage of its federal Title 1 money. So states and districts may not offer enough to attract larger firms. For example, when Hawaii offered less than $700 per student, Princeton Review decided not to provide services there. "In that particular case, it was obviously not profitable," Kutno says.

In addition, while providers were under the impression that each district would set a per-student offering price for tutoring, many districts have told providers that they will pay only an hourly rate for a child's tutoring. So rather than receive a flat per-child payment, a number of providers are paid only for the time the child uses rather than the amount of time the child signs up for, which has made it difficult for providers to gauge how much they will make in a given district. Some providers claim this practice is in violation of the law. The Education Department isn't taking sides. "This is a can of worms that ought to be worked out at the local level or with the states," said one Education Department official.

Specific Criteria: District Relations, Infrastructure, Networks

One of the toughest elements to gauge in this decision-making process is the ease with which a provider can work with a district. The biggest red flag, say providers, is whether the district itself is a provider. That alone might be enough for a private provider to look for business elsewhere for fear the district will monopolize the local market. Providers meet with the district representatives and gauge a personality fit. They also do their homework on the district's history of working with outside vendors, and they scrutinize the contract. "Sometimes [Princeton Review] spent a lot of energy on the contract negotiation [with a district] only to have something not materialize," said Kutno.

For example, once approved in Tennessee, Princeton Review sought to work in Memphis and Nashville. But when it came time to draw up a contract, each school district interpreted the regulations differently. Memphis decided to assign one provider to each school, but Nashville allowed a free-for-all among its schools and wanted to negotiate hourly rates with each provider rather than pay a flat per-student fee. Princeton Review stayed with Memphis and dropped Nashville.

Another important part of the location calculation is existing infrastructure. For example, Jeffrey Cohen had planned to work with the San Diego Unified School District in 2002–2003, but he decided to pull out. "We weren't prepared with the right folks on the street in San Diego to develop the program and the site network and the relationship with the community," he said. "In that instance, we thought it was better to withdraw and come back to San Diego when we knew we had a game plan." Chicago, on the other hand, was perfect for Catapult last year because it had been working with Chicago Public Schools before the supplemental services program. "It was just a prudent business decision," Cohen explained. Catapult started up in San Diego the following year.

Another key piece of the location puzzle is the company's personal network. Edison, for example, tapped one of its board members, Floyd Flake, a minister and former U.S. representative, for connections he had with a key educator in New York City. While Edison's Rose declined to mention the educator's name, he said she is a former high school principal in New York City and is highly regarded in Queens. "Given her background and her network, she's been able to work through our network," Rose said. "Her presence, her credibility, and her talent on the operations side are key factors in getting individual schools to want to work with us." In fall 2003, Edison signed up three thousand students in New York City, which made it the second largest provider there, behind the school district.

Uncertainties and Obstacles

Uncertainty is expensive. And its cost is reflected in higher prices. In the supplemental services world, where the price is fixed by each district, higher prices translate into fewer hours of tutoring for each child. So it's in the interest of policymakers to reduce, to the degree they can, the uncertainties and other obstacles that have emerged in the first year of the supplemental service program. Because so few districts and providers truly understand the dos and don'ts of supplemental services, they're stumbling along in a volatile marketplace. Providers say their biggest stumbling blocks are participation and school districts' administration of the program.

First, participation is wildly unpredictable. The number of eligible students varies each year. In addition, when parents do enroll their children, they choose among a number of providers, so it's nearly impossible for a provider to gauge how many parents will choose its program over the competition's. Many parents either don't know about or don't understand the program, and some are reluctant to sign up because they don't want to acknowledge that their child needs help. Scott Morchower of Club Z in Georgia said one of his toughest challenges is convincing parents that the service is free to them. Parents will often hang up on him because they think he's a telemarketer, he says. And sometimes parents simply don't want to acknowledge their child needs help. "Even when I come out to the house, they ask, 'What's wrong with my kid?'" Morchower says.

Second, administration, particularly at the district level, has been challenging. Districts wield an enormous amount of power in this program, and the federal program offers disincentives for districts to cooperate. The program is seen by districts as a punishment, and it allows districts to keep any money set aside for this program that goes unused. Providers complain that district implementation of the program has been extremely uneven. Some districts appear to be making a strong effort to implement new tutoring programs while many others' implementation has been more perfunctory.

One of the biggest responsibilities that districts have is informing parents of the program, and Los Angeles is a model district. In addition to an initial letter to parents, Liechty has mailed out colorful brochures touting a "$1000 scholarship for your child." The district is also running public service announcements on local radio and television programs. But other districts have done nothing more than write the letter required by the law and tuck it into a student's backpack. New Orleans Public Schools sent to parents a jargon-obscured letter focusing almost exclusively on how the district is complying with the law; the letter features multiple attachments and never explains that "supplemental educational services" means free tutoring.

Districts also throw up more subtle obstacles that impose hidden costs on private providers. As Princeton Review experienced in Nashville, a number of districts have decided to pay providers an hourly rate rather than a per-child rate, so they don't have to pay for the times when the student fails to show up. The cost of tutoring space is another hidden cost in many districts when a provider can't operate at the school, or they charge an impossibly high rate to do so, as they do is Los Angeles. "This is Los Angeles," Liechty says. "Most vendors can't afford it. We have not had one, yet, lease. I couldn't afford it either." But he says rent is a fair use of the district's competitive advantage.

The district contracting process can also be an onerous one in which districts haggle over the rates providers charge even though the law is designed to allow providers to set their price and let parents choose. And some providers say that districts are not actually setting aside the money they are required to by law. "We've seen districts where the federal per-pupil allocation says it's $1,800 and the district will say it's $1,100," said one provider. "What happens to that other $700?" The provider added, though, that fewer districts appear to be holing away extra money for themselves in the 2003–2004 school year.

Perhaps most significant is the districts' role as both a provider and administrator of the program, which produces an obvious potential for conflict of interest. The concern is that because districts have the most direct access to parents, they have an unfair advantage over other providers. Jeffery Cohen of Catapult witnessed letters by a district that automatically sign parents up for the district's program unless a parent affirmatively decided to go with a different provider. "There's not a level playing field," he says.

Some providers also say that allowing districts with failing schools to be providers is bad policy because such districts have already proven themselves to be failures. Failing districts cannot be providers, but districts that house failing schools can. Liechty says he does his best to administer all 26 tutoring programs fairly. "We try to be as transparent as possible so far as treating everybody equally," he says. Yet, he acknowledges that the district has an inside track with parents because the public schools are a known quantity. "We don't hide that," he says. "There's no question the district is going to have an advantage." Plus, the money going to private providers comes out of a pot of federal money that districts have historically counted on for their own. "You can't just expect teachers to roll over and give you $3 million," Liechty adds.

There are some small signs that district monopolies may recede with time. In New York, 88 percent of the children who took advantage of the program in 2002–2003 signed up with the school district, according to a recent study by Advocates for Children, a New York–based non-profit. In the 2003–2004 school year, however, only 65 percent did.

To overcome these obstacles, most large providers are going around districts by beefing up their own public education and marketing. Catapult runs public service announcement ads that simply explain the supplemental service program prior to the district's enrollment period for supplemental services. Then, during the enrollment period, Catapult touts its own program with leaflets or promoters who go door-to-door, to shopping malls, and, when allowed, to the school. Edison has also hired recruiters.

Most providers, however, remain optimistic and hope to be well positioned to take advantage when participation reaches its highly anticipated tipping point. "We're really talking exponential growth," says Rob Cohen of Princeton Review. "I really feel good about how things are proceeding, and I think there are some real opportunities here." Also, many large providers, like Edison and Princeton Review, know that other divisions of their company will benefit from relationships with more public schools. There are skeptics, though. "I don't ever want to be dependent on a government program," says a cautious Morchower of Club Z. "If they pull the plug on me, where am I?"

Emerging Issues

As this program matures, the issues it will face are likely to be less about participation and more about access and quality. On the access side, the program may eventually have to worry about overenrollment as well as getting services to non-urban schools. On the quality control side, there are looming questions about who should be monitoring the quality of tutoring—and how best to do it.

Access

What happens if more children sign up for tutoring than the district can pay for? The law requires the district to prioritize students based on how far they are behind academically. Those who are furthest behind are at the top of the eligibility list. But turning away kids who are in perpetually failing schools is not an ideal public policy outcome. So as the program catches on, providers, school districts, and the federal government will need to think through how to handle such a situation beyond what's already outlined in the law. They could start by lifting the 20 percent limit on school-choice spending from federal Title I money.

In addition, children from rural schools may be left out. In some rural areas the only option is online tutoring, and the belief that online tutoring is a panacea for rural schools isn't true. Not only does that notion assume Internet access and computer ownership among poor rural families, but it also assumes that online providers will be a successful format for all children—or any children. It's also not clear that online providers are interested in serving sparse rural communities. At SMARTHINKING, Smith's approach to marketing so far has been the same logical choice as his competitors: Go where the children are. "It's just not cost-effective to do outreach in a rural county," he says.

There's also no guarantee that tough-to-educate children will actually receive tutoring. Providers in a free market reserve the right to refuse services to children whom they deem to be too difficult. In Colorado, Laura Hensinger, a senior Title 1 consultant for the state education department, said she's run into providers who say they won't provide services to anyone whose parent won't attend tutoring with their child. Another refused to work with children who used drugs or are in gangs. And in New York City, Advocates for Children, a non-profit research and advocacy group, found that services are sorely lacking for children who don't speak English or are in special education.

Quality Control

Quality control may be the toughest challenge ahead, and officials at all levels of government are just beginning to struggle with it. The most basic challenge is deciding what success means for tutoring. It's tough to isolate the effect of a few hours of tutoring a week, especially when these children are in schools that are under great pressure to improve. If a student's scores go up, how do you know it's the tutoring and not a new reading curriculum? Or an attentive parent?

How does the Education Department define success in this program? "I wish I had a sound bite on that," says one Education Department official. He says ideally, districts would compare the performance of their students who take advantage of the tutoring to those who don't, but he acknowledges, "In the real world, is anyone going to have the fiscal resources to do that?" He added that at the very least, the federal government should establish a guide for states to help determine what a provider must show to prove it is delivering results.

Right now, the provider determines how success will be measured, and it's up to the states to look over each provider's shoulder. With such loose and undefined enforcement, each provider defines success differently. In reviewing provider applications, Colorado's Hensinger has seen the range—from improved performance on the provider's self-fashioned tests to increased school attendance.

If quality control is going to happen, it will probably be at the state level. Some states are beginning to think about quality control, but the process is currently more art than science. In Colorado, Hensinger says her office is in the process of developing a state monitoring system because right now "it's practically impossible" to weed out bad providers. That monitoring program, she says, will probably include some kind of paper-based reporting in which providers submit their results, in combination with visits from state education department officials. Still, that's not a terribly systematic process. And while the best monitoring for quality control would, in theory, happen at the district level, the current incentives in the law aren't conducive to an impartial quality-control assessment.

In addition, districts remain concerned about how well after school tutoring programs will mesh with the school's curriculum. (See chapter 9 of this book.) Princeton Review has established a modular program that adapts to state standards. Edison plans to establish ways for teachers and tutors to communicate about an individual student's progress. Still, many, and probably most, providers work solely from their own curriculum, and beyond truly basic skills like addition and multiplication, students are unlikely to learn much from a tutoring program they see as irrelevant to their classwork.

Implementation

Before policymakers worry about quality control, they need to make sure the program is being implemented in the first place. The federal government's primary focus right now is implementation. One of the Education Department's top concerns is making parents aware of the program because if no one takes advantage of the tutoring, it doesn't matter how good or awful a tutoring program is. In the fall of 2003, the department developed public service announcements that ran in major cities to help seed the market. The department has also commissioned research groups like WestEd and AIR to study implementation efforts in select districts with an eye toward developing implementation models that other districts can emulate.

In addition, the department is monitoring specific districts' efforts at implementation in a "non-systematic way," says an Education Department official. When providers or parents complain, the federal government will investigate. Still, he says, often the issue is whether the district is truly implementing the spirit of the law, not whether it's following the law's basic requirements. "It's not black and white what full implementation means," the official said. "It's a kind of gray area."

In the end, there are limitations to the kind of federal and state enforcement that can be accomplished without willing participants. And as the program matures, we may find that what's really needed is not even so much monitoring and quality control, but buy-in. "A lot of this is going to succeed or fail not on whether they implement the law, but how well they implement the law," said one Education Department official.

Concluding Thoughts

As policymakers forge ahead, this baseline survey of the supplemental services marketplace highlights many areas in which the new federal program needs considerable work: (1) improving participation levels; (2) quality control; (3) data collection; and (4) general enforcement of compliance with the law.

Poor participation is the program's most immediate challenge, and it's the area in which both providers and the federal government have exerted the strongest effort to make improvements. When it became clear they could not rely solely on districts to educate parents about the program, both the federal government and providers decided to do it themselves. But the district's failure to educate parents points to a major problem in the program's incentive system. So long as districts get to keep any tutoring money that goes unspent, they have no reason to encourage parents to avail themselves of the tutoring program. Until those incentives are altered, districts can be expected to drag their feet.

Quality control seems to be an afterthought. It's a huge responsibility that the federal government is dropping on the states, without being explicit about it. Though the federal government expects the states to monitor for quality control, it has given the states no guidance in how to determine a good or a bad provider. In fact, the federal government hasn't even decided what constitutes a successful tutoring program. Without these most basic guidelines, there can be no expectation that states will do high-quality quality control—or will do any at all. The current let-a-hundred-flowers-bloom approach to quality control is wholly incapable of ensuring meaningful tutoring for these children.

Perhaps the most important building block for quality control—both of the tutoring programs and the supplemental services program as a whole—is data collection. And for an administration that has been so strong on data collection and accountability in the rest of its elementary and secondary education programs, surprisingly little data are being collected on supplemental services, a totally untested program.

At the very least, the Education Department should know how much it spent on the program in the 2002–2003 school year and how many children are eligible for the program in a given year. But in order to gauge whether the supplemental services program is working or not, the department ought to be collecting information on a host of measures. To name a few:

- How many children are actually signing up with different types of tutoring providers: large corporate, school districts, community-based non-profits?
- Are new tutoring organizations starting up solely because of this program, and if so how many?
- What is driving parents' decisions to participate or not participate?
- What is driving parents' decisions in choosing one tutoring provider over another?
- How do the children who participate in tutoring fare academically?

The other troubling finding of this chapter is that no one has determined who should be in charge. The federal government's approach is largely to let the states innovate. The states don't know what to do because they don't have enough direction from the federal government. So, the real responsibility falls to the districts, which are closest to the purse strings. Yet, districts tend to be the most reluctant partner in the process. If this program is to work, the federal government must make some tough decisions about who is responsible for what and be explicit about it. And to be fair, if it turns out that the states (or districts) are really responsible for coordinating, implementing, and monitoring this program, there must be some acknowledgment that this effort is time and labor intensive. If the federal government wants robust implementation and quality control, it should pay for some, if not all, of it.

As this marketplace matures, two big winners among the providers are likely to emerge: corporate providers and school districts. They have the greatest number of resources; the greatest capacity to reach parents and children;

and the economies of scale to absorb the unpredictability inherent in this marketplace. Ultimately, the two groups may join forces, which would look a lot like the Los Angeles Unified School District. "I think the largest provider nationwide will be schools," says Rob Cohen of Princeton Review. "They have all the teachers. They have all the buildings." Cohen says this is a good thing. Though he acknowledges that providing the services directly to children is more profitable, he may be able to get a greater market share of a new market that sells materials to public schools than he can in the current marketplace. And it may be a way to ensure that the districts have incentives to both participate and monitor private providers.

In this Darwin-meets-public-education school reform, performance will (one hopes) matter a lot, too. That detail is not lost on large providers. "Those that will rise to the top will be those who are getting results," said Huntington's Miller. "Did the [state test] scores improve, and if they did, which provider did the student work with?"

That's the ideal, anyway.

Notes

1. This situation speaks to one of the many conflicting incentives in the supplemental services program—the better the tutoring program, the more likely the tutoring provider will lose business in subsequent years. When the students' performance improves enough to get their school off the failing list, those students are no longer eligible for tutoring.
2. Catapult's calculations are based on the maximum amount that districts could spend on the program—20 percent of what is known as "Part A" of the Education Department's Title 1 program. Part A of Title 1 represents the bulk of federal funding a district receives for "educationally disadvantaged" children. Federal officials estimate the actual numbers to be somewhat smaller. Edison's estimate, which looks toward the 2004–2005 academic year, takes into account projected demand for services. Edison also calculated its numbers based on a more conservative assumption of supply—that 15 percent of the Title I Part A money would go toward supplemental services.
3. At press time, the Education Department had yet to complete its tally of 2002–2003 participants, so Catapult's numbers were the only ones available.
4. The American Institutes for Research, which provides research services for a wide range of policy issues, has established a Supplemental Educational Services Quality Center to evaluate the program as part of its contract with the U.S. Department of Education. WestEd is one of the country's regional educational laboratories, which evaluate education policy, including a major contract with the Education Department to evaluate supplemental services.

4

Options for Low-Income Students: Evidence from the States

Robert Maranto and April Gresham Maranto[1]

When, as in the case of ESEA, a law unprecedented in scope has to be administered through state and local instrumentalities, on an impossible time schedule, by an understaffed agency in structural turnover, beset by a deluge of complaints and demands for clarification of the legislation at hand, as well as cognate legislation already on the books; the wonder is not that mistakes are made—the wonder is that the law is implemented at all.
—Stephen K. Bailey and Edith K. Mosher, 1968[2]

Introduction

The 2002 reauthorization of the Elementary and Secondary Education Act (ESEA), popularly called No Child Left Behind (NCLB), offers a revolutionary break from traditional U.S. education policy by permitting students in low-performing schools ("schools needing improvement") to move to other public schools where space is available, and to use their school's Title I funds to pay for tutoring, or, in edspeak, "supplemental services." But whether NCLB lives up to its promise depends on the efforts of state and local education officials to implement it.

Do state education departments designate sufficient numbers of schools needing improvement in sufficient time for parents to take advantage of their newfound school choice? Do states do so early enough that students can switch schools *before* rather than *after* school starts? Do states designate sufficient numbers of competent supplemental services providers? Do state education authorities ensure that local education authorities inform Title I parents of their options clearly and quickly?

We present data from e-mail and phone surveys of 60 state Title I officials, journalists, and education analysts in fall 2003 to examine whether the states designate schools needing improvement, and how much the states push school districts to implement the school choice and supplemental services provisions of NCLB. From interviews and other data, we've graded 41 states and the District of Columbia on their efforts to implement the choice-related provisions of NCLB. Implementation is naturally uneven at this preliminary stage. Some states seem to have made a good effort to approve supplemental services providers and to designate improvement schools in time for parents to choose alternative schools before school starts. Further, some states push local school districts to clearly communicate the new options to Title I parents. Others do not. Indeed, evaluation of state implementation in January 2004 found that the typical state rated only a D+, when efforts were measured on an 8 point scale. Only Hawaii, New Jersey, and West Virginia scored so well as a B-, leaving much room for improvement. In particular, roughly half the states do not list the schools needing improvement before school starts; thus Title I parents in those schools have limited ability to choose alternative options.

Given the broad scope of NCLB and its sharp break with past policies, many states are probably doing about as well as can be expected in the second year of the law's implementation. Still, whether the states make progress depends on the efforts of the U.S. Department of Education to push states to move ahead in the face of school district reluctance, or outright opposition. Even more crucial, NCLB's long-term success may depend on the degree to which journalists and state and local activists pressure school districts to fully implement the law.

Implementing NCLB: First Reports

NCLB is the most significant federal education legislation since the 1960s. Among other things, NCLB requires annual proficiency testing in reading and math for grades 3–8 and forces states to publish results of school-level testing broken down by subgroup (ethnicity, special education, free lunch status, and English-speaking status). Schools that fail to meet adequate yearly progress (AYP) for one or more subgroups for consecutive years are designated "schools needing improvement." Title I parents in such Title I schools can send their children to other public schools during the first year of improvement status, and in the second year of such status can use Title I money for supplemental services. In short, for the first time, school accountability and school choice may play a role in ESEA.[3]

Early evaluations suggest that the states are implementing NCLB. For example, *Education Week* reported that in 2003–2004 every state (and Washington, D.C.) planned to measure each school's AYP, compared with only 30[4] states in 2002–2003. Similarly, 43 states are publishing results from their tests in each area required by NCLB, a huge increase over the 16 of the previous year. States have identified more schools needing improvement, an estimated fifty-two hundred. As U.S. Secretary of Education Rod Paige states, "[e]very single school in our nation now has an accountability plan that covers every student. This is revolutionary. This alone is a powerful change of culture."[5] In addition to *Education Week* reports, the Educational Commission for the States (http://www.ecs.org) provides links to each state's required NCLB consolidated plan and rates each state's progress on issuing regulations regarding 40 NCLB requirements ranging from standards in key academic areas to inclusion of subgroups.

Journalists and scholars have examined the politics of developing account-ability measures and labeling schools as needing improvement. If states fail to develop reasonably demanding standards, then few or no schools will be found in need of improvement.[6] As we report below, only a few of our informants expressed such concerns. In contrast, states with the highest stan-dards risk looking the worst, and may have to spread limited political and material resources trying to improve too many schools at once; thus states may start with high standards and then relax them to meet political demands.[7] Some states have apparently lowered standards to avoid difficul-ties with NCLB requirements.[8] For example, Ohio redefined its criteria for failing schools, decreasing them from 760 to 212.[9]

While NCLB demands a wealth of data from schools on their perform-ances, states still struggle with how to analyze these data and reconcile their own assessment systems with those required by NCLB. This poses chal-lenges, as several respondents lamented. For example, one said:

> This gets very, very complicated. We merged our state and federal accountability sys-tems and the various lists of schools got on to each list by different criteria, so when we merged them it artificially inflated the number of schools on the [needing improve-ment] list. There were two different criteria, the Title I AYP criteria as opposed to what the state put in place, and the state's criteria were, I don't want to say lenient, but for a school to be even in the pool they had to score below a 40 in a norm referenced test, and if they scored below that they had to meet two growth factors, and so that did not identify a lot of schools. But we had a lot of other schools identified under Title I cri-teria for two years, that made the state standards but not [AYP]. We're so glad we're out of that because it was so complicated and confusing when we had to merge the systems.

Roughly half the states (23) use their own criteria as well as those mandated by NCLB to assess their schools.[10] The timing of a state's "testing window" also creates difficulties, as states with spring testing seasons struggle to report complicated AYP data to schools and parents by the start of the school year. As noted below, some states use preliminary rather than final school accountability designations, or use last year's designations to determine parent choice and supplemental services options. Finally, though NCLB required first reporting by the beginning of the 2002–2003 school year, it did not specify timing for subsequent reports, and the U.S. Department of Education has not yet pressured states to designate schools needing improvement before the school year begins.[11] Some complain of lax enforcement.[12]

These early works focus on the standards and accountability provisions of NCLB to the near exclusion of parental choice. Prior work does not examine the degree to which states and school districts provide for student transfers and tutoring.

Will States Implement the Parental-Choice Provisions of NCLB?

Like a Rube Goldberg mousetrap, the complicated school choice provisions of NCLB require the following difficult steps:

1. A state must develop accountability measures and apply those to its schools, finding that at least a few schools fail to measure up.
2. The state must approve capable supplemental services providers in sufficient numbers.
3. The state must disseminate the list of schools needing improvement to its local school districts and to the news media in time for parents to choose schools.
4. The school district must inform Title I parents in schools needing improvement of the school's status in an unambiguous manner, and must inform them of alternative public schools quickly enough for students to switch schools before the start of the school year.
5. The school district must inform Title I parents in schools needing improvement of supplemental services providers, and how to choose them.
6. Title I parents must choose to use (or not use) their school choice or supplemental services rights.

Each step is highly problematic. As noted above, there is currently little research on how states implement any of them, save for Step 1, school assessment and accountability. Obviously, if a state develops poor measures of school success, then parents may face the unpleasant prospect of moving their child from a school officially needing improvement to a public school that is no better. Assuming states measure school performance, other pitfalls remain. First, state education officials may not fully understand NCLB.[13] Notably, the U.S. Department of Education did not issue rules and regulations regarding how school districts should notify the parents of Title I children in Title I schools until December 2002.[14] As a Colorado state education official in the current study complained, "There were first-year implementation problems; we did not get U.S. Department of Education guidance and regulations until December of 02, so everyone was working on conflicting information on what the law actually said." If they do understand these NCLB requirements, states may nonetheless attempt to delay implementation; even if states don't delay, local districts might.

Regarding Step 2, if a state approves few or no supplemental services providers (or poor ones), parents cannot take advantage of this provision of NCLB. Pinkerton et al.[15] report that some school districts complain that private tutoring drains resources and that parents resist a longer school day. Some districts act as their own providers. Not surprisingly, states that best implement the supplemental services provisions are those with similar plans already in place. Rural states, in contrast, face special difficulties, and our informants state that they often rely on Internet providers.[16]

Step 3 requires the state to release data on school performance in midsummer or before; else it comes too late for parents to choose alternative schools—at least until the spring semester or the next school year. After all, parents informed in October face the difficult choice of whether to uproot their children after school has already started, sending them to an unknown school where they may start out weeks behind. In effect, *school choice delayed is school choice denied*. Yet many states do delay, and as noted above, the U.S. Department of Education has not pressured states to speed this process.[17] Our results show great variation in the timeliness of data release, with some delays seemingly politically motivated.

Steps 4 and 5 hold possible pitfalls. If no adequately performing alternative schools have space to accommodate additional children, then parents lack real alternatives. For example, a Maryland informant reports that for the 2002–2003 school year Baltimore had thirty thousand children eligible for school choice, but only 194 places for those children, even though the school district had lost roughly half its enrollment over the previous three decades: "So it's got half the enrollment and yet they could not find room to put these transferred kids—it's ridiculous!"[18] In 2002 only 10 percent of eligible students in Title I schools in Chicago requested transfers, yet half were denied, allegedly for lack of space.[19] In rapidly growing school systems like Los Angeles, where children already attend overcrowded schools on staggered schedules, districts may not be able to offer alternative schools.

School districts do not always inform parents of their school's status as a school needing improvement in a clear, understandable way. For example, an informant in Michigan reports that "the politically correct term now is 'high priority schools,'" implying that schools needing improvement are *more desirable*. As Benigno reports, in its letter to parents, one Colorado improvement school explained its status thusly:

> All schools in District ____ are committed to excellence through continuous improvement. ____ Elementary is no exception. Our school has been identified for "School Improvement" by Federal Title I guidelines. We are excited by this opportunity to focus on increasing student achievement on the CSAP assessments.[20]

Even a careful reader might think this school had won an award rather than a sanction. An official we interviewed agreed that "some districts have used a misleading terminology," so the Colorado education department is "clarifying that for districts."

Ideally, school districts should also list alternative schools and supplemental services providers. In Benigno's Colorado sample, 13 schools offered their Title I parents no alternative schools, and 21 offered only one option. In contrast, 12 schools offered two options, and 20 offered parents three or more.

Finally, for the school choice and supplemental services provisions of NCLB to work, we would expect some parents to take advantage of those options (Step 6). Even if schools make a good-faith effort to inform parents of their choices, parents may refuse those options, particularly transferring to different schools. But if such decisions occur, they will reflect the wants of Title I clients rather than a lack of choice forced on them by education bureaucrats.

Methods

The rest of this chapter summarizes results from e-mail and phone surveys of state Title I coordinators, supplemented by phone interviews with journalists and members of the State Policy Network, an association of state level think tanks promoting free market-based public policy reforms. From October 8 to November 21, Title I coordinators from all 51 states (as noted above, we treat the District of Columbia as a state) received a short e-mail survey regarding the implementation of NCLB. Originally we contemplated a longer survey, but early interviews showed that few informants could discuss the details of how districts inform parents of their options; hence we ask little about the actual letters that districts use, and instead focus on how states oversee the parental choice process. Before e-mailing each Title I coordinator, we called to confirm his or her e-mail address, explain the purpose of the research, and give assurances that he or she would be identified only by state and organization. We contacted non-responding states three times, until a total of 23 states had completed the e-mail survey. (In one state two officials responded, fortunately with essentially the same responses.) We then phone surveyed eight Title I coordinators or subordinate officials who were reluctant to fill out the e-mail survey but were willing to talk by phone; thus data from state education officials could be recorded for 30 of 51 states (58.8 percent). Where possible, we recorded data from state officials rather than other respondents. To enlarge the data set and deepen insights, we also interviewed 18 education journalists from major daily papers in 18 states. Third, we interviewed 11 education analysts, nine from the State Policy Network and two from unrelated school reform groups familiar with the implementation of NCLB in 10 states. Phone surveys continued into February 2005. From these three sources, we coded data for 43 of 51 states, 84.3 percent. Sixteen states had two or more respondents, while for 27 states a single respondent supplied data. We coded additional data from state education department websites to fill in certain responses left blank by respondents, particularly the numbers of supplemental services providers and the dates on which states released lists of schools needing improvement.

For most states many of our variables come from a single informant; thus we cannot in all cases have high confidence in the results. We e-mailed an early draft of this chapter to informants, and five provided feedback used to modify the final draft.

Testing Step 1: Do States Label Schools as Needing Improvement?

For parents to have new options under NCLB, states must be willing to designate low-performing Title I schools. Accordingly, we asked respondents to designate the number of schools "needing improvement" for the 2003–2004 school year. All state informants and most other informants were able to do so. With a few exceptions, states do label sufficient *numbers* of schools as needing improvement, though of course this cannot speak to the accuracy of those designations. For 2003–2004, respondents from 35 states indicated that their states had designated a mean of 135.3 schools as "needing improvement"; 7.1 percent of public schools in those states.

Hawaii listed 33 percent of its schools as needing improvement. Kentucky had not formally released its list as of the survey, but informants indicated that about 31 percent of Kentucky schools would be labeled as failing, followed by Georgia (29 percent), Illinois (17 percent), Oregon (16 percent), and Alaska (13 percent). With the possible exception of Oregon, the percentage of schools needing improvement per state seems to have face validity; thus these states seem to be making a good-faith effort to implement standards. The percentage of schools designated as needing improvement correlates with state-level fourth-grade (1998) National Assessment of Education Progress (NAEP) reading scores at $-.37$ (p $=$ .07; n $=$ 26), suggesting that states with more schools needing improvement really do have lower student achievement.

Only a few of our informants feared that states or local districts would "game" accountability rules. One from Utah feared that:

> There's a lot more public pressure and much more of a spotlight on those schools than there ever was before, but I also speculate about whether it will promote more gaming of the system, finding ways to highlight good data or self-serving data and bury the not-so-promising data. Someone in a district suggested to me that it's not that difficult for a district to create an alternative school *code* [in the accountability database] and call it an alternative school, and dump all the unfavorably performing kids there. I have not been able to nail that down, but in a computer system I can see how that could happen.

Notably, Utah is one of several states considering whether to opt out of NCLB.[21] Similarly, respondents from Kentucky and Washington state suggested that the states used confidence intervals to decrease the numbers of schools needing improvement. Since often only 30 or so students in a given subgroup are tested in a given school, results may reflect the random variation normal to small samples (such as one student having a bad day) rather than systematic changes. The same statistical issues trouble accountability measures for small schools.[22] Small schools are particularly common in rural states. A Nebraska informant pointed out that only 159 of the state's 517 school districts had even one subgroup with as many as 30 students—thus the state lacked data to categorize large numbers of schools as needing improvement. Accordingly, states convinced the U.S. Department of Education to permit statistical confidence intervals to broaden the range of scores accepted as passing for small subgroups and to protect confidentiality while enhancing reliability.[23]

Yet such provisions can be abused. An informant insists that Kentucky used confidence intervals to halve the number of schools needing improvement, circumventing the accountability provisions of NCLB:

> If a Kentucky school has 17 African Americans and three, 18 percent of them reach proficiency, using this confidence interval formula the margin of error is plus or minus 28 points, so the school would be evaluated [at the high end of the interval] as if 46 percent had scored sufficiently, so grading on a curve will make it much more difficult to determine how a school is really doing.

Twenty-six states use confidence intervals, though, presumably few are quite so broad.

Finally, all informants stated that states release data on school performance to school districts before the public sees it, typically to permit districts to appeal. A Nevada journalist expressed concerns about this:

> We raised questions about the appeals process and the fact that it was being kept secret. Districts were allowed to appeal the designation before it was made public, and the theory was you do not want to stigmatize these schools in public, but my take is it's like a kid failing a test and then appealing before the parents get the grade.

Moreover, some states are not doing enough to identify schools needing improvement. Arkansas (which failed to respond to this survey) and Wyoming designated *no* schools as needing improvement for the 2002–2003 school year.[24] An informant states that Wyoming still has no schools needing improvement. Within the current data set, Florida, Maine, Missouri, Mississippi, North Carolina, Nebraska, and West Virginia designated fewer than 1 percent of their schools as needing improvement under NCLB.

In fairness, North Carolina, Mississippi, Nebraska, and presumably some other states identify only Title I schools on their NCLB needs improvement list. They use different accountability measures for distinct state accountability programs. Further, in some cases a small number of schools needing improvement may reflect actual school improvement. Three separate North Carolina informants (from government, media, and a school reform group) insisted that the number of schools needing improvement trended downward because of actual academic improvements resulting from the longevity and relative strength of the state's accountability plan. Florida also has a well-regarded state accountability plan. Many informants noted that school accountability plans took years to become part of school culture, and reflected complex compromises between standards-setting states and standards-opposing local districts. For example, a Massachusetts respondent expected the state's schools needing improvement to decline through "some mix of modified standards and better academic performance. It's taking quite some time for things to be hammered out. With the statewide standards people are finally starting to pay attention to it because it's what's tested."

Notably, these data could be located for only 35 states. At least nine states (Arizona, Illinois, Kentucky, Louisiana, Michigan, Nebraska, Utah, Virginia, and Vermont) had not released their lists of schools needing improvement by mid-November 2003, though informants in some of these states offered unofficial estimates, employed in these analyses. Kentucky, Mississippi, and Louisiana held regularly scheduled gubernatorial elections in 2003, while New Jersey and Virginia held closely contested state legislative races. With the exception of New Jersey, *none* of these states cooperated with this research, though private-sector informants supplied data for Virginia, Kentucky, and Mississippi, putting them in the data set. Virginia and Kentucky informants insisted that their states' late release of data for 2003 was intentional, so that the listing of schools needing improvement would not affect state elections. Possibly, this also explains Louisiana's late (November 20) announcement of its schools needing improvement, though no subjects there agreed to serve as informants. In short, only two (40 percent) of the five states holding state elections released their data by November 1, compared to 32 (80 percent) of 40 others. Ironically, this is a positive finding, suggesting that political elites and the public take school performance seriously.

Respondents from 18 (42.9 percent) of 42 states reported that the number of schools needing improvement in their states had increased or would increase from the 2002–2003 school year to the 2003–2004 school year, while 11 (26.2 percent) saw or expected a decrease and seven (16.7 percent) expected stable numbers. Of the 27 respondents willing to say why they expected a change in the numbers, eight (29.6 percent) cited better data, nine (33.3 percent) noted changed standards, seven (25.9 percent) cited improved performance, and three (11.1 percent) noted other factors. In particular, many of those citing better data or changed standards expected the schools needing improvement to increase with the requirement for greater percentages of students from subgroups to take and pass standardized tests. In short, despite the problems with NCLB's accountability provisions noted above, most informants see them as working, a point we will return to below.

Virtually all respondents suggested that NCLB is having a substantial effect on public schools. Twenty-seven of the 30 state officials (90 percent) thought NCLB harder to implement than its predecessor. Yet 19 of 27 (70.4 percent) thought NCLB likely to improve education in their states in the long run;

three thought it would harm education and five respondents picked a neutral option. In phone interviews, several state education officials suggested that although NCLB was difficult to implement in the near term, in the long run it would bring school improvement. Interestingly, a states' percentage of improvement schools correlates with respondent's beliefs that NCLB will improve education at .32 (p = .09; n = 29). Many education policy elites apparently are willing to accept short-term pain for long-term gain.

These figures may be somewhat inflated by the desire of savvy bureaucrats to please the interviewer. On the other hand, other informants agree that NCLB will improve public education, chiefly by forcing schools to emphasize achievement. Moreover, responses were not uniformly positive. Rather, state officials and other informants saw positive and negative features of NCLB. For example, 20 of 34 (58.8 percent) respondents agreed that NCLB would "divert resources from more promising reforms." Similarly, 29 of 36 respondents (80.6 percent) thought that NCLB would increase paperwork, though a few disputed this. For example, a Colorado SEA official insisted:

> It is stupid to say the law is going to require more paperwork. It is requiring more *accountability*. How you do that accountability is simply an internal decision. You want to create more paperwork? Fine. Create more paperwork. But you can have more accountability without paperwork. In terms of notification maybe there's more paper, but I've been hard-pressed to say that, especially when people define paperwork as meaningful activity that makes people think more about how to communicate with parents and do follow-up.

Whatever the paperwork implications, 24 of 36 informants agreed that NCLB "motivated districts to improve low-performing schools more quickly." States seemingly see NCLB as a lever to push districts to improve. As officials from three states put it:

> It's easy to cast aspersions at this law for a variety of reasons, and yet my colleagues nationwide, I don't hear them when we get together off the record saying "how can we wait for this to go away?" I hear them saying "how can we make this thing work?" . . . The law isn't perfect but, we're moving the best we can to move our kids toward standards and above within the parameters of the law.

> Of course school districts do not think, "Oh thanks for telling me I'm on the list," especially with all the little subgroups, . . . but certainly it will motivate them to make improvements to get off the list because they don't like being on the list.

> School districts are starting to be smart about what it is they may have been obligated to do, but did not have the follow through about before. I find most districts are being very smart about this process. As much as they hate this heavy handed accountability, it has actually moved some people along. . . . What I see is a shift in how people are looking at the achievement of their kids, so a district thought of as a high-performing district now has to look at a subgroup that is not performing well, looking at populations

that have been in the past overlooked. We have never in the past focused on the achievement levels of all kids.

Similarly, a Mississippi informant suggested that the state used NCLB to push "mule-like" districts to improve:

> I think some of the superintendents don't know quite what to do. They're scared. . . . There's this one school that it took me a month to get the superintendent to let me get into. From the accountability list he saw this [labeling] coming, and finally he got a new principal in this school, and I was thinking, "if you had gotten this guy sooner you might not be on the list." This superintendent is notorious for sticking his head in the sand, and if he had moved sooner he would not have gotten the school on the list. . . . A lot of the schools really close ranks, too. It is hard to get in some of these schools. I figure if they're this closed to the media, they're probably that way with the parents too.

Seemingly, the accountability provisions of NCLB have positive impacts.

Interestingly, several state education officials suggested that states relatively far along in implementing the 1994 version of ESEA, which required states to develop standards, were also relatively far along in implementation of NCLB, a finding similar to Pinkerton's case studies.[25] As of April 2002, 19 states were in full compliance with the 1994 ESEA, 28 in partial compliance, and 4 states and the District of Columbia out of compliance.[26] We found a .35 correlation (p = .05, n = 32) between ESEA compliance status and how difficult informants thought NCLB was to implement: states already in compliance found NCLB less challenging. Similarly, a Texas journalist saw no trouble with new requirements since NCLB "used Texas as a model, so there was already a sort of system in place that you could fine tune." In addition, data show a modestly positive, though not statistically significant relationship between compliance with ESEA and belief that NCLB would improve education.

Regarding Step 2, informants and state education department web sites provided data on supplemental services providers for every state save Arkansas. The 50 states approved a mean of 31.4 providers, ranging from 0 (Nebraska, Florida, and Wyoming) to 200 (Georgia). Notably, informants from these states indicate that no Title I students are yet eligible for supplemental services because no Title I schools failed to make AYP for three straight years; hence states saw no need to approve providers. Nine states approved 1–5 providers; 16 approved 6–19; 12 approved 20–50, and 10 approved more than 50. States approved a mean of about 7.6 supplemental services providers per million residents, with Vermont leading at 66.7. Seemingly, most states have implemented this part of NCLB. Of course, though states may approve supplemental services providers, local districts might block their use. For example, a Massachusetts informant said that Boston public schools charge providers for use of rooms in school buildings. Further, a number of informants lamented that children in rural areas were unlikely to benefit, save perhaps from distance learning operations of questionable use. Informants thought that supplemental services were not yet widely used: most willing to give estimates thought that less than 2 percent of eligible children took part. Still, many thought that in the long run tutoring might substantially raise the test scores of Title I students. A Los Angeles informant reports that more than 10,000 students (out of 140,000 eligible) used supplemental services in the city. Indeed, Los Angeles public schools promoted supplemental services, contrasting their hostility to school choice. More than twenty thousand New York City students used the free supplemental services.[27]

Steps 3 and 4: Do School Districts Inform Parents of Their School's Status?

As explained above, Title I parents of children in schools needing improvement must be informed of their school's status and of alternative options in time to use those options. As table 4.1 shows, Steps 3 and 4 are problematic because only nine states (20 percent) release the list of schools needing improvement to the public before August, and another 16 (35.6 percent) release the data in August. Thus, roughly half of the 45 states on which data

Table 4.1. "When was the list of low performing schools for the 2002–2003 school year released to the public?"

Timing	Number	Percent
Before May 2003	4	8.9
May 2003	1	2.2
June 2003	1	2.2
July 2003	3	6.7
August 2003	16	35.6
September 2003	6	13.3
October 2003	3	6.7
November 2003	3	6.7
After November 2003	8	17.8
Total	45	100*

*Total percentage of non-missing cases. This does not include non-respondent states Arkansas, Idaho, Kansas, South Carolina, South Dakota. Wyoming has not yet designated schools needing improvement.

could be found do not inform the public as to the number of schools needing improvement before school starts!

Eight states (17.8 percent) still had not released the numbers as of mid-November 2003. As noted above, all state education department respondents said that they released the data to school districts before the public saw it, typically to give the districts a chance to appeal. In fairness, Mississippi, Nevada, Oregon, and New York City report releasing the data early for Title I schools needing improvement, so that eligible parents could find out about their options before school started. Perhaps other states and local districts do this as well, though informants did not report such behavior in interviews.

Public bureaucracies typically get better at implementing complex laws over time. It is therefore lamentable that only 8 of 32 respondents (25 percent) reported releasing the list of improvement schools earlier in 2003 than in the previous year; 13 (40.6 percent) reported a later release time, and 11 (34.4 percent) reported no change. Most informants that reported later release times cited the difficulty of reporting on larger numbers of subgroups, a tendency also noted by Pinkerton et al. As noted above, NCLB specifically required disclosure of school performance before school started in 2002–2003, but it did not require this for subsequent years.

Similarly, respondents report that Title I parents in schools needing improvement have relatively little time to choose alternative schools. Ten (27 percent) report that the typical district in their state permits eligible parents less than two weeks to choose schools; 14 (37.8 percent) allow two weeks to a month; seven (18.9 percent) report one-two months; three (8.1 percent) say more than two months, and three permit no choice. Thus more than a third of reporting states allow parents two weeks or less to choose alternative schools, or still do not offer parental choice. Notably, an informant reports that New York City initially permitted parents only days to select alternative schools but, after the press reported the "nine-day fiasco," extended this to one-two months. As noted above, Wyoming still does not designate schools needing improvement. Informants indicate that Kentucky and Utah refused to offer parents a transfer option. As an informant in the latter state lamented, "Utah missed its deadline for alerting parents; and the Feds, when they found out about it, I was surprised they were not taking stronger action." In fairness, two state informants insist that the U.S. Department of Education gave contradictory advice as to when the school choice and supplemental services provisions of NCLB kicked in.

Of course, even when parents have adequate time to make a decision, they may not be adequately informed. As is described above, districts do not necessarily have incentives to inform parents of their options to choose different schools; thus states need to monitor district communications to parents to assure clarity. A Nevada informant complained that Clark County schools sent Title I parents misleading communications about their options under NCLB:

> This year the news came two weeks after school started. They sent out 8,000 letters and they got 200 takers, but the letters that went out, one warned of the consequences of losing friendships, missing family dinners—as if anyone has time for family dinners any more—and all those other dangers. But what about the plus side? That you are more likely to be in a school with less crime? Or studying under a teacher with an advanced degree?

A Maryland informant said that in Baltimore the letters informing parents of their options were "pretty much a sham": "They sent out these letters, but they were bureaucratic. It was an example of typical school bureaucracy nonsense deliberately designed to make it difficult for parents to make the choices . . . they *talked* a good game about how this was going to be an open process." On a more positive note, a Mississippi journalist saw no ill intent:

> I think that in general [education administrators] tend to write over peoples' heads. Sometimes I'll see letters and I don't understand this. How's someone without a high school diploma going to understand this? You've got educators writing them and they're not thinking, "how can I help people read these?" They're going to have to get better at that the more they communicate with the parents.

Possibly, over the long term NCLB will indeed improve communications with parents, particularly if states monitor district behavior.

Twenty states in the database apparently do nothing to monitor district and individual school letters to parents in schools needing improvement, while 19 states report monitoring the letters. In addition, Oregon's Department of Education began doing so after the press reported that a prominent school district misled its parents. A reporter recalls, "We got copies of the letter and we said this is bullshit, and we called the state and they said that's illegal and the letters now are good. I've seen them all." Only 22 (57.9 percent) of the states where data could be found apparently provide (or have contractors provide) model letters showing districts how to inform parents of their options under NCLB; 16 do not. Not surprisingly, these actions (monitoring district letters, and providing model letters) correlate at .39 (p = .02, n = 38): states that do the one tend to do the other.

Informants suggest that states offering interdistrict and intradistrict school choice give parents more time to select schools, though the data set does not indicate a quantitative relationship.[28] Informants in Albuquerque, Portland,

Boston, Denver, Seattle, Charlotte-Mecklenburg, and Memphis suggested that preexisting open-enrollment policies made the school choice provisions of NCLB relatively easy to implement, while at the same time limiting their impact. As one respondent put it, school choice in Portland seems "up 15 percent or so from what's usual . . . which has made the schools and school district more acutely aware that they don't have an iron grip on these kids, but it's not a humongous difference." Seattle and Denver informants suggested that some parents were confused as to the differences between NCLB-mandated school choice and preexisting intradistrict school choice. Informants in Seattle and Boston felt that NCLB-mandated school choice helped few families because the better schools were already over capacity. Notably, Memphis and Portland informants thought that their districts did a good job informing eligible Title I parents of their options, holding meetings and making a good-faith effort to find spots for students.

In contrast, states without inter- and intradistrict choice may have more difficulty. As the Maryland informant quoted above observed, Baltimore City Public Schools had a number of schools with empty seats, yet the system was apparently unable to find space for Title I transfer students. In some cities, the poor quality of all public schools limits options. A New Jersey informant lamented "Newark has only a few high end elementary schools that are packed to the gills, so there's no room at the inn, and even the schools listed as not needing improvement are not always much better than the other schools, so there's no big pickup in school choice here." Similarly, the Portland informant thought it likely that in fall 2004, all of the city's 10 high schools would fall short of AYP for the second straight year, precluding parental choice. In an unusual twist, a New York informant suspected that some successful schools were put on the needs improvement list so they would not have to accept incoming transfers.

Seemingly, states already used to and perhaps supportive of public school choice find NCLB-mandated school choice policies somewhat easier to implement. Of course, such states can offer students in schools needing improvement a wider range of options, including those across school or district boundaries. Yet interviews and quantitative analyses show no relationship between the number of charter schools per capita and the amount of time parents had to select their NCLB-related options. Notably, North Carolina respondents report that charters were overrepresented among schools needing improvement, because many serve at-risk students. In addition, a substantial literature suggests that first-year charter schools often have start-up problems, and in most states a large percentage of charters are in their first or second years.[29]

Grading the States

Overall, how well do states ensure Title I parents in failing schools their rights to education alternatives? There are many reasons expect mediocre performance. State education officials may themselves resent federal mandates. No matter their views, state officials frequently have little influence over politically influential local school boards and superintendents. For example, as an Oregon informant put it:

> There's a much stronger tradition of state leadership in the South. It's not like that out here. We don't ask questions until two years after the fact. There's not a central repository for the information out here. You'd think those things would be tracked, wouldn't you? It's very different from [southern city]. It's been interesting to come out here and talk to the state education people and say "you never ask anyone anything about what?" Here the districts say "that's none of your beeswax."

Similarly, a Colorado state education official unable to track down the number of NCLB student transfers complained that "because we are a local-control state, districts have a way of just balking when you ask them for more information."

Further, the novelty of NCLB, particularly its school choice elements, may make it particularly challenging to implement.

Table 4.2 summarizes how well individual states implement the school choice and supplemental services provisions of NCLB. Through our surveys and interviews, we were able to grade 42 states,[30] based on the following:

1. *Timely Announcement: SEAs inform the school districts and the public of schools needing improvement in a timely fashion, as shown in table 4.1.* We award states 2 points for listing their schools needing improvement before August (as nine states do), 1 point for doing so in August (16 states), and 0 points for announcing their list in September or later (21 states), presumably after school has already started.
2. *Parent Notice: Parents have adequate time to select alternative schools*, as is discussed above. The 10 states that allow parents more than a month to make their choices get 2 points; the 14 states that allow two weeks to a month get one point, and the 19 states that allow parents less than two weeks or no choice at all get 0. (This correlates only weakly with Timely Announcement because some states release data early for Title I schools likely to have to offer parental choice.)
3. *Oversight of District Letters: States make an effort to see that school districts inform parents.* The 19 states that monitor district letters for clarity get

1 point on oversight; the 22 states that do not monitor get 0 points, and the one state which began to monitor the letters after pressure from the news media (Oregon) gets .5 points. Second, for the variable Model Letter, the 22 states that provide a model letter to school districts to guide their efforts to inform parents get 1 point; the 20 others get 0. As noted above, these variables are correlated.

4. *Supplemental providers: States must approve adequate numbers of supplemental services providers.* As we note above, states approved a mean of 7.6 supplemental services providers per million residents. For the implementation index, those 15 states that approved fewer than 3 supplemental services providers per million people get 0 points; the 15 states that approved from 3 to 7 supplemental services providers per million people get 1 point; the 13 states with more than 7 approved providers per million people get 2 points.[31]

States were issued a letter grade, ranging from A to F, based upon the number of points earned under the evaluation results. States received an A for earning 8 points out of a total of 8 points; a B+ for 7 points; a B− for 6 points; a C+ for 5 points; a C− for 4 points; a D+ for 3 points; a D for 2.5 points; a D− for 2 points; and an F for earning less than 2 points.

Overall rankings provide little reason for satisfaction. No state earned a perfect 8, though Hawaii, New Jersey, and West Virginia scored 6 (B−), and 11 other states earned a 5 (C+). The mean score overall was 3.48 (D+) of a possible 8.0, a clear indication that much work remains. In particular, Arizona, Maryland, Virginia, Wyoming, and Utah bring up the rear, scoring badly on most or all items. Notably, for all of these states save Wyoming, we had to rely on media or think tank informants, who might be more negative (and know less) than state officials. Only 3 of 30 states in which the primary informant was a state official scored a 2 or less on the NCLB index, compared to 6 of 12 in which the primary informant did not work for the state. Of course, if state government informants exaggerate their success to make their states look good while private sector informants have greater objectivity, then our state ratings may in fact be inflated. This means that the typical rating would, in reality, be lower than we suggest here.

Further, the identity of state informants may itself indicate their level of NCLB implementation. Utah Title I officials declined to participate in the survey, describing their work in implementing the parental choice provisions of NCLB as too preliminary to discuss. (A private sector informant concurred with this assessment.) The Title I offices in Maryland, Arizona, New Mexico, and Virginia changed leadership during the study period, which

Table 4.2. An Evaluative Ranking of States on NCLB School Choice and Supplemental Services Provisions

State*	Grade	Total	Timely Info.	Parent Notice	Dist. Letter	Model Letter	Suppl. Provider
Hawaii	B−	6.00	2	2	1	1	0
New Jersey	B−	6.00	0	2	1	1	2
West Virginia	B−	6.00	1	1	1	1	2
Alaska	C+	5.00	1	0	1	1	2
Colorado	C+	5.00	1	1	1	1	1
Delaware	C+	5.00	1	1	1	0	2
Dist. Of Columbia	C+	5.00	1	0	1	1	2
Missouri	C+	5.00	2	1	1	1	0
North Carolina	C+	5.00	2	1	1	1	0
North Dakota	C+	5.00	0	1	1	1	2
Ohio	C+	5.00	1	1	1	1	1
Pennsylvania	C+	5.00	1	1	1	1	1
Texas	C+	5.00	2	2	1	0	0
Washington	C+	5.00	1	2	1	1	0
Connecticut	C−	4.00	1	0	1	0	2
Florida	C−	4.00	2	0	1	1	0
Georgia	C−	4.00	1	0	0	1	2
Indiana	C−	4.00	1	1	0	0	2
Massachusetts	C−	4.00	0	1	1	1	1
Michigan	C−	4.00	2	0	0	1	1
Oklahoma	C−	4.00	1	1	0	1	1
Alabama	D+	3.00	1	1	1	0	0
California	D+	3.00	2	0	0	0	1
Illinois	D+	3.00	0	2	0	1	0
Montana	D+	3.00	1	1	0	0	1
New Hampshire	D+	3.00	0	2	0	0	1
New York	D+	3.00	0	2	0	0	1
Nevada	D+	3.00	0	0	0	1	2
Rhode Island	D+	3.00	1	2	0	0	0
Vermont	D+	3.00	0	0	0	1	2
Oregon	D	2.50	0	2	.5**	0	0
Tennessee	D	2.50	0	.5***	0	1	1
Kentucky	D−	2.00	0	0	0	0	2
Maine	D−	2.00	0	0	1	1	0
Mississippi	D−	2.00	0	0	0	0	2
Nebraska	D−	2.00	0	2	0	0	0
New Mexico	D−	2.00	1	0	0	0	1
Arizona	F	1.00	0	0	0	0	1
Maryland	F	1.00	0	1	0	0	0
Virginia	F	1.00	0	0	0	0	1
Utah	F	0.00	0	0	0	0	0
Wyoming	F	0.00	0	0	0	0	0

* Arkansas, Iowa, Idaho, Kansas, Louisiana, Minnesota, and South Dakota state departments of education never responded to repeated requests, and Wisconsin and South Carolina declined to take the survey. We were unable to find alternative informants with sufficient information, so we could not rank these states.

** The SEA checked letters after pressure from journalists.

*** Though the state as a whole reports giving parents little notice, a second informant states that Memphis, with about half of the failing schools, gave parents substantial notice by relying on the previous year's accountability measures.

may have affected their ability to complete the survey and, more important, to implement NCLB. A long line of research suggests that leadership changes disrupt program implementation.[32] Perhaps other non-responding state officials faced similar challenges.

NCLB: No Choice

Respondents divided evenly (19 to 19) as to whether NCLB would "increase pressure for school choice." All informants agree that the parental choice provisions of the law have little effect at this time. Few could estimate the number of students switching schools because of NCLB, and those who could typically put the numbers in the low hundreds or below. Save in New York City, no informant estimated that more than 3 percent of eligible Title I students statewide switched schools. Consistent with other observers, informants in rural states suggested that the long distances between schools limited options for switching schools.[33] Even where distance is not a factor, loyalties might be. As a Vermont informant states, school choice has "been less of a true option":

> There is some very strong close community allegiance, if you will, to the school. So if I live ten miles away from another school and my school has been identified [as low performing], it's going to take more than just that identification for me to take my kid and send them ten miles away to a place where despite the fact that we're neighbors, it's not my hometown. My family has played basketball against that town since forever, perhaps my grandparents did. . . . There is that kind of allegiance and pride in the community schools, and more than a little bit of local control, that idea of Yankee independence and self determination just runs a little bit deeper in some of these smaller communities, and they are loath to say "I'm going to load my kid in a bus and send them ten miles away because someone in the *state* says my school is in need of improvement."

Similarly, an Oklahoma informant said in some towns "there were media reports that schools were failing, and interviews with parents saying, 'No. We love our school. We don't want to leave.' " A Delaware state education official suggested that "if you have the right communications with your parents [school choice] is not going to be an issue, and if you don't then it should be an issue . . . we do have some schools like that." In a more urban state, Massachusetts, an informant observed: "Parents take the view that I like my congressman, but I hate Congress. I think they genuinely like what they see in their schools, and it is a huge hassle to move a kid, to have the child adjust to a new set of kids, teachers, principals, everything. I suspect that most parents do not want to do that." Quite possibly, even if states and school districts made serious attempts to facilitate parental choice, in the short term relatively few Title I parents would take advantage of their new options.

Of course, the relatively low grades most states earn on NCLB-related choice indicate that school choice has not yet had a true test. Until states do more to push school districts to fully implement the parental choice provisions of NCLB, we cannot know whether growing numbers of eligible parents would in fact choose different schools. There are indications that they would.[34]

The Politics of NCLB's Parental Choice: Has This Idea's Time Come?

In summary, our informants report that states take the standards and accountability provisions of NCLB quite seriously. Even in the face of political pressure, states declare large numbers of schools in need of improvement. Indeed, in some respects this may reflect the desire of states to exert control over what they see as shirking districts, continuing a long-term trend.[35] Moreover, most informants think that NCLB will improve schools—primarily by focusing improvement efforts on low-performing schools and low-performing subgroups within schools—because schools will be motivated to avoid "labeling."

In contrast, states have made little progress implementing the parental choice provisions of the law. Only about half of states ensure that Title I parents receive notice of their school choice options before the start of school, and even in these cases such notice frequently comes only days before. A like number oversee how school districts communicate NCLB options to Title I parents; this despite indications that many local schools are less than forthcoming in their communications to parents. (On the plus side, most states have approved reasonable numbers of supplemental services providers.) In interviews, many informants could readily describe the arcane regulations governing AYP but had only superficial knowledge of NCLB's parental choice requirements.

Why do states implement school standards but not school choice? In part, this reflects NCLB's main focus on standards and accountability. Implementing these alone requires considerable effort, leaving state departments of education few bureaucratic resources left over for parental choice. Politically, standards attract great notice because the possibility of earning an unfavorable label affects employees and clients of all schools, while the school choice and supplemental services provisions directly affect only Title I parents in Title I schools. This is particularly true because of the reporting requirements attached to NCLB, which attract significant media attention. Twenty-nine of 37 respondents (78.4 percent) agree that NCLB increased involvement from the news media and interest groups in school reform. For example, state officials from Nevada and Oklahoma, respectively, state:

> In terms of how often my phone rings and there is a reporter on the other end, I think the media is getting this big shock of all these schools that are identified. Even though the nature of the school has not changed at all, suddenly it's been labeled as needing improvement and that gets a lot of attention.
>
> I have certainly seen it covered on television where I had not seen that in the past. In the past I might see it in newspapers, but not TV.

Informants from several states noted that NCLB's reporting requirements led local newspapers to print much heralded special editions summarizing school test scores and labels, something previously unthinkable. Thus it is no wonder that parental choice gets less attention from politicians, the press, and from state departments of education.

More broadly, all school reform is *political*, and several informants noted the political pressures attending to NCLB. For example, one state education bureaucrat who did not want his/her state identified said:

> I don't want to say much because this has been incredibly controversial in our state. [Republican] Senator _____ served on the reauthorization of this...and we have a Democratic governor, so this has been a very, very controversial piece of legislation and so to some degree I am waiting to see how this all settles out here in [state] and across the country.

Over the long term, whether states push districts to fully implement NCLB depends largely on the national political climate and on state dynamics. As a long line of political science research shows, in the fragmented U.S. political system, policy change typically occurs gradually, and from many directions at once.[36] As Hochschild argues, after years of elite and public debate dating back to the *Nation at Risk* report, standards and accountability are now *politically acceptable:* thus NCLB's standards and accountability requirements are education policies whose political time has come.[37] It is not clear that the same can be said of school choice.[38]

Accordingly, the best hope for pushing SEAs and local school districts to implement school choice provisions of NCLB lies with gradually changing the political climate. The U.S. Department of Education, which has mainly focused on other NCLB provisions, needs to pressure states to push districts to inform eligible parents of their school choice and supplemental services options, in part by requiring documentation of how districts inform parents, and of how many parents use their new options.

Of equal importance, private-sector actors need to monitor how state and local governments enforce NCLB. Some journalists are already pushing states to implement the law. As noted above, press reports in Oregon and New York seemingly shamed public officials into implementing the choice provisions of NCLB. A think tank report by Benigno may have had a similar impact in Colorado.[39]

In addition to such pressures from reporters and analysts, parent activists may push districts to implement choice. Helped by government grants, the Black Alliance for Education Options (BAEO) publicizes eligible parents' school choice options in Detroit, Philadelphia, Dallas, and Milwaukee.[40] Additional grants could expand such activities. Finally, more might follow the example of Title I parents in New York and Albany, who have sued their school districts to ensure their rights to school choice and supplemental services.[41]

Just as school desegregation took time and involved many political actors,[42] it may take several years of U.S. Department of Education pressure, crusading education reporting, and parental lawsuits to guarantee implementation of the parental choice rights set forth in NCLB. Only then are states and local school districts likely to get a passing grade on the implementation of NCLB's parental options, and only then can we know whether parents really desire such options.

Notes

1. We thank Andrea Costello, Villanova University, and the many informants—most of them public servants—who took time out of their busy days to participate in this research. The usual caveats apply.
2. Stephen K. Bailey and Edith K. Mosher, *ESEA: The Office of Education Administers a Law* (Syracuse: Syracuse University Press, 1968).
3. Krista Kafer, "A Small but Costly Step toward Reform: The Conference Education Bill" (2002). Accessed on November 12, 2003, at www.usatoday.com/news/e98/e1382.htm. See also, Robert Maranto and Laura Coppeto, "The Politics behind Bush's No Child Left Behind: Ideas, Elections, and Top-Down Education Reform," in *George W. Bush: Evaluating the President at Midterm*, ed. Bryan Hilliard, Tom Lansford, and Robert Watson (Albany: State University of New York Press, forthcoming).
4. We include Washington, D.C., henceforth treated as a state for simplicity.
5. Lynn Olson, "In ESEA Wake, School Data Flowing Forth," *Education Week*, December 10, 2003. Available at http://www.edweek.org/ew/ewstory.cfm?slug = 15NCLB.h23.

6. Eric A. Hanushek and Margaret E. Raymond, "Lessons about the Design of State Accountability Systems," in *Brookings Papers on No Child Left Behind*, ed. Paul E. Peterson and Martin R. West (Washington, D.C.: Brookings Institution Press, 2003). See also, Frederick M. Hess, "Refining or Retreating? High Stakes Accountability in the States," in *Brookings Papers on No Child Left Behind*, ed. Paul E. Peterson and Martin R. West (Washington, D.C.: Brookings Institution Press, 2003); and James W. Popham, "The 'No Child' Noose Tightens—But Some States Are Slipping It," *Education Week*, September 24, 2003. Available at wysiwyg://527/http://www.edweek.org/ ew/ewstory.cfm?slug = 04popham.h23.

7. Hess, "Refining or Retreating?"

8. David J. Hoff, "States Revise the Meaning of 'Proficient,' " *Education Week*, October 10, 2002. Available at http://www.edweek.com/ewstory.cfm?slug = 06tests.h21. See also, Richard Innes and Jim Waters, *Improbable Rise in CATS' Scores: What's the Real Story?* (Bowling Green, KY: Bluegrass Institute for Public Policy Solutions, 2003); and Popham, "The 'No Child' Noose Tightens."

9. Chester E. Finn, "Leaving Many Children Behind: Congress Passes Bush's Education Reform, and School Districts Ignore It," *Weekly Standard* 7, no. 47 (August 26, 2002).

10. Olson, "In ESEA Wake, School Data Flowing Forth." See also, William Erpenbach, Ellen Forte-Fast, and Abigail Potts, *Statewide Educational Accountability under NCLB: Central Issues Arising from an Examination of State Accountability Workbooks and U.S. Department of Education Reviews under the No Child Left Behind Act of 2001* (Washington, D.C.: The Council of Chief State School Officers, 2003).

11. Erpenbach, *Statewide Educational Accountability*.

12. Innes, *Improbable Rise*. See also, Alexander Russo, "Flunking Out: Bush's Pet Education Bill Is in Serious Trouble," *Slate* (August 28, 2003). Available at http://slate.msn.com/toolbar.aspz?action = print&id2087654.

13. Hoff, "States Revise the Meaning of 'Proficient.' " See also, Olson, "In ESEA Wake, School Data Flowing Forth"; and Elizabeth Pinkerton, Nancy Kober, Caitlin Scott, and Barbara Buell, *Implementing the No Child Left Behind Act: A First Look Inside 15 School District in 2002–03* (Washington, D.C.: Center on Education Policy, October 2003).

14. Code of Federal Regulations, Title 34, Part 200, 20.36, http://www.ed.gov/legislation/FedRegister/finrule/2002–4/120202a.pdf.

15. Elizabeth Pinkerton, Nancy Kober, Caitlin Scott, and Barbara Buell, *Implementing the No Child Left Behind Act: A First Look Inside 15 School District in 2002–03* (Washington, D.C.: Center on Education Policy, October 2003).

16. NCLB requires districts to spend 20 percent of their Title 1, Part A allocations on transportation (to alternative schools) or on supplemental services, with at least 5 percent going to each, and the remainder decided by the district. Daniel Pryzbyla, "No Child Left Behind: Unlike the Ostrich, NCLB Has Its Head in the Sand," *EducationNews.org*, December 4, 2002. See also, Dan Joling, "In

Alaska, New School Rules Don't Jibe with Rural Reality," *Philadelphia Inquirer*, April 15, 2003, p. A2.

17. Erpenbach, *Statewide Educational Accountability*.

18. See also, Liz Bowie, "Few City Families Accept Transfers to Better Schools," *Baltimore Sun*, July 10, 2003, p. A1.

19. Russo, "Flunking Out: Bush's Pet Education Bill is in Serious Trouble."

20. Pamela Benigno, *No Child Left Behind Mandates School Choice: Colorado's First Year* (Golden, Colo.: Independence Institute, Issue Paper 9, June 2003), p. 8.

21. Greg Toppo, "States Fight No Child Left Behind, Calling it Intrusive," *USA Today*, February 12, 2004, p. D14.

22. Thomas J. Kane and Douglas O. Staiger, "Unintended Consequences of Racial Subgroup Rules," in *Brookings Papers on No Child Left Behind*, ed. Paul E. Peterson and Martin R. West (Washington, D.C.: Brookings Institution Press, 2003), pp. 152–176. See also, Tom Loveless, "Charter School Achievement and Accountability," in *Brookings Papers on No Child Left Behind*, ed. Paul E. Peterson and Martin R. West (Washington, D.C.: Brookings Institution Press, 2003), pp. 177–196.

23. Erpenbach, *Statewide Educational Accountability*.

24. "Adequate Yearly Progress: A State Snapshot," *Education Week*, September 2003, p. 37. Available at http://www.edweek.org/ew/ewstory.cfm?slug= 01ayp_s1.h23.

25. Pinkerton et al.

26. "1994 ESEA: The State of State Compliance," *Education Week*, April 17, 2002, p. 29. Available at http://www.edweek.org/ew/ewstory.cfm?slug=31eseabox. h21&keywords=ESEA.

27. Michael A. Fletcher, "N.Y. Suit Claims Denial of Rights in School Law," *Washington Post*, January 28, 2003, p. A4.

28. Data on state-level school choice policies come from Krista Kafer, *School Choice, 2003* (Washington, D.C.: Heritage Foundation, 2003).

29. Robert Maranto, "How the Best Laid Schemes Go Astray: the Agony and (occasional) Ecstasy of Charter Start-ups," NCSC Review, no. 2 (April 2003): 14–17.

30. Where one variable in the index was missing, we set its value to 0; where two or more were missing we did not calculate the index.

31. Save for Oversight and Timely announcement, and Oversight and Model Letter, the variables making up the grades do not intercorrelate. States that score well on one dimension often score poorly on another. Naturally, the index itself correlates with all its constituent variables at .30 to .72. Grades fail to correlate with other education variables, such as NAEP results or implementation of the 1994 ESEA. Notably, more Democratic-voting states have somewhat higher scores.

32. Jeffrey L. Pressman and Aaron Wildavsky, *Implementation* (2nd ed.) (Berkeley: University of California Press, 1979). See also, Frederick M. Hess, *Spinning Wheels: The Politics of Urban School Reform* (Washington, D.C.: Brookings Institution Press, 1999).

33. Dan Joling, "In Alaska, New School Rules Don't Jibe with Rural Reality," *Philadelphia Inquirer*, April 15, 2003, p. A2.
34. Fletcher, "N.Y. Suit Claims Denial of Rights in School Law."
35. Michael W. Kirst, "Who's in Charge? Federal, State, and Local Control," in *Learning from the Past: What History Teaches Us About School Reform*, ed. Diane Ravitch and Maris A. Vinovskis (Baltimore: Johns Hopkins University Press, 1995), pp. 25–26.
36. John W. Kingdon, *Agendas, Alternatives, and Public Policies* (2nd ed.) (New York: Harper Collins, 1995). See also, David R. Mayhew, *Divided We Govern* (New Haven, Conn.: Yale University Press, 1991).
37. Jennifer Hochschild, "Rethinking Accountability Politics," in *Brookings Papers on No Child Left Behind*, ed. Paul E. Peterson and Martin R. West (Washington, D.C.: Brookings Institution Press, 2003), pp. 116–119.
38. Terry M. Moe, *Schools, Vouchers, and the American Public* (Washington, D.C.: Brookings Institution Press, 2001).
39. Benigno, "No Child Left Behind Mandates School Choice."
40. http://www.baeo.org/home/index.php.
41. Fletcher, "N.Y. Suit Claims Denial of Rights in School Law."
42. Gerald N. Rosenberg, *The Hollow Hope: Can Courts Bring About Social Change?* (Chicago: University of Chicago Press, 1991).

5

Florida: Confusions, Constraints, and Cascading Scenarios

Jane Hannaway and Kendra Bischoff[1]

This chapter examines the early experience of Florida in implementing the choice provisions of the landmark No Child Left Behind (NCLB) act. The centerpiece of the act is its accountability focus, intended to result in universal proficiency in math and reading by 2014. By the 2005–2006 school year, states must have accountability systems in place with annual performance objectives and must assess student performance in grades 3–8 annually and in grades 10–12 at least once. To ensure that no students are left behind in the march to proficiency, states are further required to disaggregate their test results by poverty, race, ethnicity, disability, and limited English proficiency.

In the meantime, students attending Title I schools deemed "in need of improvement" have options. Students in schools not making adequate progress for two consecutive years have the option of choosing a more successful public school in the district, with transportation paid by the district. If schools do not make adequate progress for a third year, they are required to use Title I dollars to purchase supplemental educational services (SES)—tutoring—for their students using state-approved public or private providers. Districts are required to spend up to an amount equal to 20 percent of their Title I dollars for these choice-related provisions. This chapter focuses on the early implementation of these two choice provisions in Florida.

Florida is a year behind many states in implementing the choice and supplemental services provisions of NCLB because there were no schools in 2001–2002 that had two consecutive years of not making adequate progress. School choice was not triggered until the 2002–2003 performance was recorded and 45 schools with two years of inadequate progress emerged. So the supplemental services provision, a consequence of not making AYP for three years, takes effect for the first time in the 2004–2005 school year.

Why is Florida an Interesting Case?

For many states, developing an accountability system with annual testing and consequences for schools that do not perform well is a new challenge; and the mandatory inclusion of choice programs is an even steeper challenge. But Florida is a front-runner in implementing both a statewide accountability system and a statewide choice program. Because Florida is further along these two learning curves we might expect it to provide the best-case scenario for early implementation of the provisions of NCLB. Alternatively, we might expect the state's experience and the local learning that has taken place to pose additional hurdles if the path the state has taken for accountability and choice does not map well onto the federal directives.

Below we review Florida's policy history in school accountability and school choice, present a profile of education in Florida, and then compare the provisions of NCLB with those of the state. We then examine the implementation of the NCLB provisions in Florida by looking at the experiences of two different types of districts—one large and urban, the other small and rural. We extract three observations from our analysis. First, basic differences in the state accountability system and the NCLB accountability requirements create conflicting signals about school quality. There is a risk that confusion could lead parents to discount information on school quality, undermining both state and federal efforts to improve schools. Our second observation is related. Information systems that are effective for administratively run efforts to improve schools may be very different from information systems effective for school choice efforts. And third, if Florida holds to its standards, NCLB could create a cascading scenario of demands that it may not have the capacity to handle. In short, NCLB school choice could be crushed by its own weight or lead to very restricted choice options because of a limited supply of acceptable alternatives.

The Florida Policy History—Accountability and Choice

Accountability. Florida has a relatively long history in student assessment and school accountability. As early as 1971, the legislature passed the Educational

Accountability Act and, in the next year, the first statewide assessment in reading took place in grades 2 and 4 and tests in mathematics and writing were developed. By 1975 all third-, sixth-, and ninth-grade students were being tested in reading, writing, and math. By 1978, four grades (3, 5, 8, and 11) were tested, and students were required to pass a functional literacy test to graduate from high school. This regime continued with relatively minor adjustments throughout the 1980s.

In the mid-1990s, the bar was raised. The earlier testing had focused heavily on basic skills and competencies. In 1995, the Florida Commission on Education Reform and Accountability recommended changes to heighten educational expectations for students. The recommendations were accepted by the State Board of Education and, as a consequence, the Sunshine State Standards were adopted, and the Florida Comprehensive Assessment Test (FCAT) was developed. In that same year, 158 schools were identified as "critically low performing" by the state, and a process of remediation began.

Conceived in 1999, the current A+ Plan for Education, the state's accountability system, is built on the foundation of the FCATs and the Sunshine State Standards and what was perceived to be the effective remediation of the "critically low-performing" schools. Testing using the FCAT began in 1998 in grades 4 (reading), 5 (math), 8 (reading and math), and 10 (reading and math). The first test results were not used for accountability but were shared with schools to construct a performance baseline. School accountability began with release of the 1999 test results and a comprehensive accountability plan was codified in 1999 legislation. According to the plan, Florida schools receive a report card and are graded on a scale of A to F, primarily on the basis of student test results and participation rates.

These school performance grades provide information to both parents and educators about individual school achievement and progress. But perhaps more importantly, they also come with tangible consequences. Schools that receive an A or improve by one grade level on the A-F scale receive a bonus of up to $100 per student. More than $122 million was made available for school recognition in 2002. For schools that do not perform well, there are also consequences. Low-performing schools receive assistance including approximately $1,000 per student and technical assistance in the form of reading and math coaches.[2] If a school receives an F in two out of any four years, students in those schools are eligible for Opportunity Scholarships, equivalent to the state per student allocation, which would allow them to choose any public or qualifying private school in the state with transportation included. In effect, the accountability plan in the state comes with a "kicker" in the form of a voucher.[3]

Table 5.1. School Grades Distribution 1999–2003

Year	A	B	C	D	F	I*	N**	Total
1999								
n	202	313	1230	601	76			2422
%	8	13	51	25	3			100
2000								
n	579	266	1165	397	4			2411
%	24	11	48	16	<1			100
2001								
n	592	412	1122	307			66	2499
%	24	16	45	12			3	100
2002								
n	894	553	725	185	64		109	2530
%	35	22	29	7	3		4	100
2003								
n	1230	569	527	141	35	12	80	2594
%	47	22	20	5	1	<1	3	100

Source: Florida Department of Education.
*I=Incomplete.
**N=Not rated.

Looking at school performance grades statewide, it appears the accountability plan is a success.[4] Table 5.1 shows the number of schools by grade from 1999 through 2003. As can be seen, the number of schools receiving an A grade has increased dramatically, from 8 percent of schools in 1999 to 47 percent in 2003. And the number of schools receiving D or F grades decreased from 28 percent in 1999 to 6 percent in 2003.

At least to some degree, this state-calculated success appears to be supported with recent national test results. Florida was the only state that showed a statistically significant increase in the percentage of students who scored at or above "proficient" on the 2003 National Assessment of Education Progress reading exam at the fourth grade. For the first time, grade 4 reading scores in Florida exceeded the national average. Statistically significant reading increases at the eight grade and significant improvements in math, however, were not achieved.[5]

Choice. Florida has three distinct voucher-based choice programs established by the legislature in the last few years. The first is the Opportunity Scholarship Program, noted above, which is part of the state's accountability system. The second is the McKay Scholarships for students with disabilities,[6] and the third is a tuition tax-credit scholarship program.[7] As Governor Jeb Bush noted in his 2003 State of Education Address, "More than 24,000 Florida students are using a voucher this year for educational opportunities that would otherwise be beyond their reach. This year 11,462 students participate in our Corporate Tax Credit Scholarship program; 12,113 receive McKay Scholarships; and another 619 receive Opportunity Scholarships." In addition, the state has charter schools serving tens of thousands of students.[8]

The Opportunity Scholarship Program has the greatest voucher potential, and is most relevant to the discussion here because it is part of the state's accountability plan, but it has not been widely implemented. In 1999 two schools were deemed eligible for Opportunity Scholarships, and 72 schools had one F on the books. If those F schools did not improve, there was the possibility that more than thirty-five thousand students would receive vouchers the next year. This did not happen. Indeed, no schools received a second F in 2000, and it was not until 2002 that students in 10 additional schools became voucher eligible. Some researchers claim that, even though there have been relatively few vouchers awarded, the threat of vouchers led to higher school performance.[9] But other explanations, including a grade stigma triggering socially driven remediation mechanisms and the additional resources allocated to low-performing schools, are alternatives that have not been adequately investigated.[10] Still, the voucher program is an integral part of the state's accountability system. We look at its provisions in more detail later in this chapter as we compare them to the NCLB provisions.

Florida's Education Profile

The structure of K-12 education in Florida and the demographics of the student population also make it an interesting case for examining the NCLB choice provisions. Florida has more than 2.5 million students from prekindergarten to grade 12, and most of the state's 67 countywide school districts are larger than average. The average U.S. school district serves only 3,297 students; the average in Florida is 10 times larger, 37,316 students. Though the smallest district in Florida has 1,012 students, 26 districts have more than 25,000 students apiece, making them among the largest in the country (see table 5.2). Similarly, the average school sizes (enrollment) in Florida are well above the national average; 674 vs. 441 at the primary level, 1,069 vs. 612 at the middle school level, and 1,565 vs. 753 at the high school level.[11] The relatively large number of schools in a district provides, theoretically anyway, a reasonably large range of options for students wanting to exercise school choice. In addition, the large average school enrollment means a sizable number of students would likely be eligible for choice in each school affected by the NCLB choice provision.

Table 5.2. Distribution of school districts by Size—Florida and U.S.

	Florida		U.S.*
	N	%	%
100,00 or more	7	10	<1
25,000–99,999	19	28	1
10,000–24,999	10	15	4
5,000–9,999	12	18	7
2,000–4,999	14	21	20
1,000–1,999	5	8	18
999 or less	0	0	48

* Size was not reported for 1.5% of schools.
*Source: U.S. Department of Education, National Center for Education Statistics,
2001–2002.*

Florida has a diverse student population; fully half of its more than two
and one-half million students are minorities. According to the Florida NCLB
Accountability Workbook, 24.16 percent are black, 20.95 percent are
Hispanic, 1.98 percent are Asian/Pacific Islander, 1.99 percent are multira-
cial, and .28 percent are American Indian/Alaskan Native. In addition, 11 percent of students have limited English proficiency, 15 percent are students
with disabilities, and 43.7 percent are economically disadvantaged, up from
37.6 percent just 10 years ago.

While Florida showed gains on the 2003 national assessment, the performance of the state is not high. Only 32 percent of fourth graders scored
at or above "proficient" in reading. Florida ranked 28th among the states,[12]
and the performance of minority students in Florida was considerably lower
than of white students.[13] Both black and Hispanic students, however, have
scored somewhat above the national average for each group since 1998, and
of further importance, the gains in Florida from 1998 to 2003 for these students have exceeded the national gains over the same period.[14]

A Comparison: Florida A+ Plan and NCLB

The basic concepts and strategies that undergird the Florida A+ Plan are the
same as those for NCLB. Both call for annual testing of all students in reading and math in most grades and both link student performance to consequential actions by the state, including allowing students in "schools in need
of improvement" the opportunity to transfer to other schools (see table 5.3).

Table 5.3. Comparison of NCLB and A+

	NCLB	A+
Testing	All students in grades 3–8 and at least once in grades 10–12 in reading and math.	All students in grades 3–10 in reading and math; writing in grades 4, 8, and 10.
Consequences	Districts with schools identified as not making adequate yearly progress (AYP), as the state defines it, for 2 years must offer students in the school the option of moving to a new public school; schools not making AYP for 3 years must offer the opportunity for supplemental services with Title I dollars. District must develop and implement a school-improvement plan for low-performing schools. If schools continue to not make AYP, NCLB requires districts to undertake more severe interventions.	Schools that receive a grade of F (on an A-F scale), primarily on the basis of student test performance, in two out of four years must offer students an "Opportunity Scholarship" (equivalent to the state's contribution per student) that can be redeemed at any public or eligible private school in the state. Districts must provide technical assistance to schools that are low performing and schools that receive an A or that improve more than one grade level are given financial rewards.

Source: Florida Department of Education.

Despite these basic similarities, however, the A+ Plan and NCLB differ in ways that likely make the simultaneous operation of both systems confusing.

A Confusing Picture

The A+ Plan and NCLB differ in how they define and calculate school progress, and the differences are consequential. The A+ Plan uses a point system—based on both the percent of students *scoring high* on the FCAT and the percent making *learning gains*—to establish school grades. More specifically, A+ classifies students into five achievement categories: 1 (low) to 5 (high). Schools earn a point for each percent of students achieving 3 or above in reading and achieving 3 or above in math. They also receive a point for the average of the percent scoring 3 or above and the percent scoring 3.5 or above in writing.[15] In 2002, the A+ Plan also began rewarding schools for annual *learning gains*. Schools earn one point for each percent of students who make gains in reading and for each percent who make gains in math.[16] Additional points are given for reading gains by students in the lowest 25 percent in levels 1, 2, or 3 in the school. In short, the A+ Plan scoring system incorporates explicit incentives for schools to give special attention to the lowest performing students. Indeed, in order to be an A school, the learning gains of students in the lowest quartile must be within 10 points of the gains for all students. The weight given to learning gains means that the average level of performance in some B and even some C schools can be higher than in some A schools.

NCLB calculates progress differently, even though it is based on the same FCAT exam and performance targets set by the state. Indeed, in many ways NCLB ratings are simpler. Florida set its NCLB performance objectives in reading at the twentieth percentile of school performance in 2002. This translates into 31 percent of students scoring at or above 3 in reading on the FCAT and 38 percent in math.[17] The performance objective in reading increases to 48 percent in year 3 (2004–2005), 65 percent in year 6 (2004–2005), 82 percent in year 9 (2009–2010), and 100 percent in year 12 (2013–2014). In math, the jumps in corresponding years are: 53 percent, 68 percent, 83 percent, and 100 percent.

There are four major differences between NCLB and A+. First, though A+ focuses heavily on *learning gains* as well as achievement levels, NCLB focuses only on achievement levels. Even if students in a school make large gains, it would not register in the NCLB performance accounting unless the established target were met. Under NCLB, either you make it or you don't.[18] Second, while A+ gives special weight to academically low-performing students in developing a school grade, NCLB calculates separate scores for multiple subgroups of students: white, black, Hispanic, Asian American, American Indian students, and students who are economically disadvantaged, have limited English proficiency (LEP), or are disabled (DIS). Third, the test participation criteria are higher and broader in NCLB. In NCLB, 95 percent of enrolled students must be tested. In A+, a 95 percent participation rate is required for receiving an A, but for other performance grades participation need only be 90 percent. And fourth, NCLB requires the testing of all students, including those not yet proficient in English and those who are disabled, though it allows alternate assessments for some of these students.[19] In contrast, A+ requires the participation of only "standard curriculum" students, though speech-impaired, gifted, hospital/homebound, and limited English-speaking students with more than two years in an ESOL program are considered to be in the standard curriculum.[20]

The differences in the ratings assigned to schools by the two accountability systems are dramatic (see table 5.4). Eighty-seven percent of the schools in Florida did not make AYP in 2002–2003 according to the NCLB criteria![21] Though most of the schools that passed were A schools, 75 percent of the A schools in Florida failed. Such results might suggest that Florida's student

Table 5.4. Florida schools–AYP status by A+ grade, 2003

	A	B	C	D	F	N*	Total
Pass AYP							
#	309	40	16	—	—	16	381
%	25	7	3			20	15
Fail AYP							
#	934	526	518	139	35	63	2215
%	75	93	97	100	100	80	85
Total	1243	566	534	139	35	79	2596
	48	22	21	5	1	3	

*Not previously rated.
Source: *Preliminary data provided by: NCLB Accountability Report, Florida Department of Education.*

performance objectives are set too high. But this is an unlikely explanation because baseline proficiency requirements are set at the standard twentieth percentile of student achievement in the state (31 percent for reading and 38 percent for math), per NCLB.

The disaggregation of subgroup data appears to have particularly important effects on NCLB school performance results in Florida. Florida's NCLB provisions require that, for each school, subgroups with at least 30 students be included as separate categories in accountability reporting. For many states with more homogenous populations and smaller schools, the minimum cell size stipulation provides a loophole in the law.[22] Schools can easily omit "at-risk" students from accountability reports if the subgroup population falls below a critical cell-size number, a number that varies from state to state. Given Florida's diverse student body and large average school size, Sunshine State schools are likely to have more subgroup hurdles to clear, providing one explanation for the state's low AYP success rate.

The NCLB subgroup requirement is also the likely culprit in producing the disparity between state and federal accountability results. Students with disabilities, students who have limited English proficiency, and black students most often failed to perform adequately on the FCAT exam (see figure 5.1). Students with disabilities did not meet the math standards in 87 percent of non-AYP schools and did not meet reading standards in 75 percent. Similarly, students lacking proficiency in English failed to meet math requirements in 78 percent of non-AYP schools and failed reading standards in 85 percent. Though it is discouraging to see a pattern of failure for subgroups, it points out what is not detailed in the A+ accountability plan. Although it may take some time and adjustment, these federal guidelines may force schools to concentrate on problems specific to low-performing students.

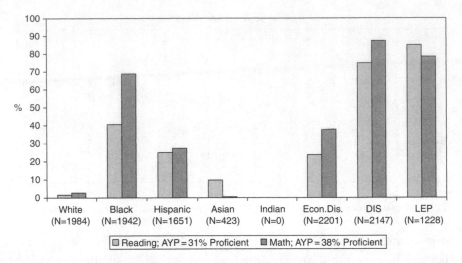

Figure 5.1. Percent of non-AYP schools failing by subgroup

N = Number of schools in subgroup calculation. (Only schools with at least 30 members in a subgroup were included.)

Data provided by: Florida Department of Education, Florida NCLB Accountability Report.

Implications for choice. The apparently conflicting school ratings associated with A+ and NCLB have possibly important implications for the effective working of a choice system in Florida. In order to reap the benefits that might result from giving parents choice over the school their child attends, parents must have reasonably complete and accurate information about the value of their options. Information is at the very core of market-oriented models.

In fact, there have been complaints about confusion just in the A+ system since the school grade was changed to be a combination of level of achievement and learning gains. While A-F school grades appear simple and transparent on the surface, parents have to unpack them in order to understand the quality dimensions of a school. Unpacking the A+ grade is not a trivial task. For example, a news account in Miami recounted the experience of one high school that earned more points on the percent of students scoring a 3 or above on math and reading than any high school in South Florida. The school also had the second-greatest improvement in the county for its lowest scoring students, yet failed to get an A because the gains for its lowest quartile were 11 points lower than the gains for students overall and the requirements specify 10 points as the limit.[23] In the same news account, a PTA president not surprisingly said, "I think there is a real lack of understanding about how these school grades are put together."

When we include the AYP ratings in the information that parents must digest to determine school quality, it would be a wonder if parents were not confused. Florida schools often have up to 30 criteria to meet to make AYP.

Table 5.5. Count of AYP criteria not met by school grade (2002–2003)

# criteria	A	B	C	D	F	I	N
1–5	769	260	138	17	4	5	34
6–10	185	160	148	40	15	3	25
11–15	29	80	103	27	8	1	7
16–20	1	30	81	24	4	2	
>20		6	46	33	4	2	

Source: Florida Department of Education.

Missing just one leads to failure. Table 5.5 shows the number of criteria that schools in different A+ grade categories failed. Some schools failed to meet AYP simply because less than 95 percent of their students were tested. Testing of even 94 percent would lead to failure though all other criteria were met. Note that the number of criteria not met by a majority of schools that failed to make AYP is relatively small.

The 2002–2003 school year was, of course, the first year of AYP ratings and only the second year with the A+ grade combining level of achievement and learning gains. As time passes, parents may become better acquainted with the accountability ratings. The accountability measures of the two systems may also come into closer alignment, and therefore become less confusing, if the state is successful in incorporating more of the learning gain elements of A+ into the AYP measure. "NCLB just does not give schools enough credit for learning gains built into A+," commented one state official. The state proposed learning gains criteria in the submission of its original NCLB plan to the U.S. Department of Education, but these were not accepted. The state is now work- ing to compile data in an attempt to show that including learning gains in AYP will not undermine the intent of the law; that is, that measures of gains do not have the effect of allowing lower performing students to bypass high standards.

Interestingly, state administrators appear not to be much fazed by the dif- ferences in A+ and NCLB, and the same may be true for school level admin- istrators. Commissioner Jim Horne has said, "No Child Left Behind's AYP measure simply sharpens our focus on improving education for specific groups of students." One state official explained, "A+ and NCLB are two different kinds of snapshots of the school . . . NCLB helps schools diagnose beneath the surface of the A+ parameters to see where they have pockets of need that have not been addressed." Principals of Florida schools that the senior author visited are probably also not much fazed. In what appears to be a sea change in school management, principals in Florida are now typically armed with three-inch–binder notebooks detailing the performance of indi- vidual students and subgroups of students on subscales of different tests.

Reorganizing the data to focus on different groups and tracking progress would not be difficult.

But an information system good for administrative purposes may differ from an information system good for school choice purposes. Both A+ and NCLB build in strong incentives for schools to attend to all students and to give particular attention to at-risk children. The measures do not allow schools to ignore the low-performers or the students whose parents are not able to make demands on the school, nor do they allow schools to mask the performance of particular groups of students with school averages. And the incentives seem to work; at least they appear to get the serious attention of state and school administrators and teachers. Apart from formal accountability, the data provide schools and administrators with information that before was largely unavailable. But parents, and probably especially parents of students in low-performing schools or low-performing groups, may have difficulty sorting through the multiple and apparently conflicting messages about the quality of their child's school. These performance information systems are designed to assist parents in their decisions to select an appropriate school for their child; but confusion may diminish the perceived relevance and value of available information. In short, sending confusing signals may create the risk that parents discount performance information, and it may thereby undermine the core theory behind much of the reform efforts.

What's ahead. As noted above, nearly 90 percent of the schools in Florida failed to make AYP in 2002–2003. But only 45 schools in 14 districts did not make AYP for two years and thus were required to offer choice. Forty-five schools in 14 districts is fairly manageable, according to state officials who are reviewing the school improvement plans of the districts. But what will happen in subsequent years?

Many of the over 2000 schools that failed to meet NCLB requirements, especially those not performing satisfactorily on only a few criteria, may well make AYP in 2003–2004 and not have to offer choice. Figure 5.2 shows the percent of A schools that failed to make adequate progress by NCLB subgroup. Performance of disabled and limited English-proficient student groups was particularly problematic. There were also problems with the math performance of black students. In addition to giving more concerted effort to the low-performing groups, schools may also be helped by new federal rules on students with disabilities that allow more local flexibility in measuring and counting the scores of students with significant cognitive disabilities. In addition, the state is considering some changes related to the testing of students lacking proficiency in English and in February 2004 the U.S. Department of Education also provided some new flexibility for such testing under NCLB.

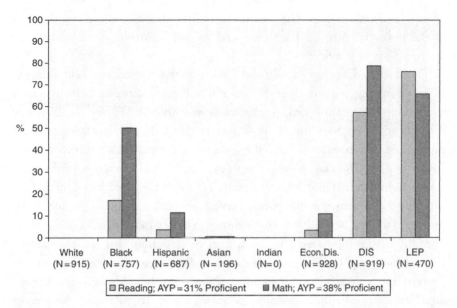

Figure 5.2. Percent of non-AYP A schools failing by subgroup

N = Number of schools in subgroup calculation. (Only schools with at least 30 members in a subgroup were included.)

Data provided by: Florida Department of Education, Florida NCLB Accountability Report.

But the possibility of widespread school choice being required by NCLB in Florida in 2004–2005 is real and cannot be ignored. The governor and State Board of Education are determined to hold to their standards and not lower proficiency measures as some states have seriously considered. Even if all the A schools made AYP in 2003–2004, more than twelve hundred schools could remain as inadequately performing, and about half of the schools in the state are Title I schools. Students in the failing Title I schools must choose a school that has received at least a C grade on the A+ accountability plan and is making adequate progress. How many eligible schools will there be, and will they be in close enough proximity to be feasible alternatives? If a large number of A schools do not make AYP in 2003–2004, the state could have the odd situation of A schools, presumably the best performers in the state, not open as options for students seeking higher performing schools. There simply may not be enough adequately performing schools where they are needed for a viable choice system to operate.

Offering supplemental education services (SES)—tutoring—may be more widespread and implemented earlier than originally thought. Technically, only the 45 schools currently offering choice should be worried about supplemental services in 2004–2005. But the likely absence of a sufficient number of eligible school choice options may force districts to move to earlier use of supplemental services. The Florida Department of Education is well aware of the potential demand for these services and is currently establishing an approved list of providers.

Thus far, the Office of Family and Community Outreach has held an informational meeting for interested entities at which applications and informational addendums were distributed. Applications were due on January 5, 2004, and the state approved 56 of the 71 applicants in March. In an effort to increase the number of faith-based providers the application process was re-opened in the late spring. State officials will meet with districts to discuss responsibilities, time lines, and implementation assistance as well as request that participating districts submit action plans. Finally, public service announcements will be aired and provider fairs will be held over the summer to help parents decide.

Many of the interested entities appear to be school districts themselves. Consulting firms, universities, Internet-based education services, community centers, and non-profits with an educational focus have also expressed interest. The approval rubric exhibits the state's intent to compile a financially sound and effective group of providers. Although an approved list of supplemental services providers will surely aid districts in their efforts to comply with regulations, many issues about the effectiveness of the providers and the availability of options in urban areas and sparsely populated rural areas are bound to emerge.

In the section below, we examine the implementation of school choice in two districts in Florida. We chose a large urban and a small rural district in order to get a picture of similarities and differences in the issues that emerged in the implementation of the choice provisions in different contexts.

Implementation of NCLB Choice: A Look at Two Districts

The NCLB legislation requires only that parents be given a "reasonable choice," meaning that they have at least two schools from which to choose. Beyond that, school districts are free to develop their NCLB choice plans in whatever ways make the most sense for them educationally and financially. The U.S. Department of Education provides little guidance on choice plans and the state, at least at this time, requires only that districts comply with the two-school minimum, thereby leaving districts with considerable discretion. For example, districts are able to identify which schools are eligible to be "receiving" schools so long as the schools are performing sufficiently well. The best schools need not be eligible. State officials suspect that at least some districts will attempt to protect their premier schools by not including them as choice options. In addition, some districts are reportedly considering redesigning their economic survey so that their high schools are not eligible for Title I funds, and consequently not subject to the AYP provisions. Districts also have responsibility for determining how to go about informing parents of their options; and they do so, at least for now, with little state guidance. The case studies below, of urban Miami–Dade County and rural Jefferson County, illustrate some of the challenges that districts face in their inaugural year of implementing NCLB choice and how local conditions shape their responses.

Urban Case: Miami-Dade

Miami–Dade County Public Schools is the largest district in the state of Florida and the fourth-largest nationally. With an enrollment of 371,691 students in more than 400 schools, the district is a massive education system in a diverse urban environment that is spread out over two thousand square miles. The student body is 10 percent white, 29 percent black, and 59 percent Hispanic. Eighteen percent of the students are enrolled in Exceptional Student Education (ESE) services, 25 percent have limited English proficiency, and approximately 61 percent are economically disadvantaged. [24]

Miami–Dade County has been and continues to be at the forefront of Florida's progressive education policies. The district already offers an impressive number of options to exercise school choice, which for parents must be both liberating and daunting. Miami supports 71 magnet schools, 25 charter schools, 14 "controlled choice" schools,[25] and 4 satellite schools. Enrollment in these schools in 2002–2003 totaled 12 percent of the district's student body, before including A+ and NCLB choice.[26] Additionally, the district plans to initiate a federally funded Voluntary Public School Choice Program in 2005, which will broadly restructure and redefine education in the district.[27] The program is already recruiting and enrolling students. In light of these numerous possibilities, it is no wonder that parents, students, and even administrators have difficulty deciphering the system, determining eligibility, and maneuvering through the application processes. Though not every school can offer every program, the meshing of accountability measures and provisions creates a complex web of options that parents must sort through in an attempt to select the best educational opportunities for their children.

The overlap among programs has created some unusual situations for the district. For example, one controlled choice arrangement in Miami-Dade includes three schools, one of which was an F school eligible for A+ Opportunity Scholarships redeemable at any public or participating private school. A private school in the neighborhood reportedly was actively encouraging parents to choose the F school so they could receive a voucher and then attend the private school with tuition covered by the state. The district realized what was happening and told parents that, if they knowingly chose the F school, they would not be eligible for a voucher. Another unusual situation, that is at least theoretically possible, is that a student receiving an Opportunity Scholarship could redeem it at a school that did not make AYP. Recall that 75 percent of the A schools in Florida did not make AYP, so it is not necessarily an unreasonable choice. But if schools that did not make AYP are "receiving" schools for other choice programs, the competitive pressure brought on by NCLB choice may be diminished.

Because Miami-Dade has extensive experience with school choice and because it is a dense and diverse urban center, it presents an interesting and perhaps unusual case in which to consider NCLB choice. At least in 2003–2004, the impact of NCLB on choice appears to be marginal at best. As the Assistant Superintendent for School Choice and Parental Options explained, "NCLB is not the first trigger for choice . . . with all the other programs simultaneously going on in Dade, the effects of NCLB are negligible."

Nine schools in the district—five elementary, two charters, and two high schools—were identified for NCLB choice. Of the 7,546 students eligible for NCLB choice, only 321 exercised it. According to the district's school improvement plan, parents may choose any school within their established NCLB zone that has made AYP, and their children will receive transportation to the school. Students may also choose a school outside their zone, but they are then responsible for transportation. Because the district is divided into only three zones, mapped onto high school feeder patterns, there are a large number of possible choices, assuming that schools made AYP.[28]

Interestingly, two of the schools in the district identified for NCLB choice are charter schools. So in this case, parents are already exercising choice. The district was unsure how to handle this atypical circumstance and received little guidance from the state. It decided to offer parents the option of returning their children to their originally assigned school if it had made AYP. Only if it did not would other options be open to them. The district has not moved to revoke the charters of these schools, but the schools are under intensified supervision and are required to develop goals and school improvement plans.

Both high schools identified for NCLB choice in the district are also identified as eligible for A+ Opportunity Scholarships, which allows both public and private school options. The experience of Miami-Edison Senior High

School shows the extensiveness of choice in the district. The school is in a community characterized by the Caribbean and South American roots of many of its residents. It serves a racially diverse and multicultural population of whom approximately 83 percent are Haitian/Creole immigrants, 22 percent have limited English proficiency, and over 60 percent qualify for free or reduced-price lunches. FCAT results show that 84 percent of tenth-graders are in Level 1 in reading, and 66 percent are in Level 1 in mathematics. Edison faces serious educational challenges, evidenced by the fact that it received an F grade twice and also failed AYP for the past two years. Parents have a number of options, and they exercise them. Fully 32 percent of the student body takes advantage of choice. In addition to A+ Opportunity Scholarships and public school transfers under NCLB, magnet schools and McKay Scholarships are also possibilities. The data from 2003–2004 show that out of 883 students who chose to leave Edison High School, 491 took advantage of the magnet program, 223 received Opportunity Scholarships, and 60—just 2 percent of the student body—participated in NCLB choice.[29]

In addition to the availability of various choice programs in Miami-Dade, the low take-up rate on NCLB choice may be related to timing. The school system found out in June 2003 that the nine schools would have to offer federally mandated choice for the 2003–2004 school year. The district turned this information around quickly and had letters out to parents by July 1 in English, Spanish, and Haitian Creole. It gave parents until August 1 to make a decision and informed schools of new transfers in the first week of August, about three weeks before the first day of school. At least for this inaugural year, parents were informed about their NCLB option well after being informed about other options, such as Opportunity Scholarships. The A+ test results were out in June[30] and parents were required to register for Opportunity Scholarships by July 1, before they even received notification about the NCLB rating and its consequences. Since NCLB choice is more restricted than A+ Opportunity Scholarship choice, it is surprising that any parents used it. It could be that the 60 families in Edison High School who exercised NCLB choice simply missed the deadline for Opportunity Scholarships.

The letter the district sent to parents affected by NCLB explained that they had the option of leaving their child at their school or transferring to another public school that had made AYP. An application was also attached, and a phone number was provided for assistance. There were not, however, any specific transfer options listed, although parents could come to the district office to discuss options. A real concern is that parents may know what they are leaving but have little information about what they are choosing, and little time to become informed.

While the district had to react quickly to the new NCLB provisions in 2003–2004, the rush was manageable. The number of affected schools was small, and the district had procedures in place for A+ notification of parents and for making logistical arrangements for school choice that could be easily adapted to the NCLB situation. But the 2004–2005 school year may be different. Florida cities may experience what many other urban districts in the country faced in 2003–2004. If Miami-Dade schools that did not make AYP this year fail again in 2003–2004, the number of schools required to offer choice under NCLB will be overwhelming. Just 28 of the 400 schools in the district made AYP last school year. Without significant improvement, the 28 schools would be the only schools eligible to receive transfers from the 169 Title I schools at risk of a second year of not making AYP. Clearly the numbers won't work. The obvious result is no or very restricted choice. Thinking about the coming year, the Miami-Dade assistant superintendent said, "I'm scared . . . there's no place for the students to go." If the 2003–2004 take-up rate for NCLB choice is any indication, the number of students likely to opt for NCLB choice may be small. But the district must be prepared to accommodate students in persistently low-performing schools. Doing nothing is not an option. The fallback position for the district appears to be offering students tutoring in keeping with the NCLB's provisions, but the details are far from clear. As mentioned before, the state is currently developing a list of approved supplemental services providers.

Rural Case: Jefferson County

Located in the Florida panhandle, Jefferson has approximately thirteen thousand residents. The school district enrolls 1,485 students in three schools. Jefferson Elementary School, the only Title I school in the county, did not make AYP for the past two years and is currently "in need of improvement," even though it successfully moved from F to C in the state system in 2002–2003 and received school recognition. The student body is 27 percent white, 69 percent black, and 2 percent Hispanic. Twenty-seven percent of the students are classified as students with disabilities and 72 percent are economically disadvantaged.[31] The middle school and the high school in the county also did not make AYP, but the district directs all Title I funds to the elementary school, so the other two schools are not subject to NCLB provisions.

The district's exceptionally high percentage of disabled students casts doubt on its chances for ever making AYP for this subgroup. The district is currently lobbying its congressman, hoping to get the maximum percentage of alternative test-takers raised to accommodate its unique student population.

Unlike Miami-Dade, there are no preexisting choice programs within Jefferson County. However, there are two university-affiliated lab schools in neighboring Leon County, a parochial school in Jefferson County, and a significant number of children being home-schooled. The lab schools are both highly rated, but also have enrollment quotas and long waiting lists, reflecting the region's demand for alternative options. In 2003–2004, 137 Jefferson County students attended the lab schools, about 200 students studied at the Christian academy, and approximately 125 were taught in their homes. According to the district superintendent, the number of students receiving home education has gradually increased in the past few years and now amounts to nearly 8 percent of the district enrollment, significantly higher than the state as a whole, which has less than 2 percent of the student population being schooled at home and Miami-Dade, which has less than 1 percent.[32] Furthermore, the district has lost more students between 1999 and 2003 (23.37 percent) than any other district in the state, suggesting both a loss of resources for a problem-laden school district, and also the possibility that the lack of acceptable educational alternatives may be driving parents to find their own.[33]

When the district was informed in June 2003 that its elementary school would have to offer school choice, it considered all possible alternatives. The letter sent to parents on July 31, 2003, laid out for the parents the alternatives that the district was exploring which included transfers to neighboring districts and supplemental services. The district planned to let parents know by August 7, the first day of school in the county. The Jefferson superintendent contacted the superintendents in neighboring Leon, Wakulla, Taylor, and Madison counties, but all four turned down the transfer request. The only option available was supplemental services.

The district hastily developed an after-school tutoring program, Power Hour, run by four certified teachers. In the 2003–2004 school year, parents had the option of sending their children or not. Almost 100 students of the approximately 625 enrolled at the elementary school opted to participate in this program. It was reported that every parent who inquired about the program received services. In 2004–2005, the district hopes to have a broader menu of supplemental services providers, perhaps including Catapult Learning (formerly Sylvan Learning Centers) and the Boys and Girls Club, which has three locations, one right next to the school. Decisions will have to wait, however, until the state finalizes its approved provider list. In any case, it is highly unlikely that school choice will ever be a feasible reform strategy in Jefferson County.

Three Concluding Observations

Three observations about the implementation of the NCLB choice provisions emerged as a consequence of our analysis of the Florida experience, and these may have implications beyond Florida. First, state and NCLB accountability systems can lead to dramatically different results, even when most of the basic principles underlying the systems and tests are the same. We think this is a significant problem to the extent that it undermines parent confidence in the performance information that the different systems produce. Indeed, we suspect it could lead parents to seriously discount school performance information when attempting to determine school quality. Perhaps this is a short-term problem. That is, our concern may be misplaced if the state and/or federal systems evolve in ways that make them better aligned. Federal policymakers should take advantage of the experience of some of the more highly developed state systems as thought is given to changes in the federal system. Florida with its commitment to high standards, accountability, and choice, and with a rich data system from which to extract lessons, may provide some guidance or a location for experimentation. Giving schools credit for performance gains as well as performance levels is an example of an issue about which Florida is particularly knowledgeable.

Our second observation is related. The simple summary ratings of schools—A-F in the case of the A+ plan and making or not making AYP in the case of NCLB—mask the highly complex basis for school performance ratings. If well-informed decision makers are essential for market-based models to work well, then parents need to unpack the performance measures–no doubt a difficult task for many parents, especially when ratings differ and decisions have to be made under short deadlines. At the same time, it appears that the multifaceted ratings are well understood by school professionals and that they are effective at directing focused attention to particular problem areas in a school or district. So complex rating schemes are not necessarily bad; they have definite administrative advantages for directing effective school reform. But more attention needs to be given to mechanisms for effectively informing parents about the dimensions and relative merits of their assigned school as well as other schools open to them as they make decisions. Choosing a school is not like choosing a breakfast cereal. Placing a child in an ineffective school for even a year can have long-term consequences for the child.

Third, while there is no doubt that school choice can play an important role in reform efforts, it clearly is no panacea. And there appears to be a trade-off between high standards and practical implementation. The higher the standards, the larger the number of schools that do not make AYP, and the fewer the number of schools eligible to be receiving schools. The mathematics of the problem is simple. But the consequence is that, where we need choice the most, acceptable alternatives are the scarcest. Where choice is unworkable, the immediate solution appears to be offering supplemental services, and many of the providers may be the school districts themselves. This is not necessarily a problem. But, ironically, it could lead to Title I history repeating itself; that is, a movement away from integrated schoolwide programs to more targeted remedial assistance programs.

Analysts have noted for years that the Achilles heel of choice reforms is the supply of reasonable alternatives. In the case of NCLB choice, supply problems appear to be central. In order to see a good test of choice, we need not only to focus on accountability for low-performing schools, but also on incentives for the creation of new high-performing alternatives.

Notes

1. The research reported here is part of a larger multi-year project evaluating the Florida A+ Accountability Plan being conducted by David Figlio, Dan Goldhaber, Jane Hannaway and Cecilia Rouse. It is supported by the Annie E. Casey Foundation, Atlantic Philanthropic Services, the Smith Richardson Foundation, the Spencer Foundation, the National Institute of Child Health and Human Development, and the U.S. Department of Education.
2. Press release by Governor Bush and Education Commissioner Jim Horne, June 18, 2003.
3. Goldhaber and Hannaway, "Accountability with a Kicker: The Florida A+ Plan," *Phi Delta Kappan,* April, 2004, pp. 598–605.
4. Critics might argue that the improved grades are a result of teaching to the test, the development of test-taking skills, or grade inflation.
5. "The State of Education in Florida," remarks prepared for delivery, Governor Jeb Bush, November 13, 2003.
6. The McKay Scholarship Program became a statewide program in the 2000–2001 school year after a limited one-year demonstration. The McKay Scholarships are designated for students with disabilities who are dissatisfied with the services provided to them in their public school program. The amount of the scholarship is the total cost of educating the child in public school.
7. The Corporate Income Tax Credit Scholarship Program, instituted in 2002, is currently providing choice to more students in the state than the Opportunity Scholarship Program. Corporations are allowed to take dollar-for-dollar tax credits for donations to scholarship funding organizations. The legislation limits the amount each contributor can make to $5 million and an aggregate limit for the state to $50 million. Only students who qualify for the free or reduced-price lunch program are eligible for the scholarships, and they can receive up to $3,500

per school year. Students can use their scholarship for any public school or eligible private school in the state. At least 75 percent of the scholarship to private schools must be used for tuition and the remainder may be used for transportation, books, and supplies.

8. Charter schools offer another form of school choice. Schools districts and state universities are authorized to grant charters in the state. Currently there are 227 charter schools in Florida serving more than fifty thousand students altogether. The legislation established caps on the number of charter schools based on the population of a school district. The cap is 28 schools in districts with 100,000 or more students, 20 schools in districts with 50,000 to 99,999 students, and 12 schools in districts with less than 50,000 students.

9. Jay P. Greene, "An Evaluation of the Florida A-Plus Accountability and School Choice Program" (New York: Manhattan Institute, 2001).

10. Goldhaber and Hannaway, "Accountability with a Kicker: The Florida A+ Plan," *Phi Delta Kappan,* April, 2004, pp. 598–605.

11. U.S. Department of Education, National Center for Education Statistics, May 2003.

12. The highest performing jurisdiction was Massachusetts (47 percent); the lowest was the District of Columbia (10 percent).

13. The average scale score in fourth-grade reading in 2003 was 218; for black students, it was 198, and for Hispanic students, 211.

14. Gains by black students in Florida in fourth-grade reading exceeded the national average gains by 9 scale points; gains by Hispanic students were 8 scale points higher. See: Kathleen Kennedy Manzo and Michelle Galley, "Math Climbs, Reading Flat On '03 NAEP," *Education Week,* November 19, 2003, pp. 1, 18. See also: National Center for Education Statistics, http://www.nces.ed.gov/nationsreportcard/.

15. The biggest gains in student scores over time have been in the writing portion of the FCAT, and some think this has been the easiest test on which to show high scores. Perhaps for this reason extra weight is given for scoring high (≥ 3.5) in writing. (See Goldhaber and Hannaway, "Accountability with a Kicker.")

16. A gain can be demonstrated by (1) moving up an achievement level, e.g., 1 to 2, 2 to 3, etc; (2) maintaining a high level of achievement (3 or above); (3) showing one year of growth within levels 1 or 2. *Florida NCLB Accountability Workbook,* available at http://www.fldoe.org/NCLB/finalNCLB.pdf.

17. In addition, in order to make adequate yearly progress, schools must increase by 1 percent the percent of students who score 3 on the FCAT writing test and improve the graduation rate by 1 percent. *Florida NCLB Accountability Workbook.*

18. "Safe harbor," however, allows schools that have met the requirements for testing participation rates and the state's other indicators (writing and graduation rate), but have not met the reading and/or mathematics targets, to make AYP if there is at least a 10 percent decrease in the number of non-proficient students from the prior year for the area being evaluated. *Florida NCLB Accountability Workbook.*

19. NCLB requires that no more than 1 percent of all students tested can be counted as proficient through alternative assessments.

20. A+ participation rules are changing effective the 2003–2004 school year to include all students, including students with disabilities and LEP students. State Board of Education action, November 18, 2003.

21. Florida had the highest failure rate of any state. This is no doubt because the student population is diverse and schools are large. Therefore it is likely that the number of criteria required to be met in Florida schools is, on average, larger than the number of criteria required in most other states. Some schools will no doubt appeal their AYP status.

22. Twenty states require cell sizes above 30 and 28 states require cell sizes at or below 30. Some states have higher minimum cell sizes for students with disabilities. Lynn Olson, " 'Approved' is Relative Term for Ed. Dept.," *Education Week*, August 6, 2003, pp. 34–36.

23. Matthew Pinzer, "Paradox in School Bonus for FCAT Success," *Miami Herald*, October 21, 2003.

24. Florida Department of Education, Florida Information Resource Network, http://www.firn.edu/doe/eias/eiaspubs/pdf/pk-12mbrship.pdf and http://www.firn.edu/doe/title1/9899t1/files/t19899miamidade.pdf.

25. Controlled choice plans were established to comply with a desegregation order and were continued as a way to promote choice. Almost eight thousand students exercise choice under the open enrollment policy.

26. Miami–Dade County Public Schools, Office of Evaluation and Research: http://drs.dadeschools.net/Highlights/Highlights%2002-03.pdf.

27. The district will create eight "choice zones" in which parents will have increased options and more efficient transportation for their children. The options will include "All Academy" model schools, commuter schools, magnet schools, charter schools, and satellite centers. See: Miami-Dade County Public Schools, Office of School Choice and Parental Options at http://choice.dadeschools.net/.

28. The north zone has 12 high schools, 20 middle schools, and 78 elementary schools; the central zone has 14 high schools, 19 middle schools, and 78 elementary schools; and the south zone has 12 high schools, 15 middle schools, and 51 elementary schools. See: Miami–Dade County Public Schools, *NCLB Public School Choice Implementation Plan 2003*.

29. Miami–Dade County Public Schools, Division of School Choice and Parental Options.

30. The district, knowing which schools are at risk of vouchers, starts sending information to parents even before test results are out.

31. Florida Department of Education, http://www.firn.edu/doe/eias/eiaspubs/pdf/pk-12mbrship.pdf.

32. Florida Department of Education, http://www.firn.edu/doe/choice/pdf/hebrief.pdf.

33. Florida Department of Education, http://www.firn.edu/doe/eias/eiaspubs/pdf/pk-12mbrship.pdf.

6

Colorado: Layered Reforms and Challenges of Scale

Alex Medler

Introduction

As a state, Colorado has made a concerted effort to implement the public school choice and supplemental service provisions of the No Child Left Behind (NCLB) act. But results are uneven at the local level. This unevenness is caused by differences in scale, policy, and politics. As NCLB's sanctions affect more Colorado schools, the federal law will increase the amount of choice and the range of services available in some districts. But local differences may diminish the effects of NCLB in other districts, and they could generate conflict throughout the state.

This study has four main findings. First, although both urban and rural districts face sanctions under NCLB, the sanctions produce fewer options for children in rural areas. Second, previously existing policies at both the state and local levels affect how and whether districts comply with NCLB. Specifically, accountability systems and choice mechanisms can either facilitate or complicate efforts to identify low-performing schools and provide their students with new options. Third, some districts that have the capacity to provide choice do not want to; and, not surprisingly, they resist NCLB. And fourth, the inflexibility of the federal statute and its implementation by the U.S. Department of Education has created feelings of urgency and tension. These feelings have stimulated a great deal of work, but they have also created an impression that the federal government does not adequately accommodate or leverage existing state reforms.

The chapter is organized as follows. The next section briefly presents the context of Colorado's education system. The third section examines state-level efforts to implement NCLB, including the designation of schools that do not make adequate yearly progress (AYP), oversight of public school choice provisions, and efforts to support supplemental services. Two district-level case studies then examine local implementation. The chapter closes with a brief discussion of major findings.

The Colorado Context

Colorado's public school system serves more than 751,000 students in 1,613 schools spread among 178 districts.[1] The state's public school enrollment is 65 percent white, 24 percent Hispanic, 5 percent black, 3 percent Asian, and slightly more than 1 percent Native American. These basic numbers mask regional differences. The Denver metropolitan area has more than half the state's students and most of the largest school districts, including over four hundred thousand students in 15 school districts. The Denver district, Denver Public Schools, has more than seventy thousand students with a minority enrollment nearing 80 percent.

Meanwhile, almost 90 districts are considered rural, and more than 100 districts serve fewer than twelve hundred students. More important for choice, Colorado has more than 120 districts with only one elementary school. Great distances separate districts in the eastern plains of the state. Daunting passes divide mountain communities to the west. The resulting isolation creates obstacles to providing both choice and supplemental services. Some of these rural communities serve large proportions of low-income, Hispanic, and Native American students, as well as large migrant populations.

The Policy Environment

The state mixes a strong history of local control and decentralized governance with a growing array of accountability and school choice policies. State leaders frequently begin interviews about policy by saying, "Colorado is a strong local-control state." This is reflected in the lean design and support for the Colorado Department of Education and in the influence of local districts in most of the state's education policies and politics.

The state received about $100 million in Title I basic funds in 2003–2004, up from $77 million in 2001–2002, an increase of about 30 percent in two years. The state keeps 1 percent of its Title I funding for administrative functions, which supports fewer than eight full-time equivalents. Several larger districts report that their own administrative offices have more capacity and expertise than the state for complicated tasks like managing and analyzing performance data. The state's reluctance to increase the central capacity is exacerbated by the legislature's fiscal conservativism.

Despite Colorado's historically small central system and reliance on local districts, some new policies have created a larger role for the state through accountability while others have expanded parental control through choice. Collectively, these steps have diminished district dominance of the Colorado education system.

About 90 charter schools are spread among 40 districts. They serve nearly 4 percent of the state's public school students. Colorado offers inter- and intradistrict choice. Intradistrict open-enrollment programs vary in size and sophistication. State law mandates that districts establish open-enrollment policies. Under this law, receiving districts decide whether they have room to accommodate interdistrict transfer students. More than thirty thousand students, about 4 percent of the state's total enrollment, currently attend schools outside their district of residence.

Colorado recently passed a voucher law that was subsequently ruled unconstitutional in state court. But even if the appeal succeeds and the program eventually goes forward, it will be phased in and primarily available to students in failing schools in districts with large numbers of failing schools. In other words, voucher programs, if implemented, will most likely be concentrated in the Denver area or in larger, front-range communities.

Like most states, Colorado had a far-reaching and expanding accountability system in place prior to NCLB. NCLB requirements are added to these earlier measures. The Colorado Student Assessment Program (CSAP) includes tests that are used for several purposes. The scores are used to give schools a school accountability report (SAR), which designates them as unsatisfactory, low, average, high, or excellent. The unsatisfactory rating was established using the lowest 2 percent of public schools as a benchmark. Unsatisfactory schools face conversion to charter status if they do not improve within three years. However, the state delayed the implementation of the reconstitution provisions, and most schools that received unsatisfactory ratings in the first years of the SAR system have subsequently improved to the "low" level, thus avoiding reconstitution. The voucher program, if reinstated, would use these scores to identify eligible students. The state also has an accreditation system that differs from both the SAR and NCLB systems. The accreditation system includes student assessment results, but it also uses other measures of school quality, including evidence of teacher quality. The state hopes to improve the utility and legitimacy of its assessment system through a pilot "value added" assessment that will allow longitudinal tracking of individual student performance. Some state leaders hope to adapt the state's assessment and accountability policies to implement the pilot program on a statewide basis. The SAR system is different from the measures of AYP under NCLB in that it fails to disaggregate data by major demographic groups.

NCLB Implementation in the State

Initial Infrastructure and Attitudes toward NCLB

Colorado's effort to implement NCLB is overseen by a state-level working group that meets monthly. It is based on a similar group of education stakeholder groups that helped implement the SAR system. The group quickly grew large and established 10 working groups. To reflect the central role of the larger group and its relationship to numerous subgroups it is referred to as the "Hub" group. The Hub group gets widespread credit among education leaders for being inclusive and willing to solicit advice from all parties.

The confidence in the Hub group contrasts with state leaders' attitudes toward the federal government. Many Colorado leaders interviewed for this project portrayed Washington as inflexible and blamed federal officials for the state's problems in implementing NCLB. These perceptions of inflexibility arose most strongly during negotiations between the Colorado and U.S. Departments of Education over how the state would use its existing accountability systems to determine AYP and the time line for providing public school choice and supplemental services.

Identifying Low-Performing Schools: Designating School Improvement Status

Combining several accountability systems creates both long- and short-term complications that affect choice and supplemental services. These complications generate significant delays between the time when students take the tests and when they can enroll in choice schools or receive supplemental services. Before NCLB was enacted, troubled schools were already designated as either schools needing improvement or requiring corrective action. The previous version of federal law used performance data that differ in kind from those used in the current system. Under the old version, the state had 154 schools during 2001–2002 that needed improvement or correction. Prior to having its AYP plan approved, the state education department distributed several proposals for calculating AYP. Districts were allowed to calculate whether their schools had improved enough to escape failing status using any of the proposed systems. As a result, in the 2002–2003 school year only 87 schools remained designated as either needing improvement or corrective action.

Seven of these schools were later removed from "improvement" status for various reasons. For example, one district reallocated Title I funding to other schools in the district, making its only improvement school ineligible for that status. In addition to prompting districts to provide new options to students in troubled schools, NCLB may create incentives for districts to take resources away from them. As a result of these and similar maneuvers, only 80 of the 154 schools that had been designated as needing improvement or corrective action during 2001–2002 were again put under that designation during 2002–2003. Seventy-six schools had improvement designations and the remaining four had correction action plans. Because schools must fail to make AYP two years in a row before being designated as needing improvement, no new schools will receive that designation until the beginning of the 2004–2005 school year. Until then, the implementation of choice and supplemental services is limited to the 80 schools.

The Colorado Education Department staff announced preliminary results of AYP calculations for the 2002–2003 school year in December 2003. According to the department, approximately 50 percent of the state's schools failed to make AYP during 2002–2003—about 780 schools. Approximately 60 percent of the state's districts also failed to make AYP, with the larger districts the least likely to make AYP. If the same schools fail to make AYP in 2003–2004 it could translate into a tenfold increase in the number of schools designated as needing improvement. This expansion of schools requiring new services and additional plans would also change the role of the state vis-à-vis the entire public school system.[2]

Characteristics of Eligible Schools

The initial 87 schools under federal scrutiny in 2002–2003 served a total of 40,149 students,[3] making the public choice provisions of NCLB potentially available to more than 5 percent of the state's enrollment. Fifty-nine percent of the students in these schools qualified for free or reduced-price lunch. The 80 schools that maintained their federal designation were located in

27 districts. Denver, with 34 schools designated as needing improvement, had by far the largest number. In Denver these schools served nearly nineteen thousand students, roughly a quarter of the district's total enrollment and almost half of all students in improvement schools in the state. One district had five such schools, two districts had four, seven districts had only two or three, and 16 districts had only one.

The degree of intradistrict choice available through NCLB is related to the ratio of schools needing to improve to schools that did not earn that distinction. Districts in which the troubled schools are a small percentage of the total number of schools are more likely to have at least one higher performing school serving the same grades that children in the troubled schools could choose. Failing schools were less than 10 percent of the total schools in 10 districts; 3 districts had 11 to 20 percent such schools. These 13 districts are likely to have enough other schools to provide choice. Seven districts had 21 to 30 percent of their schools designated, 3 districts had 31 to 40 percent, and 4 districts had more than 40 percent (see figure 6.1). This means that the children entitled to public school choice in most of the districts affected by NCLB thus far have few higher-performing schools from which to choose.

Key to implementing choice and supplemental services are state decisions regarding which schools are performing poorly enough to require new options. The schools designated as needing improvement are not necessarily the state's lowest-performing schools. Of the original 87 designated schools with SAR ratings in the 2001–2002 school year, only 8 received the unsatisfactory rating on the SAR system. Sixty-seven received low ratings, and 10 were rated average. Two schools did not receive SAR ratings.[4]

Denver, which had all eight improvement schools with an unsatisfactory rating, had 13 additional schools receive an unsatisfactory rating that were not designated as needing improvement. Meanwhile, Denver Public Schools

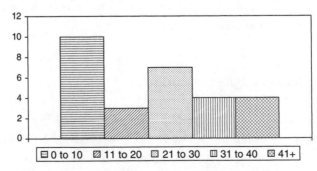

Figure 6.1. District frequency of improvement schools as percentage of all schools in district (N = 27)

had 26 improvement schools that rated higher than unsatisfactory on the SAR system. Thus, according to the two systems, schools with performance that was considered "lower-performing" than the improvement schools according to the SAR system were not labeled as needing improvement. Statewide, nine schools outside Denver that received unsatisfactory ratings were not labeled improvement schools under Title I.

There are even more dramatic contradictions at the higher end of the student performance spectrum. In Boulder, an affluent college town, nine schools failed to make AYP according to preliminary announcements in 2003—including at least one school rated as "excellent" on the SAR system and four labeled as high performing.[5] The schools included four of the district's five high schools. None of the Boulder schools that failed to make AYP were currently designated as needing improvement, and it is unclear which received Title I funding.

The latest round of designations, which is the first to use the formula for calculating AYP approved by the federal government, also creates confusion. While the majority of scores follow trends from SAR scores (i.e., most schools making AYP are also scoring at the higher end of the SAR system), there are oddities. Based on preliminary scores, 11 of the state's 53 unsatisfactory scores made AYP, and 13 excellent schools failed to make AYP (see figure 6.2).

If AYP designations remain out of kilter with other evaluations of schools, the differences could empower nascent protests against testing. Colorado teachers already report growing numbers of parents who withdraw their students from school on testing days as a protest. Parents are acting against what they see as unnecessary testing and a waste of time that could be spent on instruction. Since improvement status can be triggered by a failure to test

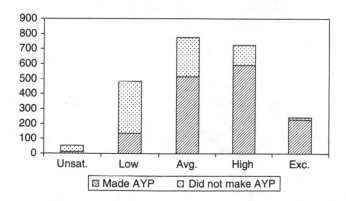

Figure 6.2. SAR and AYP ratings (2002–2003, prior to dist. appeals, rough estimates)

95 percent of students in a single school, it would take only a small proportion of parents to push all schools into that status through similar acts of
protest. In addition to making a general statement against testing, parents
would have two self-interested reasons to force a high-performing school into
improvement status. Gaining that designation would preclude their school
from being offered as a choice option to students from lower-performing
schools in the district. If students had options to choose other district
schools, getting the receiving school on improvement status would end the
mandatory provision of transportation. Parents could also try to force their
own school into such status to get free transportation to other schools.

Challenging Time Lines

The initial time lines proposed by the Colorado Department of Education
reflected constraints that have not changed with the federal directives.
Colorado has contracted with McGraw-Hill to manage the Colorado
Student Assessment Program. This multiyear, multimillion-dollar contract is
legally binding. It includes time lines for gathering, cleaning, and analyzing
data. Though the state is revisiting this contract, there may not be room to
accelerate its schedule significantly. Schools administer the assessments in
March. Moving the tests any earlier in the school year would make it impossible to evaluate the progress of each school for that year. Statutorily, districts
must make the designation of schools that do not make AYP with state-level
confirmation. Initial data from the assessments must be shared with districts
to allow them to make AYP calculations. The district's proposed status of
each school is then reported to the state before it is confirmed. An appeals
process is also available if the state and district disagree over a school's status.
Disagreements are likely, given the ambiguity of the law and a lack of data
regarding which students must be included.

   This lack of data is crucial because determining which students' scores
needed to be included in each school's AYP calculation is far from straightforward. Though NCLB is generally understood as testing all children, the
scores used to evaluate a given school are supposed to be based on students
who have been enrolled in the school long enough to attribute their performance to the school. Questions have arisen about whether the students
who were not enrolled at the school the entire year, or even from the period
since the last assessment (including the spring following the state assessment
from the preceding year) needed to be included. The state's assessment system did not track these enrollment data, and schools and districts have been

struggling to piece together information to determine which students' scores "count." The ambiguity of records and procedures could be the subject of future appeals of AYP designation between the state and districts that find new data on student transfers after initial designations have been announced.

This entire process, as proposed by Colorado, would not have produced final AYP designations until the end of December for assessments done the previous spring. That timetable would allow students to participate in open enrollment procedures only during the spring of the school year after they took the test. They would subsequently be able to enroll in the new school for the start of the next school year (17 months after taking the assessment that indicated the original school's failure). It would also delay until the middle of the second year the final decisions about whether a school had transitioned from first-year improvement status to second-year status, which is the trigger for the mandatory provision of supplemental services.

The federal government rejected these time lines and insisted that they be reworked to guarantee choice and services at the beginning of the following school year. The state is exploring ways to reconfigure its assessment system to comply with these new time lines. But it may not be able to speed up testing time lines to meet the letter of the law under NCLB for several years. As of mid-November 2003, the state had still not finalized AYP designations from the 2002–2003 school year.[6] Consequently, districts were unsure whether schools that had been in the first year of improvement status in 2002–2003 were required to provide supplemental services in the fall of 2003.

While the logistics of providing choice and supplemental services to the initial 80 schools under federal scrutiny have been challenging, as the subsequent section will outline, the scale of NCLB implementation is due to expand drastically in the start of the 2004–2005 year as the rate of schools failing to make AYP is much higher than under the previous Title I procedures. This expanding scale could exacerbate the tensions and challenges of implementing public school choice and supplemental services.

School Choice

The initial implementation of NCLB's public school choice provisions has been uneven across Colorado. Complete data on the number of children choosing new schools are unavailable, but we can draw a few lessons from this experience. Some districts have used creative non-compliance to limit choice for children in failing schools. In many rural districts, choice has been limited, or precluded entirely, by constraints of size and geographic isolation. In the larger districts, especially Denver, existing programs already provided interested children with public school choice.

One of the state's primary tasks in supporting public school choice has been to oversee district communication with parents. Outside investigators at the Independence Institute documented efforts by several districts to sidestep their obligations.[7] Their study rated the notification documents against 12 criteria.[8] No district included all 12 measures, and 22 of the 34 districts in the study included fewer than half the measured items.[9] In addition to failing to include important information, a variety of strategies were employed to reduce choice. Many schools included notification of students' rights to choice in other documents, buried it at the end of longer newsletters, or sent nothing directly to parents and instead placed advertisements in local papers. Several district letters included language to discourage parents from exercising their choice. Though the study also noted the sincere efforts by several districts to comply with NCLB requirements, one principal's efforts at persuasion were illustrative. That principal wrote: "I believe that the high marks made during the 2001–2002 school year proves (sic.) that (this school) is a successful school and moving to another school to get a quality education just isn't necessary. But the federal government did not ask my opinion . . . . I hope that you as parents will keep your children in (our school)."[10]

More disturbing were district efforts to misconstrue the meaning of the federal designation as a failing school. One district took advantage of the ambiguous tone of "school improvement status" to explain: "All schools in [this district] are committed to excellence through continuous improvement. [School name] Elementary is no exception. Our school has been identified for 'School Improvement' by Federal Title I guidelines. We are excited by this opportunity to focus on increasing student achievement on the CSAP assessments."[11]

The Title I staff at the state education department responded to the problem of inadequate notification before the next round of mailings. The state has since required that districts include their notification letters as part of their consolidated applications for federal funding, hosted statewide meetings with all Title I directors, convened regional groups of districts on the topic, released annotated model letters detailing the appropriate information to include in such letters, and threatened to withhold Title I funding. The state has not, however, yet withheld money from any districts based on their failure to comply with NCLB notification requirements.

Most districts responded positively to the state's efforts. In a rough calculation, the Colorado Department of Education staff viewing the letters characterized 18 of the 28 districts as "doing a pretty good job," and 10 as not complying. Of those 10 districts, 6 or 7 were districts in which the school designated as needing improvement was the only district school that served children in that grade. Consequently, intradistrict choice is not a real option. In these cases the communication requirements of NCLB, while mandatory, do not provide any real choosing power to the families. A legally compliant letter would awkwardly inform parents of options to which they were legally entitled—but these options do not exist, and the district is not required to provide them.

According to state education department staff, two or three other districts that could offer choice were still resisting compliance. In those cases, the staff explained, they were "making personal contact and saying, 'Excuse me, there seems to be some misunderstanding here.' The difference [in increased compliance this year] seems to be sitting down and walking everyone through it."

It is difficult to determine the number of children in Colorado exercising public school choice because of NCLB. The state now requires that each district's consolidated application for federal funding include data on students using choice through NCLB, but information is not yet available, and when it is reported, based on district behavior to date, its accuracy should be suspect. Examples from individual districts provide some information. Denver Public Schools reports that 365 students in failing schools received transportation to choice schools in the 2002–2003 school year, up from the 75 that did so in 2001–2002. In contrast, Jefferson County, the largest district in the state, reported no students exercising choice under NCLB.[12]

Rural Obstacles

Many rural districts had few options to provide. Because they are required to provide transportation only within their own districts, and getting to other districts can require long commutes in rural settings, the ability of rural families to choose schools across district lines is likely to be restricted to families with the resources to support travel.

Though officials were reluctant to go on the record, there are anecdotal reports of rural districts refusing to accept transfers from neighboring districts for fear the new students would either be low performing or would increase the size of disaggregated groups to the point that their own schools' AYP status would be in jeopardy. If these stories are true, it is possible that NCLB might inadvertently suppress choice in rural settings where it is already quite limited. However, Colorado's finance system rewards the receiving districts with additional funding for every student that enters their system through choice. The financial rewards of accepting students may yet outweigh the risks of interventions potentially incurred through NCLB.

The state has taken several steps to address the challenges of choice in rural settings. It has clarified that school systems that do not have any choice options available within the district can instead provide supplemental services in lieu of choice during a school's first year of improvement status. The state also encouraged districts to consider options for creating new programs and services within schools. Education department staff distributed a list of 15 options for expanding capacity within the district if "demand outpaces capacity." Suggestions included:

1. Improve schools that are identified
2. Create virtual schools
3. Create new schools-within-schools
4. Create incentives for high-performing schools to receive more students (i.e., give principals bonuses); and
5. Create charter and charter-like schools.

Unfortunately, most of the 15 options do not address the primary obstacle faced by districts with a small number of students in any grade. Many of the options would be difficult because a district would have to create schools or programs that would not serve enough students to be financially viable. And because districts without choice options within their district boundaries are legally within their rights to refuse to create additional options, it is unclear which, if any, of these options most rural districts will pursue when their schools fail to make AYP. Consequently, the state may have a hard time persuading rural districts that are hostile to choice to provide any. As State Board Member Evie Hudak explained, "Right from the very beginning, the rural areas have been saying that this was clearly an inner-city law—that it took no rural realities into account when it was written."

Not all rural districts necessarily oppose efforts to add options. State officials report that several small districts with no other schools serving the affected grades offered supplemental services immediately. However, rural districts also face considerable challenges in securing supplemental service providers. In an encouraging sign, charter schools do succeed in rural Colorado. Twenty-two charter schools, or 25 percent of the charters operating at the time, were located in rural communities.[13] And some Colorado charter schools find ways to operate with extremely small enrollments. But rural districts have also put up some of the state's fiercest fights against charter proposals. Small communities can be divided about the merits of creating options that divide small student populations and resources. Rural communities are also participating in a growing array of distance learning options that are increasingly sophisticated.

Supplemental Services

The state role in facilitating supplemental services is more direct than for school choice. The state reviews potential providers and endorses those that meet its established standards. State officials report challenges in deciding how to judge whether programs have been proven effective, how to insulate the vendor approval process from political pressure, and how to provide a range of services in rural settings.

Staff at the Colorado Department of Education have aggressively recruited a broad range of applicants by participating in conferences and meetings of the White House's Faith Based Initiative, recruiting recipients of Twenty-First Century Community Learning Center grants across the state, and networking with non-profit and educational service providers.

Colorado handles the approval process through an annual request for proposals for vendors. The state has conducted two competitions and approved a total of 36 vendors. In the first competition, the state received 20 applications and approved 13. Five of the approved vendors from this cohort declined to be listed after the first year. The state approved 23 of 25 applications during the second competition, leaving 31 current providers.

Experts reviewing applications expressed frustration in determining how to judge program effectiveness. As state officials explained, "(The vendor) had to show a demonstrated record of effectiveness. Providers aren't giving CSAP, (or) any standardized assessment, so it's hard to show a demonstrated record of effectiveness."

Because of concerns over program quality, the staff had proposed giving "provisional" approval to vendors without clear records of effectiveness. They hoped to follow up with any providers receiving provisional approval by conducting site visits during the year and evaluating their initial implementation. Federal officials blocked this approach. Instead, almost all applicants in the second competition were approved and a statewide evaluation that includes all practicing vendors will take place. After the evaluation, vendors may be removed for failure to perform. The end result appears to be the same as it would have been if the state had implemented its preferred strategy.

State education staff also complained of receiving frequent endorsements for particular vendors from political officials and their representatives. This informal lobbying on the part of applicants occasionally takes place in other grant applications. However, staff reported an unusual degree of political pressure in this case. (They were also quick to add that the pressure did not affect the outcome in any way.)

PROGRAM CHARACTERISTICS

I analyzed the program descriptions of the 31 vendors still offering services.[14] They differ by delivery method, grades served, base of operations, and cost. The overwhelming majority of programs involve direct contact between students and program staff. Hands-on, tutorial, or small-group delivery methods were proposed by 23 providers; five others are strictly Internet or computer based; and two use a combination of computers and hands-on delivery. Some have argued that NCLB's supplemental services provisions would be easier to communicate to the public if they were simply described as "tutoring." Based on the variety of delivery methods, and the connotation of individual instruction inherent in the word tutoring, supplemental services remains a more accurate term.

In terms of grades, 13 programs serve K-12 or an approximation of all grades, such as 1–12 or 2–12; 10 serve the elementary grades, K-5 or 1–5; 5 serve K-8; 1 serves 6–8; 1 serves 6–12; and 1 serves 1–2. The programs' bases of operation also vary. Nine are based outside the state. Twenty-two were initiated in Colorado. Five of the Colorado-based programs are run by school districts. These district-run programs are distinct from the general program available in the district's schools, and would be offered at times outside the regular school day. Districts do not run the other 17 Colorado-based programs. They vary in cost. Estimates are rough because vendors use a variety of reporting procedures on state documents. Estimates range from $250 to $1,950 per child per year.[15] Of the 31 current vendors, three cost less than $500; 17 cost between $500 and $1,000; nine cost between $1,000 and $1,500; and two programs could cost $1,900 or more.

There is no obvious correlation between the base of operations, use of computers, and costs. Operations based outside the state include national networks that operate by hiring local staff as well as using Internet-based programs. The costs of Internet-based programs, including both local and national providers, vary from $250 to nearly $1,000. The costs of programs based outside the state also vary dramatically. Offering to serve the full spectrum of grades appears to increase costs, as five of the most expensive six programs serve grades K-12.

The number and delivery method of supplemental service providers available to a district varies with geography. Many providers are willing to work with districts in the Denver metro area, but rural districts have few options. For example, 21 providers are willing to work with Denver Public Schools' students, whereas most rural districts have only four providers to choose from. On average, the districts in the Denver metro area have 7.5 potential providers, but districts outside Denver average 3.9 providers. And in most rural settings it is the same three or four providers—all of which operate online programs. Many of the Denver-area providers operate in face-to-face programs. Rural superintendents also complain that some online providers charge discounted rates to districts that sign up enough students to exceed a fixed minimum. As a result, rural schools, which have too few students to qualify for discounts, pay more per pupil. However, other rural superintendents readily admit that Colorado's small districts already receive extra state funding to help defray the cost of operating on a smaller scale.

Although the numbers of students receiving supplemental services during these first years were so low that no district reported the need to limit participation, in the event that participation outpaces funding, there will be differences in the per-pupil amount that districts can spend. The limit is established by statute as the per pupil amount of Title I basic funding the district receives. This means that a large district with a low proportion of Title I children would have less to spend on each eligible child than a small district with a large proportion of low-income children, even if the two districts each received the same total amount of Title I funding and served the same number of Title I children. The district with the least Title I funding per student can spend only $832 per year providing any one student's supplemental services. Fourteen of the 31 available programs offer services under this limit. Districts with more Title I funding per student can spend as much as $2,732 apiece, which is more than any currently available program costs. The mean limit is $1,220, which would cover the cost of 24 of the 31 programs.

State-level data on students who participate in supplemental services are unavailable. And the number of affected schools was small until 2003–2004. Because the state's release of preliminary AYP calculations was delayed until December for the 2002–2003 school year, many districts did not know which of their schools were required to provide supplemental services. However, this uncertainty is not a sign of shirking by districts. Several rural districts offered supplemental services in lieu of choice, and Denver chose to offer supplemental services to all children in schools that were in improvement status during 2002–2003, regardless of whether these schools were later determined to have made AYP. State officials are working to get districts to look at supplemental services as something all schools should want to provide. One staff person lamented, "I just wish everyone would stop calling this a sanction. It's something we should all want for these kids."

District Examples

District Case #1: Denver Public Schools

To review what we already know about the Denver system, here are some facts: The city of Denver is a single school district serving 71,000 students in 141 schools—making it the state's second-largest school district. It has the state's highest proportion of minority students, with 79 percent minority enrollment. Like most districts in the metro area, Denver experienced growth in the 1990s. It receives the largest Title I allocation of any Colorado district—more than $22 million in 2003, representing nearly a 43 percent rise over the $15.5 million they received in 2001. Denver also has the largest number of low-performing schools on all available measures. Thirty-four of the state's 80 schools under federal scrutiny are in Denver. The district with the next highest number has only five schools with improvement designations. On the initial SAR ratings, Denver had 21 of the state's 30 schools that received an unsatisfactory rating.

This district's diversity and efforts to desegregate its public schools expanded the amount of choice present in Denver before NCLB. Denver emerged from a court-ordered desegregation plan in 1997. It moved from a busing system to a strategy designed to combine neighborhood schools with magnet programs and extensive public school choice. According to district officials, approximately 30 percent of Denver students now attend a school other than the one they would attend if they were assigned by residence. Half of these students attend magnet programs or specialized schools serving specific students—such as those with particular disabilities. Another half of the students exercising choice take advantage of the district's open enrollment program.

The Denver system also has 17 magnet schools and 10 charter schools. After initially leading state efforts to fight Colorado's charter school law, district leaders have become increasingly supportive of charter schools. Denver has more students traveling across district boundaries than any other district. More than four thousand students who lived within Denver's boundaries attended schools in 24 surrounding districts during the 2002–2003 school year. Denver is also one of the districts potentially affected by Colorado's new voucher law. If appeals succeed, the district will be at the center of its implementation.

Implementing NCLB in Denver

The Denver schools with students eligible for choice and supplemental services served 18,956 students during the 2001–2002 school year.[16] During that year, Denver relied entirely on existing open-enrollment programs to provide choice. The district sent a mailing soon after the passage of NCLB, but it did not track choices of students or provide transportation differently in failing schools in this first year. For the 2002–2003 school year, Denver sent an initial mailing to students in failing schools explaining their schools' status, but again offered no additional choices or transportation. A second mailing to middle schools on improvement status was made in August 2002 that included a list of higher-performing schools that families could choose and offered transportation to these schools. According to district officials, approximately 75 students used this opportunity to enroll in higher-performing schools.

During 2002–2003, Denver moved to more complete compliance with the letter and spirit of NCLB. The district sent targeted mailings to approximately seventeen thousand families at a cost of $50,000. District officials estimate this effort required the equivalent of four staff working full time over three months. This series of customized mailings included all the elements suggested by the state education department for NCLB notification. As noted earlier, 365 students accepted the offer.

Denver also adjusted the procedures of its open-enrollment process to give students in federally sanctioned schools advantages over families in higher performing schools. In 2002, the application period was extended a month for all students. In 2003, students in sanctioned schools were allowed to apply throughout the spring and summer. The letters explained that students could apply to enroll in any district school, without the benefit of free transportation. The mailing then identified two schools for each failing school that were higher performing and for which the district would provide transportation. Each pair consisted of a magnet school and a non-magnet school. To reduce the cost of potential transfers and to avoid adjusting bus routes, the selection of schools was based, in part, on available space and existing transportation routes.

Data are not available to identify families who chose to enroll in schools other than the two for which the district offered transportation. It is likely that more than 365 students exercised choice in Denver's improvement schools under NCLB, but chose schools other than those that included transportation. The 365 students who chose the schools with transportation represented about 1.7 percent of the students exercising choice in Denver, and about 2 percent of the students who received NCLB mailings.

District leaders explain that they support school choice generally and their actions to implement NCLB provide evidence that this support is sincere. The district has repeatedly interpreted ambiguities of NCLB in ways that increase the number of students eligible for choice. Choice was offered to students attending schools that fed into SI or CA schools at later grades. Siblings of students eligible for choice under NCLB were also provided the same choices. And families whose children had not previously attended the failing school but who approached the eligible schools during the summer seeking admission also received all the choice options available to families previously enrolled at the school. Students completing the final grade of a school with improvement status could also open enroll for the following year and were offered transportation.

Supplemental Services in Denver

Three schools in Denver in corrective action status during the 2002–2003 school year had to provide supplemental services that year. The 31 Denver schools on improvement status were all in their "first year" in 2002–2003, and thus were not required to provide supplemental services until the fall of 2003. Only improvement schools that did not make AYP during the 2002–2003 school year were technically required to provide supplemental services in the fall of 2003. Because the final AYP calculations were not available at the beginning the 2003–2004 school year, Denver offered supplemental services to students in all of the sanctioned schools starting in fall 2003. This was a good-faith effort by the district to comply with NCLB in the face of the state's inability to deliver timely AYP designations. In hostile districts, it is unlikely the state's delay in designating schools will induce those districts to take the extra steps Denver undertook to comply with NCLB in the absence of final AYP designations. With hundreds of schools possibly being sanctioned, and no sign of shorter time lines for the tasks associated with AYP designation, Colorado could face growing conflict with many districts.

Denver has 21 approved vendors willing to provide supplemental services in their district. The district contracted with Catapult Learning (formerly Sylvan Learning Centers) to provide services on site at each of the affected schools if principals selected Catapult. The district provided information on all 21 available vendors to parents and allowed parents to make their own arrangements with any provider. Vendors report that, despite the low number of students requiring transportation, the district held aside the minimum amount of Title I funding for supplemental services (5 percent), and that principals then recruited a number of students who would not exceed this initial allocation. Information on the number of participating students was not available in November 2003. As with choice, Denver had a variety of supplemental service programs under way prior to NCLB. Three different programs operated by the district itself were approved as supplemental service providers.

CONCLUSION

Denver faces unique challenges because of its large size, minority population, and large number of low-performing schools. The district has recently begun a sincere effort to comply with NCLB. This effort has been helped by the choice and service programs already in place. Complications have arisen. But they are primarily the result of managing and communicating to parents about a complex bundle of services. Other complications stem from NCLB time lines that are more compressed than those for existing programs, and the problems are exacerbated by the state's delays in calculating AYP and designating each school's status. On balance, these challenges did not prevent Denver Public Schools from complying with NCLB and marginally expanding the choices and services available. But in future years, as more districts have large numbers of schools enter improvement status, the obstacles that Denver overcame could create opportunities for reluctant districts to resist NCLB.

District Case #2: Ignacio an Ethnically Diverse, Rural Community Struggles with Declining Enrollment

While Denver is a good case study because it serves so many children affected by NCLB, the Ignacio district is a worthy case because it serves so few. Ignacio is a small town in rural, southwestern Colorado near the New Mexico border. It contains the Southern Ute Indian reservation and serves a tri-ethnic community that is 37 percent white, 23 percent Hispanic, and 38 percent Native American. The district has experienced a dramatic decrease in enrollment in recent years.[17] In 1999, the district served 1,029 students. By the fall of 2003, enrollment had fallen to 764. District figures indicate a 26 percent enrollment decline in the last five years, and estimates of the decline between 2002 and 2003 alone place it at around 10 percent.[18]

Despite declining enrollment, Title I funding for the district has increased. The district received $197,407 from Title I in 2001–2002, and $239,002 in 2003–2004. This represents a 21.1 percent increase over two years. The district has four schools, and only one school serves each grade level. The district's intermediate school, serving grades 4–6, is its only school designated as needing improvement. This school failed to make AYP during the 2002–2003 school year.

Families are choosing to enroll their children outside the district. According to state records, 114 students residing in the Ignacio district transferred to schools outside the district in 2002. The adjacent districts of Durango and Bayfield received 106 students from Ignacio. While about 60 students left each of these districts to attend schools elsewhere, none transferred to Ignacio. Families enrolling their children in schools across district lines must provide their own transportation. Media reports describe families making hundred-mile round trips daily to bring their children to schools outside Ignacio.[19] And some observers believe racial conflicts are driving many of the transfers, as white families flee schools with larger Native American and Hispanic populations.[20] District officials believe that students able to exercise choice are not the low-performing students they believe NCLB was intended to serve. Instead, according to Roy Lyons, the district's Title I director and principal of the junior high, "The kids that are leaving are those that are higher performing, not the low-performing kids. If a parent walked in and said, 'You guys suck, you haven't done anything for my kid'. I'd say, 'Good luck.' But basically the parents that are leaving [are the ones whose kids] are doing well."

Lyons explains that the district is in an awkward position when it comes to creating options for children who do not have the resources to travel outside the district. "We lack capacity to create choice. . . . In a small district like this we don't have another school [serving grades 4, 5, 6]. If parents aren't satisfied, it's an open-enrollment state, they can take them anywhere they want to." This exodus began before NCLB was enacted. According to Lyons the difference in CSAP results between Ignacio and the neighboring districts was enough to trigger white flight in the district.

The district responded to NCLB by notifying parents of the intermediate school's improvement status and, in lieu of choice, offered supplemental services in the first year. According to district officials, only one or two parents responded. Like most rural districts, Ignacio had only four online providers that were willing to serve its students.

If there is a good side to Ignacio's experience with NCLB, it is that surrounding districts have not responded to the influx of Ignacio students with fears that they will undermine their own schools' AYP status. Consequently, surrounding districts continue to accept the students who are able to leave Ignacio. If allegations of flight by higher-performing students are accurate, this welcoming attitude among receiving districts could change if the types of students leaving Ignacio changed. The lessons of the Ignacio school system have implications for more than a hundred districts in Colorado. They also point to problems that may occur in all small districts, and especially in rural communities. Many rural communities consider the choice and supplemental service provisions of NCLB irrelevant. Strategies to expand options for rural students in low-performing schools, as well as efforts to improve their schools, depend on the districts' willingness and resources. These will likely need to be adjusted to address the unique challenges of small scale and geographic isolation.

Discussion

Colorado provides multiple lessons about the challenges of implementing NCLB. These lessons tell us about the implications of differences between districts, as well as challenges of laying NCLB atop preexisting accountability and choice programs.

Urban/Rural Divide

The difference between rural and urban school districts with regard to NCLB is immense. Choice and supplemental services are much more relevant interventions in larger districts and in districts with many nearby schools. Though NCLB uses the individual school as the unit of analysis to identify schools in need of improvement, the law relies on districts to implement interventions. Both the choice and supplemental service provisions of NCLB are of questionable utility in many rural settings, raising equity issues for rural America.

District Hostility to Choice

There are options for expanding choice in rural districts. But these largely depend on district initiative. Rural communities will likely respond to NLCB requirements for public school choice and supplemental services the way they have responded to charter schools. If so, NCLB will generate a few options in select communities, but most districts will do nothing.

Among larger school systems, there are opportunities for even greater disparities among districts. Part of the difference stems from local leaders' attitudes toward choice as well as the range of options and services already available. In districts like Denver, where the leadership supports choice and a wide variety of options are available, implementing NCLB is not that difficult. In districts that have resisted choice, implementing NCLB will require rigorous oversight to discourage subtle, and not so subtle, forms of resistance.

Conflicting Accountability Systems

At the state level, NCLB does not align with the accountability and choice systems already in place in Colorado. The contradictions between various systems designed to identify low-performing schools are likely to generate confusion, and they could eventually undermine support for all accountability systems. Thus far, the U.S. Department of Education has been inflexible in interpreting the requirements of federal law and unwilling to accommodate Colorado's efforts to align NCLB requirements with state-based goals and programs.

As the number of schools identified by NCLB expands (potentially exponentially), the obstacles will grow more significant, not less. There are likely to be huge increases in numbers of small, rural districts that cannot comply and large districts that could provide choice and supplemental services but choose to use the state's difficulties with identifying and overseeing NCLB to aid their resistance. The combination of uneven capacity, hostile district attitudes, and limited state-level capacity to facilitate NCLB could create a policy mess. Given the potential conflict between local, state, and federal accountability systems, this mess will add legitimacy to latent arguments that the federal government has foisted requirements on Colorado that hurt, rather than help, local efforts to improve education.

Notes

1. Unless otherwise noted, the basic statistics on Colorado schools, districts, and students are drawn from various pages on the Colorado Department of Education website. PDF addresses reflect working links as of January 5, 2004. Updated links should be available by selecting the Department's NCLB home page and by the link to data on schools and districts. http://www.cde.state.co.us.
2. During telephone interviews in November 2003, state officials predicted that by the fall of 2004, no large district in the state would make AYP. While the school

choice and supplemental service provisions are not directly affected by a district's AYP status, each of these districts would be working to create improvement plans and would require additional oversight by the state. Districts that fail to make AYP can no longer provide supplemental education services.

3. Data on improvement schools' enrollment and student demographics were taken from SAR report cards for individual schools from the 2001–2002 school year, available at the Colorado Department of Education website.

4. In the initial year of SAR reporting, small schools and schools for special populations did not receive SAR grades. They did receive report cards, but the one-word rating was not assigned. That exemption has since been lifted, and all schools in the state now receive SAR scores.

5. Amy Bounds, "Schools Fail Targets: BVSD Officials Say Schools Missed Few Federal Goals; State Standards Don't Match," *Boulder Daily Camera*, November 19, 2003, online version.

6. Preliminary designations were released in January 2004.

7. Pamela Benigno, "No Child Left Behind Mandates School Choice: Colorado's First Year," *Issue paper* no. 9 (Golden, CO: Independence Institute, 2003). The study surveyed districts with failing schools and requested the notification letters or other documents used by districts to communicate with parents about their rights under NCLB. The study reviewed documents to see if they covered required elements, and evaluated whether the letters used language to discourage parents from exercising their rights. Surveys and letters were returned from districts or schools that accounted for 82 percent of the schools under improvement status in 2002.

8. The state has required districts to submit information on the number of children exercising choice as part of each district's consolidated application for federal funding. The data from these reports have not yet been compiled or released by education officials, but they should be available in 2004.

9. Benigno, "No Child Left Behind."

10. Ibid., p. 7, school identity deleted in original report.

11. Ibid., p. 8, school identity deleted in original report.

12. Ibid.

13. Colorado Department of Education, *The State of Charter Schools, 2001–02: The Characteristics, Status, and Performance Record of Colorado Charter Schools* (Denver: Colorado Department of Education, March 2003), p. 15.

14. One provider, Dreamcatcher, lists four affiliated providers under different regional titles. These four affiliates are analyzed as one unit for the purposes of these figures and are included as one of the 31 programs still operating. Because of ambiguity in program descriptions the following figures should be considered estimates only.

15. Estimates are based on the maximum possible charge for the services offered, calculated per child per school year from information on program descriptions.

16. These calculations are based on combining information from the SAR reports for each of the 34 SI and CA schools for the 2001–2002 school year, as available at the education department website.

17. Mary Ann Lopez, "Parents Yank Children from Ignacio Schools," *Durango Herald,* November 9, 2003, online edition.

18. Ibid.

19. Ibid.

20. Ibid.

7

Michigan: False Start

David N. Plank and Christopher Dunbar, Jr.

Introduction

NCLB relies on two key elements to induce schools to improve: the clarity of the signals that schools receive about their own performance, and the credibility of the consequences that schools experience when they fail to meet their achievement targets. In Michigan, however, the clear message that NCLB is expected to send to schools has been muddied, and the sanctions foreseen under NCLB have been imposed weakly and capriciously. There is widespread confusion and anxiety about the identification of "failing" schools, and little confidence that the sanctions required by NCLB will lead to school improvement. It is possible that these are start-up issues that will be resolved with time, but today there is little reason to think that this is true. Indeed, it is difficult to see NCLB gaining much traction or leading to significant improvements in the performance of Michigan's public schools.

In this chapter we review the early implementation of NCLB in Michigan. In the following section, we describe the state policy context, with a particular focus on preexisting school choice and accountability policies. We also discuss some of the administrative and political issues that have influenced implementation at the state and local levels. In the third section, we discuss the school choice and supplemental services provisions of the law, and in the fourth we examine how these provisions have been put into effect in three urban school districts—Detroit, Flint, and a district we have agreed to call River City[1]. In the concluding section, we offer an assessment of the early implementation of NCLB in Michigan, and express some doubts about whether the law will produce significant improvements in the performance of schools serving disadvantaged students.

Policy Context and Policy Implementation

The Michigan Policy Context

Three key features of Michigan's policy environment are especially important for an analysis of the implementation of NCLB. The first is the way Michigan funds its schools. Second is the state's extant school choice policies, which are among the most comprehensive in the country. Third is the history of the state's efforts to develop an accountability system for Michigan schools.

School Funding and School Choice

Since the adoption of Proposal A in 1994, the Michigan Legislature has distributed most education revenues to local school districts on the basis of portable capitation grants.[2] When a child moves from one district to another, or from a traditional public school to a charter school, the full value of the state foundation allowance moves with her. There is no residual local share. Under this system, the only way for school districts to increase revenues is to increase enrollments, and the competition among schools and school districts for students and the revenues that come with them has steadily intensified.

The competition to increase enrollments and revenues has produced new options for parents. On the one hand, Michigan has one of the strongest charter school laws in the country. In 2002–2003, there were 184 charter schools in operation in Michigan, enrolling more than seventy thousand students. Most are located in urban districts, including more than 40 in the city of Detroit. On the other hand, Michigan's interdistrict choice law places virtually no restrictions on parents' opportunities to choose among public schools. Parents may choose schools in any school district within their own intermediate school district,[3] or in any contiguous intermediate school district. Children in Lansing, for example, can choose to attend any school in Ingham County (where Lansing is located), or in Clinton, Eaton, Jackson, Livingston, or Shiawassee Counties. The only constraint on interdistrict choice (apart from practical considerations of distance) is that districts may decide to close their schools to non-resident students. The number of open districts has nearly doubled since 1996, however; almost 70 percent of Michigan school districts are now open to non-resident students.

About 6 percent of all Michigan students are currently enrolled in charter schools or schools in districts other than the one where they reside, and these numbers have been growing rapidly (see table 7.1). The vast majority of students who participate in school choice programs are from Michigan's major

Table 7.1. Participation in school choice, 1996–2003

School Year	Number of charter schools	Number of charter school students	Charter school students as a percentage of All Michigan K-12 students	Number of interdistrict transfer students	Interdistrict transfer students as a percentage of All Michigan K-12 students	Percentage of districts accepting nonresident students	Choice and charter students as a percentage of All Michigan K-12 students
1996–1997	79	12,047	0.8	7,836	0.5	36.8	1.3
1998–1999	138	34,319	2.2	14,723	0.9	45.2	3.1
2000–2001	176	56,417	3.5	25,553	1.6	58.3	5.1
2002–2003	184	72,312	3.8	43,756	2.3	69.4	6.1

metropolitan areas, including Detroit, Grand Rapids, Flint, Lansing, and Pontiac.

HOLDING SCHOOLS ACCOUNTABLE

Like other states, Michigan has wrestled over the past decade with the task of holding its schools accountable. The Michigan Education Assessment Program (MEAP) was created in the 1970s as an instrument to determine whether schools were covering the main elements of the state's core curriculum. In the 1990s, the stakes attached to MEAP assessments were significantly increased for both schools and students. On the one hand, scores were put to work as the principal basis for school accreditation. Schools in which a significant percentage of students failed to meet state standards were publicly identified, and some were subjected to state intervention. On the other hand, the legislature established merit awards for middle and high school students who performed well on the tests, in order to raise participation rates and encourage students to take the assessments seriously. More recently, the State Board of Education developed a new accreditation system for Michigan schools (known as Education Yes!) that seeks to provide a more comprehensive and accurate account of how different schools are performing. The new accreditation system has been plagued by a number of conceptual and technical problems, however, which delayed its implementation. The first "report cards" on Michigan schools were released in January 2004.

Over the past decade, Michigan has also acquired some experience with state intervention in local schools. In 1999, the legislature replaced Detroit's elected school board with one appointed by the mayor.[4] The new board in turn appointed a chief executive officer for the Detroit Public Schools, who enjoys all of the administrative authority traditionally vested in the school board. The board retains the right to fire the CEO, but otherwise cannot intervene in the management of the school system. In 2000, the Michigan Department of Education declared the Inkster School District to be in financial and academic bankruptcy. After negotiations with the state, Inkster's school board signed a contract under which responsibility for managing the district was awarded to Edison Schools. Since 2001, under an initiative known as "Partners for Success," the Michigan Department of Education has identified low-performing schools and required them to participate in a program aimed at improving their pupils' achievement. The program assigns seasoned administrators to assist troubled schools to turn themselves around.

Implementing NCLB in Michigan

The early implementation of NCLB in Michigan has been vexed by a number of factors. Controversy and debate over its legitimacy and efficacy have consumed the first year of implementation, despite public expressions of support from Governor Jennifer Granholm and other officials. Partly as a result, scant public attention has been paid to NCLB strategies for school improvement, including choice and supplemental services. Two key obstacles account for these early stumbles. First, the state has sent weak and confusing signals to schools about the performance of their students. Second, the limited administrative and financial capacity of state government, including the Michigan Department of Education, has undermined the implementation of key provisions of NCLB.

WEAK AND CONFUSING SIGNALS

How many Michigan schools are failing? The greatest controversy in the early implementation of NCLB has revolved around how to identify schools that are not making adequate yearly progress (AYP). Disputes over this question have been addressed in very public negotiations between the Michigan Department of Education and the U.S. Department of Education, which have produced two main outcomes. The first of these has been extraordinary volatility in the number of schools included on Michigan's list of schools that have failed to meet AYP targets. The second has been a dramatic lowering of the standards against which Michigan measures the performance of its public schools.

When the U.S. Department of Education announced in summer 2002 its first list of schools that had failed to meet AYP targets, 1,513 Michigan schools were on the list. Nearly 20 percent of all failing schools in the United States were in Michigan, more than any other state. This was attributable to the state's high standards for school performance, in place since 1994. Under those standards, 75 percent of a school's students had to meet or exceed standards in four subject areas on the MEAP test in order for the school to be given a satisfactory rating.[5] The federal standards enacted in NCLB were significantly less rigorous than Michigan's, and some states did not yet have standards in place (and consequently had no schools on the federal list).

Despite assertions from Washington that states would not be permitted to lower their standards in response to NCLB, negotiations to lower Michigan's standards immediately ensued. In November 2002, the State Board of Education adopted new standards that conformed to the NCLB standards.

Under them, for an elementary school to meet its initial AYP target, 47 percent of its students would have to meet or exceed state standards in math, and 38 percent would have to meet or exceed state standards in reading. In middle schools, 31 percent of students were required to meet or exceed state standards in both math and reading. Performance on MEAP's science and social studies components was no longer taken into account.

Under the new standards, the number of priority schools in Michigan fell more than 80 percent, from 1,513 to 216. Negotiations between the Michigan and U.S. Departments of Education continued, and in July 2003 the number of priority schools was increased once again, to 760. At the time of this new announcement, however, parents and educators were assured that most of the schools being added to the list would soon be removed.[6] In January 2004, state education officials announced that 896 Michigan schools had failed to make AYP in 2003–2004, but many schools insisted that the state's calculations were in error.[7] The true number of schools that are failing to meet Michigan's NCLB standards consequently remains a mystery.

Penalties for early compliance. Under NCLB, schools that fail to make AYP for an extended period of time are subject to escalating sanctions, ranging from student transfers in the second year to reconstitution in the fifth. The idea is that schools should initially be subjected to relatively mild sanctions and given an opportunity to turn themselves around before more draconian interventions are imposed.

In states like Michigan, however, where assessment systems have been in place for some time, many schools found themselves subject to the full array of sanctions in the first year of NCLB implementation.[8] Of the 896 schools that failed to make AYP in 2003–2004, for example, 112 are already facing reconstitution, and an additional 84 have not made improvement for four years. Of the remaining schools on the list, 83 have failed to make AYP for three years, and 30 have failed for two.

There is virtually no public disagreement with the proposition that many of these schools are in serious trouble, and a variety of initiatives have been undertaken to turn them around.[9] At the same time, however, the structured escalation of sanctions included under NCLB is not being given a chance to work in these schools. Instead, many of them find themselves obliged to respond to all three levels of sanctions at once. Under these circumstances, planning for reconstitution necessarily assumes the greatest importance. The signals that parents and educators are expected to receive from the school choice and supplemental services (tutoring) provisions of NCLB are confused or overwhelmed, and other initiatives to turn the schools around are likely to be short-circuited.

FINANCIAL AND ADMINISTRATIVE OBSTACLES

As in the implementation of any complex social policy, financial and administrative problems have complicated the start of NCLB in Michigan. On the administrative side, problems with management and analysis of MEAP scores have produced long delays in identification of schools that are subject to NCLB sanctions. In addition, the radically diminished capacity of the Michigan Department of Education undermines efforts to hold schools and districts accountable for implementation. On the financial side, a persistent and deepening budget crisis has diverted policy attention from the problems of failing schools and curtailed the resources available to support intervention in these schools.

One persistent complaint about MEAP (and other state assessment programs) has focused on delays in getting test scores back to teachers and schools. Failure to return scores in a timely manner deprives teachers of potentially useful feedback, because the students who participated in the assessment under their supervision have moved on to other teachers or other schools. The prospect of sanctions under NCLB further increases the significance of prompt return of assessment results for school districts and parents. Districts need to know the status of their schools if they are to inform parents about their options, identify providers of supplemental services, and plan for reconstitution. Parents need to know the status of their schools if they are to take advantage of the opportunities for choice and supplemental services that NCLB opens to them.

For the first full year of NCLB implementation, the Michigan Treasury[10] contracted with a private company to manage and analyze MEAP data. The contract called for MEAP results to be returned to schools in June 2003, but in reality schools received their preliminary results in October, well after the beginning of the school year. In this process, more than three thousand test forms were misidentified or lost, and some results were sent to the wrong schools. In addition, more than one-third of all Michigan schools immediately filed appeals of their MEAP results, claiming errors in the data provided by the state.[11] Schools that had failed to achieve their AYP targets in 2002–2003 were finally identified at the end of January 2004.

The early implementation of NCLB has been further undermined by the radically diminished capacity of state agencies to monitor local compliance. Over the course of the past decade, the number of employees at the state education department was reduced by 90 percent, with key functions including student assessment transferred to other agencies. Cuts in budget and staffing have continued under Governor Granholm, who has simultaneously moved to return most educational functions to the department. As a result, the energies of key staff are consumed by financial emergency and administrative reorganization. Whatever capacity for leadership remains has been devoted to implementing Michigan's own fledgling accountability system. As a result, the department has exercised almost no oversight over local implementation of NCLB. According to one senior official, "We're relying on the public trust and the good faith of schools to do what they need to do out of the interest of children."[12] Pressure to comply with key provisions of NCLB must therefore come from the federal government or from parents and other local actors.

Administrative obstacles to the implementation of NCLB are exacerbated by Michigan's current budget crisis, arguably the worst since World War II.[13] Schools have been obliged to cut their budgets in each of the past two years, and the prospects are grim for 2004–2005 as well. A growing number of districts are on the verge of bankruptcy, and this number includes many of the districts that face the stiffest challenges under NCLB.

Not surprisingly, the state's inability to fund its current commitments to K-12 education has intensified frustration with the new mandates and expectations associated with NCLB.

SUMMARY

Taken together, the implementation problems identified here have had two main consequences. In the short run, they have significantly blunted the potential impact of NCLB on Michigan schools. Parents do not have the information that they need to make good choices on behalf of their children, and as a result schools do not feel the pressure that might oblige them to improve their performance. In the long run, the variety and severity of these problems have undermined confidence in the reliability and legitimacy of the judgments about Michigan schools on which NCLB relies. Unless they are confident that the labels assigned to their schools are accurate and meaningful, and that changes in the ways they manage their schools and classrooms will lead to predictable changes in those labels, educators (and to some extent parents) will not make the changes in behavior that would be necessary for NCLB to produce sustained improvements in student achievement.

School Choice and Supplemental Services

In Michigan, the school choice and supplemental services provisions of NCLB are something of a sideshow. They are being implemented in a policy context in which the sharpest instruments available for change, including school

choice, have been significantly dulled by previous use. In addition, administrative and technical obstacles encountered in the process of implementation
have called the legitimacy of NCLB sanctions into question and weakened the
incentive of state and local administrators to comply with the law's more
demanding requirements. As a result, those administrators have responded to
NCLB's choice and supplemental services provisions with a manifest lack of
enthusiasm, making it difficult for parents to understand or exercise their
options under these provisions.

School Choice

As noted above, Michigan has an increasingly active and competitive market
for schooling, with about 6 percent of public school students already attending schools other than those to which they would traditionally have been
assigned. This is particularly true in the state's metropolitan areas, where most
of the schools subject to NCLB sanctions are located. Many urban districts
have adopted open enrollment policies, under which parents (including non-
resident parents) may enroll their children in any district school, subject only
to space limitations. In addition, parents in metropolitan areas may choose
schools from a wide array of charter schools and nearby school districts.

Under NCLB, the parents of children who attend schools identified as
failing must be informed of that fact and advised that they have the right to
select a more successful school within the district. By definition, therefore,
NCLB does not expand the array of options available to Michigan parents;
the set of schools that is open to them under NCLB is a small subset of the
schools that they could choose before the law was adopted.

It is possible that some Michigan parents were not previously aware of the performance of their children's schools or of the alternatives available to them. By the
same token, it is possible that the prospect of transportation provided by the district will reduce the marginal cost of choosing different schools sufficiently that
previously trapped parents will feel able to move their children. For now, however, there is virtually no evidence to suggest that the advent of NCLB has
increased the incidence of non-traditional choices among Michigan parents.[14]

Supplemental Educational Services

The supplemental services case is more complicated. The Office of Field
Services in the Michigan Department of Education developed a supplementary

services application process that requires prospective providers to demonstrate how their program will improve MEAP scores in reading and mathematics.[15] By January 2004, the department had approved 44 providers, including three intermediate school districts, ten local school districts, and two individual public schools. The list of approved providers also includes some large private-sector companies like Sylvan (now known as Catapult Learning), Kumon, and Edison Schools, along with a variety of local firms.[16] With a large and growing number of Michigan schools under federal scrutiny, there is a potentially huge market for supplemental services in the state, but that market has been slow to develop, for two main reasons.

First, state and local officials have not taken aggressive steps to ensure that parents have access to supplemental services for their children. The state education department has done little in this regard other than to publish its list of approved providers and inform districts of their obligations under the law. At present, the department has no information about which districts have funded supplemental services for students in failing schools, or how many students have received services. They expect to receive reports on the number of students who received services in 2002–2003 beginning in January 2004, and evaluate the program's success in 2006. Local districts have sent letters to parents informing them of their right to seek out supplemental services, as NCLB requires, but few have encouraged participation.

Second, some private-sector providers have reportedly been slow to enter the market for business reasons. Under NCLB, school districts must set aside 20 percent of their Title I funds to provide transportation and supplemental services for their students. The available funds fall far short of the amounts that would be needed to cover all eligible students, and so some districts have consequently engaged in protracted negotiations with potential providers to reduce their fees. Many providers have not been able to devise a business plan for local service delivery that promises them a satisfactory return.[17] For the time being, therefore, many potential providers remain on the sidelines, and the funds available for the purchase of supplemental services remain on the table.

Geography imposes further constraints. In Flint, for example, only 3 of the 44 state-approved providers have offered to provide services, despite the many eligible students in the district. Schools in outlying districts with fewer eligible students are apt to attract even fewer private-sector providers.

To sum up: because neither education officials nor private providers have moved aggressively to develop the market for supplemental services, few Michigan students have been able to take advantage of the opportunities that

NCLB promises. Clearing the obstacles to increased activity in this market should be a priority for those who seek to achieve the goals of NCLB.

The Politics of NCLB in Michigan

Despite the implementation problems catalogued above, state political leaders, including Governor Granholm, have generally remained supportive of NCLB. Speaking to the State Board of Education in March 2003, for example, Granholm strongly endorsed the law's central purpose: "Let's embrace it, let's move on it. Let us go forward at 90 miles an hour and say we are not going to leave any child behind. You have to have high expectations, and you have to have accountability. . . . Failure is not an option." In the same meeting, State Superintendent of Public Instruction Tom Watkins was more equivocal, but still supportive: "The point is this is the law of the land and we have to implement it. What we want to do is make No Child Left Behind more than just a rhetorical statement."[18]

In her response to NCLB, however, Governor Granholm embraced the central purpose of the law while effectively minimizing if not rejecting the instruments proposed to accomplish that purpose. Rather than emphasizing the sanctions that may be imposed on low-performing schools, she stressed the importance of providing additional support for schools and students in danger of being left behind.[19]

Her signature initiative in this regard is the Children's Action Network, an effort to mobilize and coordinate the efforts of an array of social service agencies in targeted schools. In budget negotiations, she has also striven to protect the categorical funding that Michigan provides for "at-risk" students, arguing instead for across-the-board reductions in the foundation allowance and additional cuts for the highest-spending school districts. She has supported the Partners for Success program, which provides technical assistance to severely troubled schools, and introduced mandatory "leadership academies" for principals of schools that fail to meet their AYP targets.

These emphases work at cross-purposes in important respects to the intentions of the law's sponsors, particularly with regard to choice. Most notably, Governor Granholm has attempted to increase the resources available to the most troubled schools rather than encouraging parents to seek out alternatives or supplementary services. Her education policy initiatives have served to make the schools on Michigan's priority schools list *more* rather than less attractive to parents. Enrollments have consequently risen rather than declined in some of the state's lowest-performing schools.

Local Responses to NCLB

Here we examine the responses of three urban districts—Detroit, Flint, and River City—to the school choice and supplemental services provisions of NCLB. Urban school districts are under intense strain in Michigan. Since the adoption of Proposal A and the expansion of school choice opportunities, their enrollments and revenues have declined steadily. At the same time, their student populations have shifted significantly, with growing percentages eligible for special education services and free or reduced price lunch.[20] All but 7 of the 216 schools on Michigan's first list of failing schools were in urban, high-poverty districts. Fully half were in Detroit.[21] Nearly 90 percent of the students in these schools were members of racial or ethnic minorities, and more than three-quarters were poor.[22]

Detroit

Detroit is the largest school district in Michigan, enrolling nearly 160,000 students. Enrollments have fallen dramatically in recent years, however, because of demographic shifts and transfers to charter schools and nearby school districts. Since 1994, more than twenty thousand students have left the Detroit Public Schools, reducing district revenues by approximately $160 million per year. More than 80 of the Michigan schools labeled as failing in NCLB's first year were part of Detroit Public Schools; approximately seventy-eight thousand of the district's students were enrolled in schools that had failed to make AYP for at least two years.

TRANSPORTATION AND PARENTAL CHOICE

In fall 2003, the school district mailed letters to the parents of students in schools that had not made AYP for two years. These advised parents that their children were eligible for transportation to a higher-achieving school within the district. The letter specifically read, "This letter is to officially inform you of the status of your youngster's school and to inform you of your right to transfer your youngster to another school that made AYP." Immediately following this sentence, however, DPS alerted parents that the district was "poised to address the academic crisis . . . and that the district intended to move their schools off the current list. Our major concern is assuring the success of our students who continue to attend schools not making AYP."

The letter identified a number of special initiatives that the district intended to implement to enable schools on the list to make AYP during 2003–2004. These included the assignment of a reading and/or a math specialist to each school not making AYP, the employment of additional consultants by the district to assist with the Open Court Reading Program, and professional development for all staff. Parents who decided to have their children remain in their current school were told that the district would work with them "to help assure the school's success during the upcoming year."

Toward the end of the letter, a couple of sentences informed parents who wanted to transfer their children that they were required to contact the district within 30 days of the date the letter had been mailed. The district further stated that it would provide a maximum of two options of schools to which their youngster might transfer. If a student wished to transfer to a school located beyond the district's established walking distance of 1.5 miles, then the district would provide transportation from a central location (which could be the neighborhood school) to a new school within walking distance.

The official responsible for overseeing these programs informed us that the district was prepared to set aside 5 percent of its Title I funding to support student transportation. When the 5 percent is spent, however, transportation ends. According to this official,

> The transportation unit is working to identify two achieving schools closest to a failing school. The parent could then choose either school A or B. A parent may not choose a school 15 miles away because they are offering a program their child is interested in taking. It is either school A or B. The law is very open and vague. It only says that you must send them to a school making AYP. This is why DPS [Detroit Public Schools] designates either school A or B. And DPS is sending students to the closest achieving school available to students.

As of December 2003, approximately nine hundred families had requested information about transferring their children to schools making AYP. Yet no students had been transferred. The same official explained that the district had not yet worked out the logistics involved with moving students to other schools and providing transportation, particularly in circumstances where the number of schools subject to sanctions (and the number of students eligible for transportation) remained uncertain.

> We have no idea how many parents may opt for the transportation. We may not get the children transported until the second week of October. [NB: No children had been transported at the end of December 2003.] We are well after the fourth Wednesday's count for state aid so how are we going to do this? In addition, some schools where parents have requested transfers from may come in having made AYP. We don't know

because we don't have MEAP scores. In this case, we don't have to transfer/transport students. It is a nightmare.

SUPPLEMENTAL EDUCATIONAL SERVICES

In May/June 2003, the district mailed seventy-six thousand letters to parents of students eligible for supplemental educational services, whose schools had failed to make AYP for three consecutive years. According to the responsible official: "There was an overwhelming response from parents when the letters were sent out initially in May. We did not anticipate the volume. My phone number and the number to the Title I office were on the letter. A huge volume of calls blocked all the phones out so it essentially wreaked havoc on the system." To handle the calls, the district hired a temporary service that provided 20 people and phone lines. The temps answered the phones and registered parents for supplemental services, collecting information on students' schools and birthdates that was cross-checked with the district's database of eligible students (i.e., students eligible to receive free or reduced price lunch who were attending schools that had not made AYP). In the end, however, only thirty-seven hundred students signed up for supplemental services during summer 2003. According to the official,

> I think parents thought they were going to get a check that would enable them to send their child for supplemental services rather than be referred to a provider. Once they found out that they would not receive the $1,352, the interest lessened. Summer Learning Academy [a district program for low-achieving students] was mandatory and it was going on at the same time. The law says that tutorial services could only begin at the end of the day. Students were going to the academy from 8:00 to 1:00 and then were expected to begin SES at 1:00 PM until whenever. This schedule was not appealing to students or parents.

In fall 2003, the district sent new letters to parents of students in schools that had not made AYP for three or four years. These families were given the option of receiving supplemental services or transportation to an achieving school, but not both. The list of supplemental services providers included programs like Sylvan (now known as Catapult Learning), which offered face-to-face instruction, and other programs featuring online services. The district set an initial deadline of September 18 for families to sign up for SES, but this was subsequently extended to October 24 to allow more parents to enroll. Officials scheduled districtwide parent meetings for October 17 and 18 to explain NCLB and options offered to parents, including where to sign up with approved providers in the Detroit area.

The official attributed the delays to the fact that the district had not received the results of the state test: "The state is holding up the MEAP data so we don't really know. A school may have made AYP this year and in doing so gives them another year. We sent out seventy-six thousand letters to parents to comply with [NCLB requirements]. The state not having this data available, puts the district in violation of NCLB mandates that parents be notified no later than the first day that school opens."

Of the approximately seventy-eight thousand students eligible for SES in the DPS in fall 2003, only thirty-seven hundred ultimately enrolled to receive services.

On the other side of the market, some providers argued that the district was creating obstacles for parents who wanted their children to receive supplemental services. According to one, for example, the district told some providers not to "stir up business because that would cause the money to soon run out." This provider also complained that information meetings scheduled by the district were set up with too little advance notice and too little opportunity for providers to inform parents about services they offered and provide parents with an opportunity to sign their children up. Other providers complained of shifting rules and deadlines, and of differential treatment for different providers. Some had the names of students referred to them by the district, while others were obliged to acquire students' names through contacts with parents. One private provider signed up a number of families only to be informed by district officials that children who enrolled directly through the provider (and not through the district) would not be eligible for services.

THE POLITICS OF NCLB: BAEO

Detroit is one of four cities across the country where chapters of the Black Alliance for Educational Options (BAEO) have been awarded $600,000 grants from the U.S. Department of Education to help inform parents about NCLB and its provisions.[23] The Detroit chapter of the Alliance began its outreach activities under the name of Project Clarion in September 2002. Its goal was to reach five thousand parents in 18 months to inform them of their right to move their children from schools not making AYP. The chapter held workshops for parents, participated in parent-teacher organization meetings, and partnered with the mayor's office and other community organizations in an effort to get the word out. Some of the workshops included representatives from the SES providers. There were also radio and billboard promotions aimed at informing parents.

According to the president of the Detroit chapter, parents were frustrated because they were unaware of the options provided by NCLB and wanted to know why they had not received this information sooner. The president also expressed exasperation, but no surprise, over her mostly futile attempts to work cooperatively with Detroit Public Schools.

When asked whether the district had worked with any community organizations (more specifically with the Alliance) to dispense information about NCLB and its implications, the Title I director indicated that the district had not. District officials are trying to comply with NCLB while keeping Detroit children enrolled in the district and keeping Title I resources under district control. The Alliance is encouraging children to take advantage of NCLB provisions that would shift Title I funds out of the control of the district. Under these circumstances, the lack of cooperation is not surprising.

Flint

Flint Community Schools is on the verge of bankruptcy.[24] Enrollments and revenues have fallen steadily in recent years as families move to the suburbs and students move to charter schools and neighboring districts. The district has closed 10 buildings in the past two years and expects to close another 10 in the coming decade. In 2003–2004, it experienced a net loss of one thousand students, with an associated fall in revenues of approximately $8 million. In response, the district has laid off staff and privatized virtually all non-instructional services. The district will cease providing transportation for students (except special education students) in 2004–2005. Sixteen of its schools were on the state's first list of failing schools.[25]

INFORMING PARENTS

In May 2003, Flint Community Schools mailed out a first letter to parents of children attending schools that had not made adequate yearly progress. That letter simply informed parents that they had the right to move their children to another school in the district, but it stopped short of providing specific directives on how this transfer would take place. The letter also (in a single sentence) made reference to "supplemental services," but it provided no explanation as to what this option meant or how it would work. At the same time, the letter explicitly assured parents that administrators believed in Flint's schools and were doing all they could to make necessary improvements. A phone number was listed in the conclusion of the letter that recommended that parents with questions call for further information. It is uncertain how many responses the district received, but no children were transported and no supplemental services were provided in summer 2003.

District Plan

Instead, in summer 2003 local education officials scheduled what they characterized as "priority meetings" with every school in the district that had been labeled as failing. A panel of administrators was assembled and charged with the responsibility to critique the school improvement plan put forward by each sanctioned school. A rubric was provided to assess the merits of the plan. Ideas were shared between the panel and the school improvement team.

The school improvement teams expressed frustration about the additional demands placed on them as a result of NCLB. They believed they had done all they could do and had made improvements. They produced data to support their claims. In discussing their student population, they asserted that they were "fighting an uphill climb to the bottom," with little prospect of success in meeting AYP targets. The superintendent echoed these concerns, proposing the creation of a local assessment model that would highlight district successes rather than district failures.

Transportation and School Choice

In May 2003, the district held discussions about the possibility of having to transport students to other schools within the district. By August, however, officials had observed no increase in the number of students moving between buildings. The district has not transported any students using Title I funds; according to district officials, no parents have requested transportation for their children. In any case, Flint plans to cease transporting *all* students in 2004–2005 because of budget pressures.

Supplemental Educational Services

In fall 2003, Flint Community Schools negotiated contracts with two supplementary services providers to provide tutoring services to eligible students, and was engaged in negotiations with a third. The contracts require providers to offer services in all 16 of the district's failing schools in the first hour after the conclusion of the regular school day, in either reading or math. This arrangement places the providers in direct competition for students in each of the schools. Payments will range from $700 to $1,000 per student.[26] The contracts require providers to deliver monthly reports on student progress to the district. The district has encouraged both providers to hire and train district employees to staff their programs, on the grounds that the teachers are already familiar with the students who will be receiving services.

A letter sent to parents in August 2003 identified the two providers the district had approved and encouraged parents to enroll their children. Approximately one thousand students had signed up to receive supplemental services by December 2003, and district officials expressed the hope that additional students would enroll. The first tutoring sessions took place in January 2004.

River City

Like Detroit and Flint, River City is struggling with declining enrollments and revenues.[27] The rate of decline has slowed in recent years, in response to a variety of initiatives launched by an energetic new superintendent, but enrollment losses in 2003–2004 were significantly larger than expected.[28] In combination with state funding cuts, this produced a substantial budget shortfall, which the district struggled to close. Only one district school was on the original list of failing schools, and as a result the district's response to NCLB was different than those of Detroit and Flint.

INFORMING PARENTS

In River City, letters were mailed to parents of students in the district's one priority school in April 2003. The letter contained information about choice options and supplemental services as well. It listed ten providers approved by the state for parents to choose from.

TRANSPORTATION AND PARENTAL CHOICE

There is no evidence that parents with students enrolled in River City's one priority school have sought to move their children to more successful schools, and the district has spent no Title 1 funds on student transportation. In fact, enrollments increased significantly after the school was identified as having failed to achieve its AYP targets, for two main reasons. First, the school is closely identified with River City's Hispanic community, and this apparently made some parents reluctant to move their children to other schools. According to the school's principal (himself Hispanic), parents and students in the community "are happy here." In the view of the principal, NCLB threatens to shift the school's focus away from the attributes most highly valued by the community: "I'm not talking about the MEAP. It's about students living and feeling good about themselves. . . . I'm trying to save lives."

Second, the school was selected as one of 18 pilot sites for the Children's Action Network initiated by Governor Granholm. Hence an array of social services are available to families with children enrolled in this school that are not available in other district schools. It appears that access to these services has attracted additional students.

SUPPLEMENTAL EDUCATIONAL SERVICES

The River City school district has not contracted with any supplemental services providers, and no Title 1 funds have been spent on tutoring. Instead, the district has continued to focus resources and attention on its own internal improvement efforts, including expanded summer school opportunities and innovative instructional programs for students in the early grades. Additional resources, including instructional specialists in reading and math, have been assigned to the district's low-performing school, and the superintendent has solicited assistance from a local university to help the staff identify weaknesses and improve academic outcomes.

DISTRICT STRATEGY

Despite apparent non-compliance with key provisions of NCLB, the River City superintendent views the law favorably. Indeed, he was frustrated when only one of his schools was placed on the state's original priority list, because he had hoped to bring pressure to bear on other schools that he believed to be in serious need of improvement. With respect to the one school placed on the list, he has made clear that this school will be reconstituted in 2004–2005 if its MEAP scores do not improve. He expressed frustration that the close ties between the school and the Hispanic community made it extremely difficult to remove the current principal and encourage needed changes, and he expressed hope that NCLB would make that task easier.

NCLB in Michigan: What Have We Learned?

Will the goals of NCLB be accomplished in Michigan? In our view, the answer depends on two key considerations: the clarity of the signals sent to schools and the credibility of consequences that schools experience when they fail to meet NCLB targets. In Michigan, as in other states, schools find themselves in a turbulent policy environment in which they must respond to a variety of urgent challenges—political and financial as well as educational—including but hardly limited to NCLB. In this chaotic setting, the signal conveyed by the incentives and sanctions at the heart of NCLB must come through loud and clear if it is to induce educators and others to behave in new and more productive ways.

The credibility and consistency of the signal conveyed by NCLB are as important as its strength. If incentives and sanctions are to produce desired changes in the behavior of educators and parents, they must be introduced in ways that make sense to those who are subject to them. In the first instance, those expected to respond to new incentives and sanctions (e.g., designation as a failing school) must accept the legitimacy and reliability of the information on which rewards and sanctions are based. In addition, they must have confidence that changes in their own behavior will produce positive consequences in terms of access to rewards or avoidance of punishment.

On these criteria, NCLB has gotten off to a rocky start in Michigan, for four main reasons. First, the integrity of the signals it sends has been called into question by public wrangling over which schools should be identified as failing. Many Michigan schools have already been on and off the state's priority schools list more than once, for reasons that they perceive as arbitrary. Under such circumstances, there is little reason to suppose that NCLB will spur educators to make the kinds of changes that might lead to sustained improvements in school performance or student achievement.[29]

Second, Michigan educators were already well acquainted with the sanctions introduced under NCLB, and as a result their effect is likely to be limited. This is especially true of the school choice provisions, which add marginally at best to the array of options already available to Michigan parents. It is also true of the central thrust of NCLB, which is to identify failing schools in the expectation that this information will encourage educators and parents to take actions that will lead to improvement. MEAP data on school performance have been widely published and compared for most of a decade, and schools (and parents) have grown accustomed to the public opprobrium or praise that comes with their scores. NCLB's focus on adequate yearly progress has generated new uncertainties and anxieties among schools that have traditionally performed well on MEAP, but in the Michigan schools that are most in need of improvement, NCLB provides no new information and thus only a weak incentive to improve.

Third, the implementation of NCLB coincides with Michigan's worst budget crisis in many years. This diminishes its impact in two ways. On the one hand, schools and districts are confronted by a host of challenges that compete for their attention, now including the need to plan for potentially severe budget reductions as well as the need to meet AYP targets, and the threat of the former is likely to reduce the urgency with which they address the latter task. On the other hand, the prospect of reduced revenues is now available for deployment as a justification for limited compliance and accomplishment under NCLB, as state and local officials struggle to maintain the integrity of the systems they administer.

Finally, Governor Jennifer Granholm and the Michigan Department of Education have made clear that their preferred strategies for achieving NCLB's goals are different from those provided for in the law. The governor's education initiatives have focused almost exclusively on providing additional support for priority schools, and virtually not at all on the threat or implementation of sanctions. The department has been careful to comply with the requirements of NCLB, and has encouraged schools and school districts to do likewise. At the same time, it has done little to push schools and districts toward more aggressive efforts to put new alternatives for parents into practice and nothing at all to monitor local responses to NCLB requirements. The law requires the department to review district efforts after two years, and this is what state education officials propose to do. For now, therefore, they possess almost no useful information about how NLCB is being put into practice at the local level.

Some of these obstacles may be overcome with time, but two fundamental problems remain. First, the assessment system on which incentives and sanctions are based has proven itself too fragile and capricious to win the confidence of educators and other audiences. In addition, the incentives and sanctions introduced by NCLB are not strong enough to produce positive changes in educators' behavior when measured against the financial and political turmoil surrounding troubled schools. Hence there are few grounds for optimism that NCLB will lead to significant improvement in the performance of those Michigan schools where children are most in danger of being left behind.

Notes

1. We have agreed to protect the identity of this district, because of the possibility that the anonymity of specific individuals could be compromised.
2. The value of the grants varies across school districts, depending on their level of educational spending in 1993–1994. Some revenues continue to be distributed under categorical programs. For a full discussion of Michigan's school finance policies, see David Arsen and David N. Plank, *Michigan School Finance under Proposal A: State Control, Local Consequences* (East Lansing: The Education Policy Center at Michigan State University, November 2003). Available at www.epc. msu.edu.
3. Intermediate School District boundaries correspond to county boundaries. Some Intermediate School Districts comprise more than one county.

4. The state superintendent of public instruction appoints one member, who enjoys a veto over some board decisions.

5. Schools could also meet the standard if 10 percent more of their students passed the tests than in the previous year, Michigan's own version of AYP.

6. "544 Schools Are Added to Problem List," *Detroit News*, July 15, 2003. The additional schools had met their AYP targets in the 2002–2003 school year, but not in the preceding year. NCLB requires schools to make AYP for two consecutive years.

7. Alexandra R. Moses, "Nearly 900 Michigan Schools Don't Meet Progress Goals," *Detroit News*, January 31, 2004. The new number includes high schools for the first time.

8. In states that did not already have assessment systems in place, in contrast, there will be no schools on the sanctions list in the first two years of implementation.

9. David N. Plank, "Business Involvement Key to Turning around Failing Schools," *Michigan Forward*, July–August 2003.

10. The previous governor moved MEAP out of the Michigan Department of Education into Treasury. Governor Granholm has recently moved MEAP back into the education department.

11. Maureen Feighan, "Districts Question 'Grades' from State," *Lansing State Journal*, November 17, 2003.

12. Alexandra R. Moses, "Few Use School Transfer Rule," *Detroit News*, February 4, 2004.

13. For a discussion see Citizens Research Council, "A Recap of the FY2004 Budget and a Look Ahead to FY2005 and Beyond," October 2003. Available at www.crcmich.org. For additional data and further discussion see Arsen and Plank, *Michigan School Finance*.

14. As noted below, some nine hundred Detroit parents have made inquiries about how to take advantage of the school choice provisions of NCLB.

15. *Michigan Education Report*, Fall 2002.

16. For the current list, see http://www.michigan.gov/mde/0,1607,7-140-6525_17014-61646-,00.html.

17. An insider in this market suggests that even $1,200 per student is too little to make the opportunity attractive from a business standpoint, and that the per-pupil funding must be increased to attract significant private-sector participation.

18. Judy Putnam, "Granholm Gung-Ho on Bush Education Plan," *Grand Rapids Press*, March 28, 2003.

19. "If those schools need new leadership, they should get new leadership. If those schools need assistance from the state in making sure the families that feed into those schools are served better, the state should do that." Ibid.

20. Arsen and Plank, *Michigan School Finance*, table 12.

21. This includes charter schools.

22. Kwanghyun Lee and Christopher B. Reimann, *Who's Attending Michigan's Priority Schools?* The Education Policy Center at Michigan State University, Data Brief #12, July 2003. Available at www.epc.msu.edu.

23. The cities of Milwaukee, Dallas, Philadelphia, and Detroit each received $600,000 from the U.S. Department of Education from a grant awarded to the Black Alliance for Educational Options to specifically inform parents in their respective cities about NCLB.

24. We would like to thank Sheila Klaas for her research assistance on the implementation of NCLB in Flint.

25. Eighteen schools were on the original list. Three schools were closed or merged with other schools, and one school was added.

26. Providers bill their services at between $40 and $50 per hour, which means that Title 1 will pay for something on the order of 20–30 hours of one-on-one instruction per pupil. Increasing "class size" or making use of online technologies could increase the number of hours of service provided to each student.

27. We would like to thank Danielle LeSure for her research assistance on the implementation of NCLB in River City.

28. A neighboring suburban district opened a new high school and recruited an additional two hundred River City students. This reduced revenues by $1.6 million.

29. For a similar argument see David Figlio, "What School Accountability Might Do," *NBER Research Reporter,* fall 2001.

8

Fumbling for an Exit Key: Parents, Choice, and the Future of NCLB

William Howell

Parents are the linchpins in any school choice initiative—whether vouchers, intra- or interdistrict public school choice, voluntary desegregation plans, or the choice and supplemental services provisions of No Child Left Behind (NCLB). What parents know about and want for their child's education critically defines the level of interest in school choice, and hence sets in motion (or not) all of the possibilities for competitive pressures and systemic change that reform-minded advocates espouse. If parents are basically satisfied with their child's teacher and school, or if they have insufficient information about alternative schooling options, or if they express little desire to disrupt their child's current education, then choice initiatives will not get off the ground.

In an effort to explain why so few children are taking advantage of the choice provisions of NCLB—either by switching out of public schools deemed "in need of improvement" or requesting supplemental services from private providers—some attention in this volume has been cast toward the obstructionist behaviors of state and local bureaucrats, superintendents, and school board members. And for good reason. All of these political actors have a vested interest in minimizing NCLB's effect on a district by keeping children in their current public schools. Still, even if policymakers are able to rework the accountability system so that political actors throughout our system of separated and federated powers freely and enthusiastically promote the act's public school choice and supplemental services provisions, widespread enrollment changes are hardly a foregone conclusion. NCLB does not mandate change, it merely presents some public school parents with new educational options. Whether these parents will take advantage of these options, and whether they can correctly assess the best needs of their children when doing so, remain very much open questions.

Curiously, several years after the law's enactment, we still do not know whether NCLB effectively meets parents' wants and wishes. To be sure, some excellent research examines parents' educational priorities within the existing public school system;[1] other scholarship, meanwhile, surveys parents' professed interest in school vouchers and charter schools.[2] Unfortunately, none of these surveys deals specifically with the options NCLB avails to families with children in underperforming public schools. And there is good reason to believe that parents' interest in policies like school vouchers (or charter schools, or magnet schools) does not illuminate the likely choices they will make in a highly restricted, intradistrict, public school choice program. If scholars across the political spectrum have settled on one truth about school choice, it is this: the fate of a program ultimately rides on the particular ways it is structured, the population it targets, and the resources it brings to bear. All of the action is in the details, and analysts who generalize from yesterday's policy initiative to today's do so at considerable peril.

The Thirty-fifth Annual Phi Delta-Kappa/Gallup poll, released in September 2003, does contain measures of public attitudes toward NCLB.[3] Much of the survey aims to reveal public attitudes toward the law itself, asking whether citizens think testing is a good way of assessing school performance; whether the federal, state, or local government should retain primary responsibility over the governance of schools; whether subjects other than math and English ought to be included in determinations of student and school progress; and whether standards should differ for special education students. Interesting though these policy items may be, they tell us very little about how NCLB actually functions in local communities. Ultimately, it does not much matter whether parents endorse the law as it is currently written, or whether they think improvements to public education are better sought via alternative policy avenues. What matters are the practical choices that parents make within a given educational context, a subject about which the PDK/Gallup poll is largely silent.[4]

Lost in the contemporary debate over accountability and choice is any serious, systematic effort to answer a central question: if given the option, who would most likely pursue the specific educational opportunities that are presented to parents with children attending schools deemed in need of improvement? This chapter takes some preliminary steps toward formulating an answer. It does not advance, or test, elaborate theories of social networks or consumer behaviors. Its aim is considerably more modest, and its formulation is inductive rather than deductive in nature. To assist policy-makers intent on expanding schooling options in the current education system, this chapter establishes some basic facts about public school parents' knowledge of and interest in their children's education generally, and in NCLB in particular.

Drawing from a telephone survey of public school parents in the state of Massachusetts, this chapter presents original findings that are organized around two topics.[5] The first involves parents' knowledge of NCLB. How much information about NCLB do parents have? Where are they learning about NCLB? Do the targeted parents have the necessary information? Or is knowledge about the new educational opportunities primarily reserved for more advantaged families attending higher-performing public schools? The second set of questions, meanwhile, concerns parents' interest in NCLB's public school choice and supplemental services provisions. How satisfied are parents with their child's current public school? Are those parents whose children attend underperforming public schools systematically less satisfied than those whose children attend schools that made AYP? Are the newly available public schooling options likely to attract many families? Or do other schooling options (charter schools, public school in other districts, or private schools) generate more enthusiasm?

Examining parents' knowledge of and interest in NCLB, two basic findings emerge:

1. Though parents claim to be familiar with NCLB, the vast majority of those who in fact qualify for the act's choice and supplemental services provisions do not know that their child's school is on the state's list of public schools that failed to make adequate yearly progress toward proficiency standards.
2. Parents with children in schools deemed in need of improvement are especially interested in pursuing alternative schooling options; this interest, however, does not derive from pointed dissatisfaction with their current schools, and it is regularly directed toward options that NCLB does not afford—specifically, private schools.

These facts, in combination, help elucidate why so few families have either sought supplemental services from private providers or requested transfers to higher performing public schools in their districts. They also suggest that demand will not rise until communications with parents improve. If law-makers are to promote NCLB's choice and supplemental services provisions effectively, they must do more than revisit the language of the law itself. They must embark on a public relations campaign that speaks directly to parents, that informs them of their new rights and options, just as it responds to their particular interests and needs.

The Survey

During the summer of 2003, one thousand public school parents in Massachusetts' 10 largest school districts were surveyed. One quarter of the stratified listed sample consisted of parents living in Boston, another quarter of parents in Springfield, another in Worcester, and the final drawn randomly from parents in Brockton, Lynn, Lowell, New Bedford, Lawrence, Fall River, and Newton.[6] The reason for focusing on these larger districts is straightforward: the vast majority of Massachusetts' 489 school districts have just a handful of elementary schools and one or two middle and high schools. Given that NCLB mandates opportunities for school transfers within, but not across, districts, few parents in underperforming rural schools can be expected to move their children to higher-performing schools. The survey, as such, focuses on the larger districts simply because it is there that NCLB stands the greatest chance of effecting change.

Surveys were conducted over the telephone in either English or Spanish and generally required 15 to 20 minutes to complete. To qualify, households had to have at least one child in a public school, and questions were directed only to parents or guardians of this child.[7] In 72 percent of the cases, the respondent was the child's mother, 22 percent the father, 3 percent a grandparent, and the rest were other relatives. (Hereafter, respondents are referred to as parents.) When families had more than one child, respondents were asked about the youngest attending a public school. As such, elementary school children were the subject of a disproportionate share of the interviews.[8] Before abandoning a telephone number, it was called a total of 15 times, usually spread out over several weeks. The adjusted response rate was 31 percent, which is roughly on par with most telephone surveys.[9] To the extent that this survey over-sampled socio-economically more advantaged families, it likely overstates the level of knowledge that parents have about NCLB; if such families were more successful at placing their child in a preferred public school, the survey also understates the level of interest in NCLB's choice provisions.[10]

From the outset, some additional caveats are in order. This chapter takes a distinctly behavioral orientation. It identifies what Massachusetts parents know about and want for their child's education *at a given moment and within a given context*. The findings herein represent a snapshot of

Massachusetts parents two years after NCLB's enactment, and lessons drawn may apply only imperfectly to other states and times. Moreover, the survey does not provide much basis on which to levy blame—either on parents, teachers, or district administrators—for perceived lapses in knowledge, much less for failings in school performance. The survey's strengths lie in specifying what parents know and want, and less in why they know or want it.

Knowledge

When asked, Massachusetts parents claim to know a fair amount about NCLB. Among those surveyed, 69 percent profess to have heard of the act; 52 percent to know about the option of switching from an underperforming school to one that made AYP; and 46 percent to have heard about the availability of supplemental services. Of those who say they have heard about NCLB, 59 percent received their information from the media, 24 percent from the school district, 7 percent from other parents, 3 percent from friends and family, and the rest from assorted sources. As conventional wisdom suggests that average citizens pay little attention to politics and lack basic information about the contents of public policy, these figures would appear to reflect remarkably well on Massachusetts parents.[11] Unfortunately, though, they do not hold up to scrutiny.

The centerpiece of the federal government's accountability system consists of assessments of public schools' annual yearly progress (AYP) toward state-mandated proficiency standards. From these determinations, penalties are directed to schools and districts, just as benefits flow to parents and students. To navigate the educational landscape, and to seize upon new schooling opportunities, it is vital that parents know the status of their child's school. Without information about whether their child qualifies for the act's choice and supplemental services provisions, parents' general awareness of NCLB does them little good.

Overall, 25 percent of the Massachusetts parents surveyed had children who attended schools that failed to make AYP. But when asked whether their child's school was on the list of underperforming schools, only 6 percent of parents responded affirmatively.[12] Something, plainly, is amiss.[13]

Using self reports to assess knowledge about policy matters is always a tricky business. Indeed, in many ways the history of survey research constitutes a long cautionary tale about the problems of taking people at their word. For a wide variety of reasons, what people say in the context of telephone surveys does not reliably match what they believe, know, or do. In this instance, parents have ample incentives to feign knowledge of matters about which they have very little information and to overestimate their ability to place their child in a successful public school—both of which effectively distort assessments of parental awareness of NCLB and the characteristics of children that the act intends to reach.

Fortunately, we do not need to rely exclusively on what parents tell us. Because the survey asked for the name of their child's school, we can use State Department of Education administrative records to verify their responses. Doing so, a more sobering view of parental awareness begins to emerge. For starters, only 49 percent of surveyed parents in Massachusetts could correctly identify whether their child's school made AYP, which assuredly represents an upper bound on knowledge, as an unknown percentage of parents guessed correctly the status of their child's school. Forty percent of parents admitted not knowing whether their child's school made AYP, and the remaining 11 percent incorrectly identified the status of their child's school.[14]

As the results in table 8.1 demonstrate, parents have markedly different amounts of information about the status of their children's schools. Unfortunately, the observed disparities point in a direction exactly opposite of what one would hope. Parents with children who attend performing public schools generally know that their child's school is not on the list of underperforming public schools, but parents with children in underperforming schools generally do not know that their school is, and hence lack the most basic information needed to acquire the NCLB benefits that they are due. Fully 57 percent of parents with a child attending a performing public school know the school's status, as compared to just 29 percent of families with a child in an underperforming school—even though districts were formally required to notify only parents of children at underperforming schools about the status of their schools. Parents with a child in an underperforming public school are 5 percentage points more likely to claim that they do not know

Table 8.1. Do parents with children at underperforming schools know the status of their child's school?

	Percent "don't know"	Percent answer incorrectly	Percent answer correctly	(N)
	(1)	(2)	(3)	
All parents	39.9	11.3	48.8	(964)
Parents with child attending performing school	36.9	5.8	57.3	(703)
Parents with child attending underperforming school	42.0	28.8	29.2	(232)

the school's status, and fully 5 times more likely to get it wrong when they claim that they do know.[15]

Part of the trouble here, I suspect, is that when parents lack facts to the contrary, they assume that their child's school meets the grade. After all, who wants to admit, especially to a stranger on the telephone, that they send their child to a poor public school? This predisposition would explain the kind of imbalances observed in table 8.1: when guessing, parents with children in performing public schools are more likely to answer correctly than parents with children in underperforming public schools. It would be a mistake, however, to dismiss this empirical phenomenon as an artifact of survey research. Indeed, immediate policy consequences are apparent. In addition to overcoming districts' reluctance to promote the act's choice and supplemental services provisions, NCLB advocates also must find ways to break through parents' preconceptions about their child's school quality. More to the point, spreading the word about NCLB's benefits entails convincing many parents that their children's public schools are not as good—at least, according to state standards—as they think they are.

Cognitive dissonance, however, does not constitute the only barrier to knowledge, for parents at performing and underperforming schools also retain different levels of information about other aspects of their children's schools. Again, using administrative records to verify parental responses, I was able to identify which parents knew the name of their child's school principal and the size of their child's school. The results break down along much the same lines as those previously observed. Whereas 58 percent of parents at public schools that made AYP were able to correctly name their child's principal, 49 percent of parents with children at underperforming schools could do so. Similarly, when asked about the size of their child's school, 46 percent of parents of children at performing schools picked the right population range, as compared to 23 percent of parents of children in underperforming schools. Either because underperforming schools are doing a poor job of communicating with parents or because parents are insufficiently involved in their child's education (or both), parents of children in schools that failed to make AYP have less information about a wide variety of aspects of their child's education than parents of children at schools that did so.[16]

Of course, attendance at an underperforming school is not the only predictor of knowledge. Systematically, minority and disadvantaged parents have less information about their child's school than do white and more advantaged parents. Take a look at the results presented in table 8.2. Fully 54 percent of whites correctly identify the status of their child's school, as compared to 44 percent of African Americans, and just 24 percent of

Table 8.2. Parental knowledge of school status under NCLB, by family/student background

	Percent "don't know"	Percent answer incorrectly	Percent answer correctly	(N)
	(1)	(2)	(3)	
Ethnicity				
Whites	34.7	11.2	54.1	(671)
African American	43.3	12.3	44.4	(140)
Hispanic	59.7	16.8	23.5	(62)
Place of Birth				
Born U.S.	37.2	10.5	52.3	(804)
Foreign born	50.4	15.8	33.8	(149)
Education				
High school grad or less	52.8	11.0	36.1	(257)
Some college	42.8	11.4	45.8	(315)
Graduated from 4-year college	26.6	11.0	62.5	(366)
Family income				
Qualify free or reduced lunch	50.8	11.1	38.1	(186)
Does not qualify	35.3	10.9	53.8	(599)
Employment Status				
Employed full time	35.8	12.5	51.8	(601)
Employed part time or less[1]	45.0	9.2	45.8	(299)
Home Ownership				
Home owner	34.1	11.3	54.6	(715)
Renter	53.4	11.4	35.3	(207)
Marital status				
Married	36.0	12.2	51.9	(701)
Single	49.5	8.3	42.2	(221)
Gender				
Male	40.0	11.2	48.8	(232)
Female	39.8	11.4	48.8	(732)
Religion				
Protestant	44.2	11.5	44.3	(257)
Catholic	36.8	11.8	51.5	(422)
Other	33.0	10.3	56.6	(82)
No religion	38.7	7.7	53.6	(96)
Refused	46.2	12.4	41.4	(95)
Attend religious services:				
Once a month or less	36.8	12.0	51.2	(414)
Once a week or more	41.2	10.8	48.0	(440)
Child attends classes for				
Learning/physical disabled	41.0	11.1	47.9	(174)
English as a second language	65.3	9.7	25.0	(62)
Gifted/talented program	26.5	13.6	59.9	(237)
None of the above	42.9	10.5	46.6	(555)

[1] Retired and disabled respondents dropped.

Hispanics. Parents born in the United States are 20 percentage points more likely to know whether their child's school made AYP than foreign-born parents. Home ownership, income, and education all positively contribute to the likelihood that parents correctly identify whether their child attends an underperforming school. More modest, but still positive, impacts are associated with marriage and employment. Plainly, those individuals who face the most discrimination, who are among the least established in their communities, and who can draw upon the fewest educational and financial resources have the lowest levels of information about their child's school. These also are precisely the kinds of families that the act purports to help.

Churches and synagogues are potentially important conduits for information about community affairs. At Saturday and Sunday services, soup kitchens, and clothing drives, congregants have ample opportunities to discuss goings-on in their communities, and to exchange insights about the quality of their local schools. Numerous scholars, what is more, have observed high levels of social capital and connectedness within religious communities.[17] Elsewhere, in the context of a targeted, urban voucher program, I found that parents who regularly attend religious services are more likely to have the necessary knowledge, interest, and wherewithal to apply for vouchers, to find access to a private school, and to remain there over time.[18] Religion and religiosity, however, do not systematically enhance Massachusetts parents' knowledge about their school's status under NCLB. Catholics, Protestants, and members of other religions are generally no more likely to correctly identify whether their child's school made AYP than individuals who claimed not to have any religious affiliation or who declined to answer the question. Parents who occasionally attend religious services are only slightly more likely to know whether their child's school is underperforming than those parents who do so more routinely.

One might expect parents with special-needs children to pay especially high amounts of attention to their child's education, and hence to the quality of their schools. Though average children may easily adapt to a wide variety of educational settings, without adequate accommodations students at the high and low ends of the distribution may suffer both personally and academically, prodding parents to monitor any and all information about their school. With regard to NCLB, however, the evidence on this score is somewhat mixed. Parents of students in gifted/talented programs are 12 percentage points more likely to know the status of their child's school than parents of students without any special needs. Parents with learning-disabled or physically disabled children, however, are no more likely to know whether their child's school made AYP. Meanwhile, limited English proficiency students come from families who are more than 20 percentage points less likely to know whether their school is underperforming.

One group of parents, however, appears especially informed about their schools: namely, those who already have direct access to the public school system. Take a look at the findings presented in table 8.3. Parents who volunteer at their child's school, who are members of a parent-teacher association, or who work in public school districts are 15 to 22 percentage points more likely to know whether their child's school is underperforming than those who do not. When considering overall levels of access and involvement, the differences are even more striking. Only 32 percent of parents who did not volunteer, who were not a member of the PTA, and who did not work for the public school district knew whether their child's school made AYP, as compared to 52 percent of parents with one of the three affiliations, and fully 64 percent of parents with two or three affiliations.[19] The probability that parents know the status of their child's school literally doubles when moving from the bottom to the top of the involvement scale.

The lesson here is plain: those who need the most information about the performance of their public schools have the least. Unaware that their child attends a school whose students qualify for new transfer opportunities and supplemental services, parents cannot be expected to take advantage of them. Poverty, language barriers, and residential instability further depress the likelihood that parents know about their child's school—and, concomitantly, further inhibit their chances of pursuing the new schooling opportunities

Table 8.3. Parental knowledge of school status under NCLB, by involvement levels

	Percent "don't know"	Percent answer incorrectly	Percent answer correctly	(N)
	(1)	(2)	(3)	
Volunteer at school?				
Yes	32.3	11.0	56.8	(475)
No	46.8	11.8	41.4	(483)
Member of PTA?				
Yes	27.3	10.1	62.7	(358)
No	46.9	12.4	40.8	(596)
Family member works in public school district?				
Yes	23.9	12.8	63.3	(187)
No	43.2	10.9	45.9	(756)
Overall level of involvement:				
None of above affiliations	54.5	13.6	31.9	(312)
One of above affiliations	40.3	7.9	51.9	(307)
Two or more of above affiliations	23.3	12.6	64.1	(322)

available to them. Who is most likely to know about the status of their child's school? Parents with children in performing schools (who do not qualify for NCLB's public school choice and supplemental services provisions); non-Hispanics, the highly educated, and the well-off (who, by virtue of residential choice, already have access to a wide array of schooling options); and families with strong personal and professional ties to the public schools (who are already involved in their child's educational life and are in a position to ensure that existing public resources are directed to their particular needs). The irony could not be sharper: those who thrive in the existing system have the information required to realize that NCLB will not help them any further, while those who struggle lack the information required to explore new schooling options that might improve their lot.

Interest

If NCLB's choice provisions are to catch on, lawmakers must ensure that parents have more than just a base level of knowledge about which schools made AYP and which did not. Lawmakers must offer alternative schooling options that actually appeal to parents, and sufficiently so that parents are willing to disrupt their child's current education in order to obtain them. In three steps, this section assesses the demand side of the equation: first, by measuring parental satisfaction with their current schools, then by examining parental interest in alternative schooling options, and finally by considering the qualities of public schools that matter most to parents. Throughout, the intended beneficiaries of choice under NCLB (namely, parents with children in underperforming public schools) are juxtaposed against the principal population that the act excludes (parents with children in performing public schools).

Parental Satisfaction with Their Current Schools

The chances that parents will explore new education options surely depend on how satisfied they are with their child's current school. Parents who are basically pleased with their child's current school, no matter how the federally mandated accountability system rates it, are not likely to request transfers to higher-performing public schools within their district. NCLB's choice provisions ought to appeal most to those parents who anxiously await opportunities to abandon schools that they themselves perceive as failing.

Table 8.4. Parental satisfaction with current public school

	All parents		Parents with child attending . . .			
			an underperforming school		a performing school	
Grade to school child attends:	(percent)		(percent)		(percent)	
A	37.2		28.7		41.5	
B	44.4		44.6		44.0	
C	13.2		16.8		10.6	
D	3.4		6.6		2.5	
F	1.8		3.3		1.3	
Total	100.0	[991]	100.0	[229]	100.0	[698]
Grade to schools in community:						
A	15.8		11.5		16.9	
B	45.4		42.8		47.6	
C	25.6		31.7		22.9	
D	7.9		6.7		8.9	
F	5.3		7.4		4.0	
Total	100.0	[932]	100.0	[216]	100.0	[657]

Number of observations in brackets.

If interest in alternative educational options thrives only in areas of widespread discontent, Massachusetts districts need not worry about children fleeing their public schools in droves. In the surveys, parents were asked to grade their child's school on an A to F scale. Their responses, presented in table 8.4, confirm those found in numerous other studies—namely, parents are basically satisfied with their children's public schools. In this survey, fully 82 percent of parents gave their public school either an A or a B, while just 5 percent gave their school a D or an F. Whatever may be objectively wrong with Massachusetts public schools, parents give them strong votes of confidence.

When focusing on the assessments of NCLB's target population, however, the story changes somewhat. Compare the results in the second and third columns. Though most parents with children in underperforming schools did not know their school's status under NCLB's accountability system, they nonetheless expressed less satisfaction with the quality of their child's education. Parents with children in underperforming schools were 13 percentage points less likely to give their school an A than parents with children in performing schools, just as they were almost three times as likely to give their school a D or an F.[20]

Though parents express relatively high levels of satisfaction with their own child's schools, the same cannot be said for the schools in their districts as a whole. Thirty-seven percent of parents gave their child's school an A, but only 16 percent gave the schools in their community the highest mark. And though just 5 percent of parents gave their child's school a D or an F, 13 percent gave their community's schools the lower grades. For the most part, differences between parents attending underperforming and performing public schools are more modest. Though 17 percent of parents with children at schools that made AYP gave their community's schools an A, only 12 percent from underperforming schools did so. At the bottom end of the grading spectrum, meanwhile, the responses of parents with children in performing and underperforming schools are virtually indistinguishable.

Two lessons are apparent here. First, parents are especially critical of other people's public schools. Just as average citizens express considerably higher levels of satisfaction with their own congressional representative than with Congress as a whole,[21] so do parents rally behind their children's schools while casting occasional aspersions at institutions their own children do not attend. In addition, however, these findings provide an early hint that NCLB's target population might refuse the particular schooling options that the act avails. Though parents at schools that failed to make AYP are less satisfied with their own child's school, they are not overwhelmingly dissatisfied with these schools, nor are they especially keen on the schools in the district as whole. In fact, NCLB's intended beneficiaries think less of their district's public schools than do parents in performing schools—a fact that does not bode especially well for political observers who hoped that the act, at last, would unleash pent up demand for new public schooling options within districts.

Switching Schools

It would be a mistake to conclude that general contentment with existing public schools translates into disinterest in alternative educational options. While questions about parental satisfaction suggest mild curiosity, more direct questions reveal considerable interest in alternative public, charter, and private schools. And once again, differences are regularly observed between those parents with children who qualify for NCLB's choice provisions and those with children who do not.

Take a look at table 8.5. Between 11 and 16 percent of parents claim that they would prefer their child attend a different public school in the same district, a different public school in a different district, or a charter school. And in all three instances, interest is higher among parents with children in schools that failed to make AYP. Though they revealed less satisfaction with

Table 8.5. Parental interest in alternative schooling options

	All parents		Parents with child attending . . .			
			an underperforming school		a performing school	
Percent prefer that child attend:[1]	(percent)		(percent)		(percent)	
Diff. Public school in same district	14.5	[995]	23.1	[230]	10.8	[700]
Diff. Public school in diff. district	15.9	[992]	18.1	[231]	15.5	[696]
Charter school	10.9	[987]	18.3	[227]	7.6	[697]
Private school	39.4	[980]	45.0	[226]	38.1	[690]
Percent able to name alternative type of school preferred:[2]						
Diff. Public school in same district	11.3	[995]	18.8	[230]	8.8	[700]
Charter school	7.2	[987]	12.0	[227]	5.5	[697]
Private school	26.5	[980]	31.3	[226]	26.3	[690]
Among interested parents, type of school most like child to attend:[3]						
Public school in same district	23.4		18.1		26.0	
Public school in different district	5.8		6.9		5.4	
Charter school	8.2		11.9		6.0	
Private school	58.5		61.6		57.0	
Don't know	4.1		1.5		5.6	
Total	100.0	[539]	100.0	[146]	100.0	[358]

Number of observations in brackets.

[1] Parents could express interest in multiple kinds of alternative schools.

[2] Parents who preferred to send their child to a different public school in a different district were not asked to name the school they had in mind.

[3] Parents had to choose one type of school for their child. Only those parents who expressed interest in at least one alternative schooling option were included in sample.

their district's public schools than did parents with children in performing public schools, and though they were less likely to know that they qualified for NCLB's choice provisions, parents with children in underperforming schools were more than twice as likely to express interest in switching public schools. One in four parents in underperforming public schools claim that they would prefer to send their child to a different public school in the same district, as compared to one in ten parents with children in performing public schools. Much the same pattern of findings applies to public schools in different districts and charter schools.[22]

Parents who preferred that their child attend a different school were asked to name an alternative—allowing us to distinguish parents with passing interests from those with stronger commitments to new schooling options. Demand, once again, appears highest among families with children in underperforming schools. As the second batch of items in table 8.5 shows, parents with children in underperforming public schools are more than twice as likely to name a preferred alternative public school in their district or a charter school than are parents with children in schools that made AYP.

The bigger story in table 8.5, however, concerns private schools. More than any other educational institution, parents appear most enthusiastic about the prospects of sending their child to a private school. Fully 40 percent of parents generally, and 45 percent of parents in underperforming schools, claim that "if cost were not an obstacle" they would rather send their child to a private school instead of their current public school. And a surprisingly high percentage of these parents have a particular private school in mind. Roughly one in three parents with children in underperforming schools both prefers that her child attend a private school and is able to name a specific school on the spot, many of which are elite boarding schools.[23]

When reflecting on private schooling options, observed differences between parents with children in performing and underperforming schools attenuate somewhat. Whereas parents with children in underperforming schools are twice as likely to prefer different public or charter schools, they are only 5 to 7 percentage points more likely to express interest in sending their child to a private school. Attending a public school with low test scores, it seems, does not appear to be an especially important indicator of parental interest in a private education.

Up until now, survey responses reflect individual comparisons between a child's current public school and one alternative schooling option. But when simultaneously placing all options before them, which type of school would parents "most like their child to attend"? Among parents interested in an alternative to their child's current public school, one stands out: private schools. On the whole, 59 percent of parents hold a private school in highest regard, while 23 percent select another public school in the same district, 8 percent a charter school, and just 6 percent a public school in another district. Ironically, parents in performing schools (who do not qualify for NCLB's choice options) are 8 percentage points more likely to identify another public school in their district that they would like their child to attend (the one option NCLB avails) than are parents with children in underperforming schools (who actually do qualify for NCLB's choice options). Moreover, parents with children in underperforming schools are slightly more likely to prefer that their child attend a public school in another district, a charter school, or a private school (none of which are available under NCLB) than parents with children in performing public schools.

These findings have mixed implications for NCLB. On the upside, while the parental satisfaction data reveal general contentment with public schools, these data suggest that many parents nonetheless remain interested in exploring alternative schooling options. Interest, what is more, appears most concentrated among parents with children attending underperforming public schools—precisely the people whom NCLB targets. On the downside, however, parents appear most excited about schooling options that NCLB does not afford. Indeed, parents were three to four times more likely to identify a preferred private school than an alternative public school within their district, a different public school outside their district, or a charter school—and when looking at parents' "most preferred" options, the differences are even greater. When reflecting on their child's education, and when relieved of financial constraints, what these parents want most is a private education.

Criteria for Choosing

By extending new schooling opportunities to families with children in underperforming public schools, NCLB gives qualifying parents greater influence over their child's education. But whether the act should enhance parental influence is another matter entirely. For starters, when selecting among a district's public schools, qualifying parents may not abide by their child's best interests. Rather than selecting a school because of its academic strengths, parents may pay special attention to such ancillary matters as its location or its racial composition.[24] Further, parents may fail to choose a school that is any better than the one their child currently attends. Given that many do not know whether their child's school made AYP, parents whose children qualify for NCLB's choice provisions may prove incapable of assessing the quality of other district schools.

To investigate these matters, the survey asked parents to rate on a 1-to-10 scale—where 1 is unimportant and 10 is extremely important—the relative significance of nine factors when selecting a school for their child. The results are presented in table 8.6. Two features of the findings deserve attention, both of which suggest a rather salutary view of parents. The first concerns the rank ordering of school characteristics. To parents, quality of teaching, discipline, safety and order, and class size are far and away the most important qualities of a school, while location, racial/ethnic composition, and the prevalence of friends are the least important. Moderately important items include programs such as physical education, a school's reputation, and extracurricular programs and sports teams.

Second, when comparing the responses of parents at performing and underperforming public schools, both the average rating and rank ordering

Table 8.6. Factors influencing parental assessments of schooling options

	All parents		Parents with child attending . . .			
			an underperforming school		a performing school	
Importance of following factors in evaluating a school:						
Quality of teaching	9.6	[997]	9.6	[232]	9.6	[702]
Discipline, safety, and order	9.4	[998]	9.4	[232]	9.4	[701]
Class size	8.7	[994]	9.2	[230]	8.6	[701]
Programs such as physical education	8.3	[997]	8.4	[231]	8.3	[701]
Reputation of school	8.1	[995]	8.5	[232]	7.9	[698]
Extracurricular programs & sports teams sports teams	7.8	[987]	7.9	[230]	7.8	[694]
Distance from house	6.8	[986]	7.3	[228]	6.6	[695]
Racial/ethnic: composition of school	6.2	[978]	6.6	[229]	6.2	[687]
Friends at school	5.8	[983]	5.9	[225]	5.8	[695]

Number of observations in brackets. The second set of items are rated on a 1–10 scale, with 1 indicating not important at all and 10 indicating extremely important

of factors are virtually identical. Both groups give quality of teaching and discipline average values of 9.6 and 9.4, and both rank location, racial/ethnic composition of schools, and friends as the least important factors when evaluating a school. The only difference—which, statistically, may be due to chance alone—concerns the relative importance of programs such as physical education (which parents of children attending schools that made AYP ranked as slightly more important) and a school's reputation (which parents of children at underperforming school deem more important). Given scholars' general skepticism of the ability of less advantaged parents to advocate on behalf of their child's educational welfare,[25] these findings are especially noteworthy. When selecting schools, parents with children at underperforming schools—who are less likely to be white, are less educated, have lower incomes, and are more likely to be foreign born—claim to care about the same things as parents with children at performing schools.

To be sure, the factors parents claim to care about most may not reflect the actual choices they would make for their child. Few whites, presumably, would admit to a stranger on the telephone that they care more about the racial composition of a school than the quality of its teaching, even if, in practice, they might choose a predominantly white school with poor teachers over a predominantly African American school with excellent teachers.

Unfortunately, we do not have any outside measures of parental attitudes or behaviors that allow us to verify the existence or magnitude of response bias. We do, however, know the names of the schools that parents purport to prefer, establishing some grounds for advancing this line of inquiry. Specifically, by comparing the characteristics of those schools parents prefer to those their children currently attend, we may further evaluate the capacity of parents to identify schools that excel academically.

The first section of table 8.7 compares average Massachusetts Comprehensive Achievement System test scores of the school that parents prefer to the scores at the school their children currently attend. Positive values indicate that preferred schools have higher average scores than current schools; negative values that preferred schools have lower scores. Because only a small number of parents prefer a different public school in their

Table 8.7. Characteristics of preferred public schools in district

	All parents		Parents with child attending . . .			
			an underperforming school		a performing school	
Differences between test scores of preferred and current public school						
Third-grade English	0.12	[57]	0.41	[29]	−0.20	[28]
Fourth-grade English	0.32	[57]	0.56	[29]	0.06	[28]
Fourth-grade math	0.33	[57]	0.62	[29]	0.00	[28]
Sixth-grade math	0.46	[26]	0.50	[10]	0.44	[16]
Differences between student bodies of preferred and current public schools						
% African American students	−2.9	[96]	−9.9	[43]	2.6	[53]
% Hispanic students	−5.5	[96]	0.6	[43]	−10.4	[53]
% White students	7.5	[96]	11.9	[43]	3.9	[53]
% students qualify free/ reduced lunch	2.1	[69]	−14.9	[20]	14.5	[40]
% LEP students	−9.8	[96]	−16.0	[43]	−4.8	[53]
Total number of enrolled students	112.7	[96]	−43.4	[43]	237.3	[53]
Percent name a public school that is underperforming:	26.4	[106]	44.1	[44]	15.9	[56]
Percent name a charter school that is underperforming:	52.0	[87]	54.2	[29]	54.7	[53]

Parents who expressed interest in an alternative public school and could name the public school are included in this table. Number of observations in brackets. Positive values in first set of questions indicate that the preferred public school within the district that parents identify has higher test scores (expressed in standard deviations) than the public school their child attends. Positive values in the second set of questions indicate that the preferred public school has a higher percentage of students with the identified characteristic than their child's current school.

district and then can name a specific institution, the findings presented in this table are based on a rather limited number of observations. As such, these results should be considered more suggestive than definitive. Nonetheless, they do reveal some intriguing, and somewhat reassuring, findings about the ability of parents to identify successful public schools.

Parents, taken as a whole, consistently identify preferred public schools that score between one-tenth and one-half of a standard deviation higher than their current public schools. When isolating those parents with children in underperforming schools, the observed differences are even higher, ranging between two- and three-fifths of a standard deviation.[26] Given the sizable literature on peer effects,[27] students at underperforming schools would likely benefit from attending their parents' preferred schools.

Beyond test scores, how do preferred public schools compare to schools that children currently attend? The answer very much depends on whether a child is enrolled in an underperforming public school. Interested parents of children who qualify for NCLB's choice provisions identify schools with lower proportions of African Americans, low-income students, and limited English proficiency students, and higher proportions of white students. They also select schools that are slightly smaller, on average, than the schools their child currently attends. Among parents with children in performing schools, minor differences are observed with respect to the percentage of Hispanic, white, African American, and limited English proficiency students. Such parents, however, do choose schools with lower proportions of Hispanic students and higher proportions of low-income students. They also tend to express interest in larger schools than those their children currently attend.

But take a look at the last two rows of table 8.7. When asked to name a specific public or charter school that they would prefer their child attend, a remarkably high percentage of interested parents actually select another underperforming school—an option that NCLB forbids. Fully one in four parents select a public school that is deemed underperforming, and one in two select a charter school that failed to make AYP. While parents with children in performing and underperforming public school are equally likely to select a charter school that failed to make AYP, striking differences emerge when parents choose among a district's public schools. Parents with children in underperforming schools are almost three times as likely to select another underperforming school as are parents with children in performing public schools. Using NCLB's evaluative criteria, fully 44 percent of parents who qualify for transfers want to send their child to another school that is no better than the one their child currently attends—even though the test score and demographic data suggest that preferred schools house higher-performing and more advantaged students.

Two basic findings stand out here, and both speak positively of parents whose children are enrolled in underperforming public schools. First, though parents who qualify for NCLB's choice provisions navigate their educational landscape with less information, they nonetheless purport to care about the same features of schools—foremost among them being academics—as parents whose children attend performing public schools. Second, when selecting an alternative public school for their child, interested parents in underperforming schools consistently identify schools with more advantaged and higher-performing students. To be sure, many of the chosen schools themselves failed to make AYP. And without data on the quality of the teachers or the resources at these institutions, it is difficult to assess whether the schools themselves are any better. Still, if their student bodies are any indication, these preferred schools nonetheless outperform the public schools from which interested parents wish to withdraw their children.

Concluding Thoughts and Policy Recommendations

As some of the other chapters in this volume make clear, there are ample reasons for criticizing state determinations of annual yearly progress. NCLB largely disregards the independent contributions of teachers, principals, and programs to a child's education. Its accountability system holds schools accountable for the performance of multiple subgroups while failing to account for student mobility rates, and hence is predisposed to reward racially homogeneous schools that attract higher-performing students and to punish heterogeneous schools that cater to lower-performing student bodies. And by measuring student achievement strictly, and solely, on the basis of standardized tests, the act disregards important aspects of student learning.

This chapter, and the survey on which it is based, deliberately does not comment on NCLB's language or design. Instead, it takes as given state determinations of school performance in order to scrutinize the choices and preferences of parents within a given educational context. It provides an early assessment of parental knowledge of and interest in new educational opportunities, and the challenges faced by advocates of choice and accountability who aim to boost parental control over and involvement in children's education.

The survey results reveal considerable interest in new public and private schooling options, especially among parents whose children attend underperforming public schools. Though parents who qualify for NCLB's choice provisions give their schools high marks, they nonetheless appear less satisfied than parents with children in performing schools, they are more likely to prefer to send their child to an alternative public, charter, or private school, and most have in mind a specific school that they would prefer their child attend. Furthermore, when choosing among alternative schools, these parents consistently identify institutions whose students score higher on standardized tests.

Given such interest, why have so few parents transferred schools under NCLB? (Statewide, less than 1 percent of eligible parents have opted to switch out of a public school deemed in need of improvement). In addition to the structural issues identified elsewhere in this volume, lack of knowledge appears critical. Only one out of every four parents with children in underperforming Massachusetts public schools successfully identified the school's status, and hence grasped the most basic information required to take advantage of NCLB's choice and supplemental services provisions. Whether the onus of blame lies with parents or schools, information simply is not getting to those individuals who need it most.

To raise awareness of NCLB's accountability system and increase the number of students who seize upon its educational benefits, three policy changes are recommended:

1. First, and most obviously, state and federal governments should not rely on districts to disseminate information about which schools have made AYP, and which students hence qualify for transfers and supplemental services. If parents are to take advantage of new educational opportunities, they first must know about them. State and federal governments need to find ways to communicate directly with parents to ensure that they do.
2. Second, when disseminating information about NCLB, special accommodations must be made on behalf of non-English-speaking families. The poor knowledge revealed among parents of children attending underperforming schools was matched only by foreign born and parents lacking proficiency in English. Only one in three parents born outside of the United States, and one in four parents of a limited English proficiency child, knew whether or not their school was underperforming.[28] If these families are to seize upon NCLB's choice provisions, state and federal governments must find ways of effectively communicating with them.
3. Finally, and perhaps most controversially, parents with children at underperforming public schools should be allowed to select any other public

school in their district, not just those public schools that made AYP.
Almost 50 percent of qualifying and interested parents claimed that they
preferred another underperforming public school; and if the test score
comparisons between these schools are any indication, they were not mis-
guided in doing so.[29] If choice is to catch fire, as many NCLB advocates
hope, parents must be granted a wider array of schooling options than the
law currently affords.

Other policy reforms, of course, might also be entertained. For instance,
if choice advocates truly want to satisfy parents, they should add private
schools to the menu of available education options. By overwhelming margins, parents prefer private schools over any other alternative schooling
option. Plainly, however, efforts to include private schools in publicly funded
choice schemes are bound to confront serious, and perhaps insurmountable,
political obstacles. Each of the three recommended reforms, meanwhile, is
more easily implemented. For the most part, they simply require modest
financial commitments and rule changes. Were they adopted, NCLB would
stand a considerably better chance of meeting parents' current knowledge of
and interest in school choice, and would promote greater participation in the
program than witnessed up until now.

Appendix A: Multivariate models of parental knowledge about child's school

	Correctly identify school status		Correctly identify principal's name		Correctly identify school size	
	(1a)	(1b)	(2a)	(2b)	(3a)	(3b)
Attends underperforming school	-1.06*** (0.24)	-1.01*** (0.24)	-0.56** (0.23)	-0.27 (0.24)	-1.07*** (0.25)	-1.01*** (0.27)
Parent Characteristics						
African American	0.20 (0.33)	0.06 (0.34)	-0.20 (0.30)	-0.26 (0.32)	-1.22*** (0.36)	-1.17*** (0.37)
Hispanic	-1.19* (0.64)	-1.30** (0.66)	-0.07 (0.38)	-0.12 (0.44)	-0.45 (0.47)	-0.50 (0.47)
Born in United States	0.42 (0.30)	0.39 (0.30)	0.36 (0.27)	0.55** (0.31)	0.24 (0.30)	0.21 (0.31)
Education	1.29*** (0.50)	1.05** (0.51)	1.20** (0.49)	1.22** (0.53)	1.02** (0.50)	0.83 (0.51)
Work full time	0.35* (0.21)	0.39* (0.21)	-0.24 (0.21)	-0.30 (0.21)	-0.52*** (0.20)	-0.55*** (0.21)
Own home	0.32 (0.26)	0.30 (0.26)	0.18 (0.26)	0.21 (0.26)	0.16 (0.25)	0.20 (0.25)
Married	-0.02 (0.24)	-0.01 (0.25)	0.16 (0.25)	0.20 (0.23)	-0.14 (0.26)	-0.17 (0.26)
Female	0.13 (0.23)	0.15 (0.24)	0.33 (0.23)	0.38 (0.24)	-0.05 (0.23)	-0.06 (0.22)
Freq. attend relig. services	0.05 (0.36)	-0.03 (0.36)	0.02 (0.32)	0.35 (0.33)	-0.24 (0.35)	-0.28 (0.35)
Catholic	0.19 (0.29)	0.39 (0.31)	-0.11 (0.25)	-0.26 (0.29)	0.13 (0.28)	0.17 (0.30)
Protestant	-0.05 (0.34)	0.06 (0.35)	-0.07 (0.28)	-0.29 (0.31)	0.23 (0.32)	0.27 (0.32)
Child Characteristics						
Special needs	0.07 (0.20)	0.09 (0.20)	-0.15 (0.20)	-0.12 (0.19)	-0.08 (0.19)	-0.02 (0.19)
Elementary school	0.02 (0.20)	0.07 (0.21)	0.88*** (0.21)	0.98*** (0.21)	-0.04 (0.21)	-0.04 (0.21)
Boy	0.22 (0.20)	0.25 (0.20)	-0.08 (0.19)	-0.13 (0.19)	0.29 (0.19)	0.29 (0.19)
Parental Involvement						
Volunteer at school	0.37* (0.21)	0.41* (0.21)	0.66*** (0.20)	0.57*** (0.21)	0.38* (0.21)	0.45** (0.21)
PTA member	0.62*** (0.22)	0.58*** (0.22)	0.33 (0.23)	0.56*** (0.23)	0.25 (0.22)	0.20 (0.23)
Work public school district	0.52** (0.27)	0.55** (0.26)	-0.18 (0.24)	-0.06 (0.23)	0.18 (0.24)	0.22 (0.24)
Constant	-2.00*** (0.55)	-1.44** (0.65)	-1.49** (0.56)	-1.66** (0.66)	-0.66 (0.53)	0.12 (0.63)
Pseudo-R^2	.12	.14	.10	.16	.11	.13
Log likelihood	-474.13	-467.62	-479.66	-447.06	-467.87	-458.04
Number of observations	781	781	781	781	775	775
District fixed effects included	No	No	No	Yes	No	Yes

Weighted logit models estimated with robust standard errors reported in parentheses. * $p < .10$, two tailed test; ** $p < .05$; *** $p < .01$. The dependent variable is coded 1 if respondent correctly identified status of school (models 1a and 1b), the principal's name (2a and 2b), or the school size (3a and 3b), and 0 otherwise. All explanatory variables rescaled 0–1. Given high number of missing values, income not included in models; most estimates, however, appear unchanged when it is added.

Appendix B: Multivariate models of parental satisfaction with child's public school

	Give child's current public school an "A"				Give public schools in community an "A"			
	(1a)		(1b)		(2a)		(2b)	
Attend underperforming school	−0.50**	(0.24)	−0.55**	(0.25)	−0.50*	(0.30)	−0.42	(0.32)
Parent characteristics:								
African American	0.17	(0.31)	0.09	(0.33)	−0.00	(0.36)	−0.01	(0.35)
Hispanic	−0.29	(0.45)	−0.40	(0.46)	−0.37	(0.56)	−0.38	(0.61)
Born in United States	−0.24	(0.29)	−0.23	(0.29)	−0.20	(0.36)	−0.22	(0.34)
Education	0.52	(0.48)	0.23	(0.48)	0.94	(0.65)	0.58	(0.67)
Work full time	−0.41**	(0.20)	−0.43**	(0.20)	−0.74***	(0.25)	−0.76***	(0.26)
Own home	0.31	(0.25)	0.39	(0.25)	−0.36	(0.34)	−0.35	(0.33)
Married	−0.32	(0.25)	−0.25	(0.26)	0.70**	(0.34)	0.75**	(0.35)
Female	−0.33	(0.22)	−0.32	(0.23)	0.11	(0.30)	0.17	(0.30)
Freq. attend relig. services	0.44	(0.35)	0.36	(0.33)	−0.93**	(0.39)	−1.00***	(0.38)
Catholic	−0.13	(0.26)	−0.09	(0.27)	0.29	(0.32)	0.32	(0.33)
Protestant	0.44	(0.31)	0.40	(0.31)	0.56*	(0.32)	0.54	(0.33)
Child Characteristics:								
Special needs	−0.01	(0.19)	0.00	(0.19)	−0.11	(0.23)	−0.05	(0.25)
Elementary school	0.38*	(0.21)	0.40*	(0.21)	0.71**	(0.28)	0.75**	(0.29)
Boy	−0.30	(0.19)	−0.30	(0.19)	0.02	(0.24)	0.08	(0.24)
Parental Involvement								
Volunteer at school	0.04	(0.20)	0.07	(0.21)	0.06	(0.26)	0.12	(0.26)
PTA member	0.35*	(0.21)	0.23	(0.21)	0.17	(0.27)	0.17	(0.28)
Work public school	0.11	(0.23)	0.18	(0.24)	0.00	(0.29)	0.00	(0.28)
Constant	−0.16	(0.52)	0.15	(0.62)	−2.18***	(0.65)	−1.66**	(0.75)
Pseudo-R²	.04		.07		.07		.10	
Log likelihood	−500.25		−486.94		−306.27		−296.36	
Number of observations	781		781		773		773	
District fixed effects included:	No		Yes		No		Yes	

Weighted logit models estimated with robust standard errors reported in parentheses. * p < .10, two tailed test; ** p < .05; *** p < .01. The dependent variable is coded 1 if parent gave either the child school (models 1a and 1b) or the public schools in the community (models 2a and 2b) an "A" and zero otherwise. All explanatory variables rescaled ... values in ranges are not included in models, most estimates, however, appear unchanged when it is added.

Appendix C: Multivariate models of parental interest in alternative public and private schools

	Interested in public school alternative to current public school		Interested in private school alternative to current public school	
	(1a)	(1b)	(2a)	(2b)
Attend underperforming school	0.36 (0.24)	0.27 (0.25)	0.36 (0.22)	0.30 (0.24)
Parent characteristics:				
African American	0.11 (0.30)	-0.07 (0.34)	-0.01 (0.30)	-0.04 (0.32)
Hispanic	0.18 (0.40)	-0.02 (0.41)	0.89** (0.41)	0.77* (0.41)
Born in United States	-0.30 (0.27)	-0.38 (0.27)	-0.42 (0.26)	-0.47* (0.26)
Education	-0.35 (0.47)	-0.21 (0.49)	0.57 (0.46)	0.51 (0.48)
Work full time	0.03 (0.21)	0.00 (0.23)	0.38* (0.20)	0.42** (0.21)
Own home	-0.49* (0.28)	-0.57* (0.29)	0.18 (0.27)	0.20 (0.27)
Married	0.23 (0.25)	0.42 (0.29)	-0.11 (0.24)	-0.07 (0.25)
Female	0.07 (0.24)	0.09 (0.24)	0.00 (0.21)	0.00 (0.22)
Freq. attend relig. Services	0.22 (0.33)	0.12 (0.36)	0.38 (0.33)	0.28 (0.34)
Catholic	-0.08 (0.28)	0.08 (0.31)	-0.06 (0.18)	-0.22 (0.28)
Protestant	0.11 (0.30)	0.22 (0.32)	-0.12 (0.20)	-0.26 (0.30)
Child Characteristics:				
Special needs	-0.12 (0.20)	-0.16 (0.21)	0.12 (0.19)	0.16 (0.19)
Elementary school	0.56** (0.23)	0.68** (0.24)	0.30 (0.20)	0.29 (0.21)
Boy	0.36* (0.20)	0.39* (0.21)	-0.06 (0.18)	-0.09 (0.19)
Parental Involvement				
Volunteer at school	0.09 (0.22)	0.06 (0.23)	-0.12 (0.20)	-0.15 (0.20)
PTA member	-0.12 (0.24)	-0.15 (0.23)	0.03 (0.22)	-0.04 (0.22)
Work public school	-0.35 (0.25)	-0.36 (0.24)	-0.06 (0.23)	-0.06 (0.24)

Appendix C: Continued

	Interested in public school alternative to current public school		Interested in private school alternative to current public school	
	(1a)	(1b)	(2a)	(2b)
Constant	-1.03* (0.55)	-1.48** (0.68)	-0.90* (0.52)	-0.82 (0.60)
Pseudo-R^2	.06	.10	.04	.06
Log likelihood	-449.79	-430.43	-503.22	-494.72
Number of observations	781	781	781	781
District fixed effects included:	No	Yes	No	Yes

Weighted logit models estimated with robust standard errors reported in parentheses. * $p < .10$, two tailed test; ** $p < .05$; *** $p < .01$. The dependent variable in models 1a and 1b is coded 1 if respondent expressed interest in alternative public school in district, alternative public school in another district, or in alternative charter school, and zero otherwise. The dependent variable in models 2a and 2b is coded 1 if respondent expressed interest in alternative private school, and zero otherwise. All explanatory variables rescaled 0–1. Given high number of missing values, income not included in models; most estimates, however, appear unchanged when it is added.

Notes

1. Mark Schneider, Paul Teske, and Melissa Marschall, *Choosing Schools: Consumer Choice and the Quality of American Schools* (Princeton, N.J.: Princeton University Press, 2000). See also, Terry M. Moe, *Schools, Vouchers, and the American Public* (Washington, D.C.: Brookings Institution Press, 2001).

2. Moe, *Schools, Vouchers, and the American Public.* See also, Public Agenda 1999. "On Thin Ice: How Advocates and Opponents could Mislead the Public's Views on Vouchers and Charter Schools." Report available online at: www.publicagenda.org

3. Lowell Rose and Alec Gallup, "The 35th Annual Phi Delta Kappa/Gallup Poll of the Public's Attitudes Toward the Public Schools," *Phi Delta Kappan* (September 2003): 41–56.

4. While the PDK/Gallup poll contains some measures of parental satisfaction, the results basically confirm conventional wisdom—namely, that most parents are happy with their child's current public school. And unfortunately, because the analyses conducted on the poll are rudimentary at best, the findings offer little insight into how various populations with children attending various types of schools systematically differ in their knowledge of and interest in new forms of school choice.

5. To conduct the survey, the author gratefully recognizes the financial and administrative support of the Pioneer Institute in Boston, Massachusetts, Kit Nichols, Elena Llaudet, Kathryn Ciffolillo, and Stephen Adams provided especially helpful feedback and support. Opinion Dynamics in Cambridge, Massachusetts, administered the survey.

6. So that they reflect a random draw of parents in the sampled locales, findings presented in this chapter rely upon weights that account for the sizes of the district populations.

7. In a handful of cases, questions were directed toward parents of children who attend private schools. The results presented below do not change when these cases are excluded from the sample.

8. Students in grades kindergarten through 12 constituted 13.6, 10.7, 9.7, 8.6, 8.2, 6.0, 6.7, 8.7, 5.7, 6.7, 6.2, 6.1, and 1.6 percent of the sample, respectively. In 1.5 percent of the cases, the respondent did not know the student's grade.

9. This estimated response rate assumes that the incident rate among non-compliers (people who did not stay on the telephone long enough for us to determine whether they had children attending a public school) is the same as the incident rate among compliers. If the incident rate among non-compliers is lower, which is likely given the subject of the survey and the population we targeted, then the true response rate is higher than 31 percent.

10. Given data constraints, comparisons between the population sampled and the population targeted are less than straightforward. Neither of the two available data sources identifies the specific characteristics of parents of children who

attended public schools in the 10 largest districts. From the National Center for Education Statistics (NCES), one can obtain information on the profile of residents (but not public school parents) in the 10 largest districts. And from the Massachusetts Department of Education, one can obtain information on students (but not parents) in the 10 largest districts. Unfortunately, as of this writing, individual level data from the 2000 Census are available only for Boston and Massachusetts as a whole. The available data, nonetheless, suggest that the survey contains the right approximate proportion of African Americans, an undersample of Hispanics, and an oversample of whites. (Given the varying methods of collecting demographic data, race/ethnicity provides the cleanest of comparisons). In the survey, 73 percent of parents are white, 17 percent African American, and 7 percent Hispanic. NCES records show that 59 percent of residents in the 10 largest school districts are white, 14 percent are African American, and 16 percent Hispanic. Department of Education records, meanwhile, show that 36 percent are white, 26 percent African American, and 29 percent Hispanic. Given that Hispanic families tend to have more children, department figures probably overstate the extent to which Hispanics are underrepresented in the survey. Nonetheless, the magnitude of the observed discrepancies is sufficiently large to warrant concern. The problem, I suspect, derives from the use of a listed sample (which contains a disproportionate number of more stable and white individuals) and the fact that data were collected from telephone surveys (which tend to undersample minorities generally, and Hispanics in particular). Those Hispanic parents who are included in the survey, it is fair to assume, probably speak better English, completed more education, and are more likely to own their own home than the larger population of Hispanics targeted. To the extent that this is true, then the survey will overestimate knowledge of NCLB among Hispanics in particular, and among public school parents more generally.

11. Phillip Converse, "The Nature of Belief Systems in Mass Publics," in *Ideology and Discontent,* ed. D. Apter (New York: Free Press, 1964).

12. Two accountability systems currently are in place in Massachusetts, one that was introduced at the behest of the state government, the other at the behest of the federal government. Never are parents asked about the state's older accountability system. Still, to minimize confusion, the survey includes two questions about No Child Left Behind before it asks whether a child was on the list of schools deemed in need of improvement. The wording of the informational question, then, is as follows: "According to this new law, each year states must identify the public schools that need improvement. In the fall of 2002, Massachusetts publicly announced the list of schools in need of improvement. Do you happen to know whether or not your child's school is on the list?"

13. Asked where they learned about the status of their child's school, 36 percent of parents indicated the district or school, 25 percent a newspaper or television news story, 4 percent other parents, 3 percent the Internet, 2 percent a friend, and the rest did not know the source of the information.

14. Curiously, parents who received their information directly from the school or school district were 4 percentage points *less* likely to correctly identify the status of their school than were parents who received their information from other outlets.

15. Appendix A shows that these differences hold up when conducting multivariate analyses that control for different family background and school characteristics.

16. Again, see appendix A for multivariate analyses.

17. Robert Putnam, *Bowling Alone: The Collapse and Revival of American Community* (New York: Simon and Schuster, 2000).

18. William Howell, "Dynamic Selection Effects in Urban, Means-Tested School Voucher Programs." *Journal of Policy Analysis and Management,* 2004. 22(3): 225–250.

19. The sample of parents is roughly evenly divided into these three categories.

20. See appendix B for multivariate models of parental satisfaction.

21. John Hibbing and Elizabeth Theiss-Morse, *Congress as Public Enemy: Public Attitudes toward American Political Institutions* (New York: Cambridge University Press, 1995).

22. Some of these differences attenuate in multivariate statistical models that control for a wide variety of background controls, suggesting that interest derives from the kinds of families who attend underperforming schools rather than from the status of the schools themselves. See appendix C.

23. Told that "costs were not an obstacle," most of these interested parents appeared to relish the idea of sending their child to an expensive, elite private school. Four of the top five most popular private schools identified by parents were Milton Academy, Worcester Academy, Bancroft Academy, and McDuffie, all independent schools with tuitions that eclipse the monetary values of even the most generous school vouchers offered in public and private programs around the country. Still, roughly one-third of interested parents identified Catholic and Protestant day schools that charge considerably more modest tuitions.

24. Jennifer Hochschild and Nathan Scovronick, *The American Dream and the Public Schools* (New York: Oxford University Press, 2003).

25. Bruce Fuller, Richard Elmore, and Gary Orfield, *Who Chooses? Who Loses? Culture, Institutions, and the Unequal Effects of School Choice* (New York: Teachers College Press, 1996).

26. Test scores for seventh-, eighth-, and tenth-grade students are omitted given the tiny number of observations available. All values for these grade levels remain positive for parents as a whole and for parents with children in underperforming schools.

27. Eric Hanushek, John Kain, and Steven G. Rivkin, "New Evidence about Brown v. Board of Education: The Complex Effects of School Racial Composition on Achievement," *National Bureau of Economic Research,* Working Paper 8741, 2002. See also, Caroline Minter Hoxby, "Peer Effects in the Classroom: Learning from Gender and Race Variation," *National Bureau of Economic Research,* Working Paper 7867, 2002.

28. Given the survey's undersampling of Hispanics, these findings probably *overestimate* the levels of knowledge of NCLB among foreign-born families with limited English proficiency.

29. Still, another, more practical concern supports this policy recommendation. As Massachusetts schools are held accountable for the test scores of subpopulations of students, the list of underperforming schools will undoubtedly rise, further limiting the number of schools that can accept student transfers.

9

Choice and Supplemental Services in America's Great City Schools

Michael Casserly

Introduction

The school district of Philadelphia is on the list of systems in Pennsylvania that are "in need of improvement." Only 20 percent of the city's fifth-graders met the state's reading standards in 2002. So when Paul Vallas took the reins of the long-struggling district in the summer of 2002, he pledged to dramatically raise student performance and do everything he could to meet the goals of a new federal law that President George W. Bush had signed only months before, called No Child Left Behind (NCLB).

Vallas's support for NCLB was generally shared by his colleagues in the nation's major cities. The Council of the Great City Schools, the umbrella organization for the city school systems, gave the measure its endorsement as the bill headed toward final approval. And large cities across the country moved rapidly to put the law into effect after it was signed.

But urban school leaders were also wary. NCLB was different from any federal education legislation they had seen before. The new law fundamentally changed the rules of the game. Public schools were being called on not only to educate all students, including those with special needs, but to teach to a standard that few other countries in the world had ever asked of their educational systems.

The law has been in place for two years now, and a number of trends, some predictable and some not, are beginning to emerge. First, NCLB is clearly taking shape on the ground. Second, the act is experiencing serious growing pains. Third, the intent of the act, to spur higher student achievement, has focused the nation's major urban school systems more closely on academic performance.

This chapter gives an early status report on how NCLB is being implemented in America's major urban schools. We concentrate primarily on how the public school choice and supplemental service provisions of NCLB are being implemented in the cities. A final section discusses the overall status of NCLB in city school systems and describes urban leaders' current perceptions of its goals and requirements.

Implementing the Act

The Council of the Great City Schools administered a four-page survey to its 60 member urban school districts to gather data on NCLB's implementation. Fifty cities (83.3 percent) had responded with data as of November 7, 2003.[1]

The 50 cities responding to the survey enroll more than 7.2 million students—56.4 percent of whom are eligible for a free or reduced-price lunch, 15.3 percent of whom are not yet proficient in English, and 11.7 percent of whom have disabilities. (The demographic characteristics of the responding districts are similar to the 10 cities that did not respond.)

These 50 cities operate 8,941 schools enrolling an average of 810 students per school. Some 5,924 of these schools are Title I schools and are subject to NCLB's accountability provisions. The remaining schools in these cities are not Title I schools.

Adequate Yearly Progress (AYP)

Under the terms of NCLB, school year 2002–2003 was the first year that districts had to report test data on the academic progress of all major subgroups of students. The results were used to determine which schools in 2003–2004 would undergo school improvement, corrective action, or restructuring, the three main stages of sanctions in NCLB.

In school year 2003–2004, 499 schools in the 50 cities on which we have data were in their first year of school improvement (Level I) because they had not made AYP for two consecutive years. These schools must offer students the option of transferring to better schools. Some 510 schools were in their second year of school improvement (Level II) because they failed to make

Table 9.1. Number of urban schools tagged for school improvement, corrective action, or restructuring by category and year (N = 50 cities)

Category of improvement	2002–03	2003–04*
School improvement (Level I)	543	499
School improvement (Level II)	593	510
Corrective action	305	471
Restructuring	18	215
Totals	1,459	1,695

*Numbers do not include Detroit and St. Louis because the numbers of schools not making AYP had not been finalized by their states when this survey was administered.

AYP for three consecutive years. These schools must make supplemental services available to their students, in addition to offering transfers. Furthermore, 471 schools in the 50 cities had been identified for corrective action and 215 for restructuring—the two later stages of sanctions, which apply to schools that fail to make AYP for several years in a row. In all, about 1,695 schools were tagged for improvement, corrective action, or restructuring in school year 2003–2004 (see table 9.1).

In other words, 19.7 percent of all schools and 30.3 percent of Title I schools in these 50 cities (excluding Detroit and St. Louis) are in "need of improvement."

Several city school systems, moreover, have been designated by their states for "district improvement" in the 2003–2004 school year for failing to meet systemwide targets. We know of eight such districts among the 50 that responded: Baltimore, Buffalo, Denver, Philadelphia, Richmond, Rochester, Tucson, and Washington, D.C.

The survey results also show considerable variation from city to city in the numbers and percentages of schools designated for improvement. Six cities, for instance, had no schools in 2003–2004 in the "needs improvement" categories, including Austin, Dallas, Broward County (Fort Lauderdale), Guilford County (Greensboro), Houston, and Norfolk. Anchorage, Charlotte-Mecklenburg, Des Moines, and Salt Lake City had only one each.

Other cities had large shares of their schools in various stages of improvement, corrective action, or restructuring. Philadelphia appears to have the largest percentage of its schools in this situation, 194 schools or about 74 percent of all schools in the city. Chicago has about 59 percent of its schools in school improvement; Buffalo has almost 54 percent; Baltimore has 48 percent; and Newark has 46 percent in this status. The number of schools in improvement had not yet been determined in Detroit and St. Louis when the survey was administered.

It is not clear how many urban schools are undergoing sanctions because they did not make AYP for just one subgroup or because they did not test the requisite 95 percent of students. We believe the number in the first category is relatively small. Only 13 of Chicago's 365 schools (3.6 percent) on the list for improvement were there because they failed to make adequate progress for a single subgroup, for example. We suspect that a larger proportion of urban schools are on the AYP lists because they did not meet the 95 percent testing requirement.

The wide fluctuation among cities and the numbers of their schools in "school improvement" status appears to have little to do with their relative performance. Boston and San Diego have similar reading and math scores on the National Assessment of Education Progress (NAEP), for example, but Boston has 31.8 percent of its schools in school improvement and San Diego has 18.1 percent.

The variation has more to do with the fact that Congress left it to the states to define the terms and standards under which the act would be administered.

Public School Choice

The choice provisions of NCLB are proving to be some of the most difficult for urban schools to implement. The law requires schools that have not made adequate yearly progress for two years in a row (school improvement Level I) to offer all of their students the opportunity to transfer to a presumably higher-performing school that has not been designated for improvement.

Transfer rates. Preliminary data from the cities indicate that the number of students transferring from one school to another under NCLB this school year is small compared to the total number of students enrolled in eligible schools. Even so, the number of students transferring has increased substantially over 2002–2003.

Forty-four cities of the 50 on which we have data have at least one school in school improvement and are required to offer a transfer under NCLB. Of the 1.17 million students enrolled in one of the 1,695 schools tagged for improvement in these cities (excluding Detroit and St. Louis), 44,373 students requested a transfer (3.8 percent), and 17,879 (40.3 percent of those requesting a transfer) actually moved—more than triple the number of transfers (5,661) from the previous year (see table 9.2).

Despite the increased participation in the choice program, the number of requests for transfers remains low. New York City sent out some 300,000 letters about the transfer options to parents of eligible children. Approximately 8,000

Table 9.2. Number of NCLB transfers in 2002–2003 and 2003–2004

2002–2003	2003–2004	2003–2004	2003–2004	2003–2004
Number of transfers	Number of transfers	Number of transfer requests	Number of sending schools	Number of students per school
5,661	17,879	44,373	1,695	10.5

parents requested a transfer. San Diego sent out 30,000 letters and had 484 requests. Chicago sent out 270,000 notices and had about 19,000 requests. And Cleveland sent out about 16,830 letters and had 58 students opt for a transfer.

City officials, community groups, and others have explained this by noting that some parents do not want their children taking lengthy bus trips or riding public transportation. Some parents would prefer having their children close to home. Some parents are receiving information too late to make a good decision. Some parents may not have gotten their first choices. Some may not think the available options are any better than their current situations. Some participate in other choice programs. And some may be frustrated by complicated application procedures. No one factor appears to explain the lack of movement.

But the upward trend suggests that additional time, experience, higher achievement, and better communications with parents may solve some—though not all—of the problems that districts are having with the choice provision.

We looked at four aspects of choice to gain a better understanding of why the program was working as it is, including the methods school districts used to inform parents about their options, the restrictions that districts placed on the process, the time limits on parental choice, and the capacity of receiving schools.

Methods for notifying parents. First, we analyzed the ways in which school districts informed parents about choice. All 44 districts that were required to offer transfers sent letters to parents informing them of their options. Twenty-two districts supplemented the mail with website information, newsletters, flyers, phone calls, parent and community meetings, advertisements, or media announcements. The New York City Schools, for example, posted first-class mail in 10 languages; placed automated telephone calls in 10 languages; sent flyers home in backpacks; convened regional information sessions; sought help from some 20 community-based organizations; provided materials at local PTA meetings; established a chancellor's hotline; set up a special website; and placed ads in community papers.

Still, there were parents and groups in New York and other cities who indicated that they did not get the information or that insufficient notification was provided. It is likely that a number of parents were missed. Mailing addresses are often incomplete, and the mobility rate in cities is often high. We did not find any pattern between the number of transfer requests made and the method(s) that cities used to get out information.

We also looked at the wording of the correspondence sent to parents about their options. The nature of the letters has been the subject of controversy in some cities. Several watchdog groups have charged that the letters to parents are often convoluted, jargon filled, lengthy, and self-serving. Our scan of letters sent to parents in the various cities shows a range of features. Some are better written than others. None of the letters was longer than two pages, although some cities did not articulate the nature of the choice until the second page. Most letters clarified, correctly, that the choice schools may or may not have services desirable to parents. All of the letters pointed out that transportation, if required, would be provided free by the district. And most letters had some information about the schools from which choices could be made.

Numbers of choices and restrictions. All but two of the responding districts gave parents more than one option of schools. The norm (36 districts) was to grant parents two or three options. New York City, however, offers eight choices; and Philadelphia, Jacksonville, Columbus, and Nashville offer six. Des Moines provides a choice of any elementary school in the district.

Most cities limit options by zone, geographic region, feeder patterns, or clusters. Several cities pair a school in need of improvement with two or more receiving schools from which parents may choose. Some cities also built special considerations into their options, such as the desire of parents to keep siblings together or the capability of particular schools to handle certain types of disabilities. (The survey did not ask explicitly about transfers to public charter schools.)

Several cities—Boston, Dayton, Denver, Columbus, Oklahoma City, Pittsburgh, Portland, Tampa, and San Diego—have controlled choice or open-enrollment systems either within transit zones or districtwide that allow more numerous and open-ended options than the two or three designated schools under NCLB. Students in these cities, including NCLB students, are allowed to transfer to any higher-performing school within a zone or to any eligible school in the district.

Columbus, Ohio, is an example of a city that has blended magnet schools, open enrollment, school desegregation, and several other types of school choice, at least in the first year of NCLB. Columbus Public Schools has had an open-enrollment process in place for nearly 20 years, following resolution of the district's desegregation order. Open enrollment permits parents to choose almost any school in the district, subject to space constraints. To mesh this program with NCLB in January 2003, district administrators forecast (using spring 2002 test results) the number of schools likely to be in Level I school improvement the following school year. They reserved 70 percent of the seats in all schools for open-enrollment transfers and 30 percent for NCLB transfers. Parents in NCLB-eligible schools were notified on January 21 that they had until February 28 to make three choices about where they wanted to send their children in the fall of 2003. The NCLB choices were then given priority in March and April when the general open enrollment choices were made. When the spring 2003 test data were returned to the district in August, students in three more schools had become eligible for choice, and their parents were notified that they also had the option to move. Altogether, 699 NCLB-eligible students changed schools.

The ability to mesh NCLB and open enrollment depends on one critical factor: the ability to make an educated guess about the number of schools likely to be in school improvement the following school year. It is unclear how this estimating will work out in Columbus in 2004–2005. The district has nearly 40 additional schools on the "warning list" because they did not make AYP for one year. The district will now have to estimate how many of those schools and the 21 others on the original list will improve enough to avoid sanctions in 2004 and how many will not. If it guesses wrong, it could easily face serious logistical and budget problems.

Period to choose. We also looked specifically at the timing of parent notifications. We did this in two ways. First, we examined the dates on which spring testing data were being returned to the districts, when the data were finalized, and when parents were first notified about their options. Second, we looked at how long the window remained open for parents to make their selections.

Eight districts received their 2002–2003 testing data before the end of the school year; 15 received their data in June or July 2003; 13 districts received their data in August; and 8 received their data after the 2003–2004 school year began. (Six other districts had no schools tagged as needing improvement.)

Twenty-three of the districts were given less than the 30 days specified in the law to review their test results, make corrections, and resubmit changes. Tucson was given four days, for instance. The data review process is important because states typically do not know whether a child has been in a particular school for an entire year and should be scored against the school's AYP targets or the district's.

None of the districts had final data determining their numbers of low-performing schools before the end of the 2002–2003 school year. Six districts had their data finalized by the state by the end of July. Fifteen cities received their final data by the end of August. And 23 cities did not receive their final data until after the beginning of the 2003–2004 school year.

Nine districts informed parents about their options before the end of last school year. All these districts had an open-enrollment or controlled choice plan in place and, like Columbus, made an educated guess of the numbers of students who were likely to be eligible for a transfer under NCLB. Eleven districts informed parents of their options in June or July. This process also appears to have been based on preliminary data, in this case, the districts' Title I (Phase I) reports, which are usually filed with the states in early summer.

Charlotte-Mecklenburg, which had only one school that was required to offer a transfer, was able to get its data in July and inform parents the same month by using state-provided software to scan and electronically upload test results to the state. The district could then review the data for problems while the state was analyzing the results against AYP targets.

Eight cities, however, were not able to inform parents about their options until August, and 16 cities had to wait until after the beginning of the 2003–2004 school year to notify parents about their choices.

We looked, as well, at the length of time parents had to make their selections. Most urban districts (20 cities) gave parents three weeks to a month to respond with a choice. Cleveland, for instance, gave parents from September 8 to September 30. Tucson gave parents from November 2 to December 1. Miami-Dade County schools gave parents between July 1 and the first week of August to make a selection. Clark County (Las Vegas) gave parents from September 3 to September 30. And Minneapolis gave parents between September 2 and September 26 to make a choice.

Sixteen districts left their "windows" open for a month or longer. The Portland schools left their options for choice open between October 23, 2002, and July 1, 2003. Buffalo left its window open from August 2003 until January 2004. Louisville allowed choices between April 1 and May 31. And Pittsburgh is leaving its window open through June 2004. The districts with these longer windows were often cities, like Columbus, that had open-enrollment programs they were meshing with NCLB.

Eight cities, moreover, gave parents between one and two weeks to make a selection. The Washington, D.C., schools, for instance, gave parents from August 4 to August 15 to make a choice. The Anchorage schools gave parents from September 2 to September 15. And the Jackson, Mississippi, schools gave parents from August 15 to September 1. Only two districts gave parents as little as a week. No district afforded parents less than a week.

Finally, 2 of the 20 districts that gave parents three weeks to a month to respond also had two periods during which parents could choose to have their children transfer to another school. Seattle gave parents between July 14 and August 8 to make a choice, and then another opportunity between September 18 and October 10. And San Diego had windows open between March 21 and April 18, and between September 17 and October 17.

It is hard to draw definitive conclusions from the data, but it was not clear that there was a correlation between the number of transfers and the length or number of windows. In Los Angeles, for example, the window was open for several months, but the number of transfers was small. In Palm Beach, however, the window was open for about three weeks, and the number of transfers was relatively large.

The length and timing of these windows appear to be driven by two things. Many districts were uncertain about the volume of transfers that were likely to be requested in the program's first few years. The result was that some districts were more aggressive than others in marketing the choices. And many districts did not know which schools would be eligible for choice because of delays in getting test data back from the state. The timeliness of the test data is critical, since the final numbers determine which schools are tagged for improvement, which must offer choice and supplemental services, and when parents can be notified about their options.

School capacity and choice. Finally, we looked at the issue of capacity to accommodate students in the receiving schools. The urban districts reported that they had identified 1,855 higher-performing schools (1,331 elementary, 303 middle, and 221 high schools) as potential receiving schools for the 1.17 million students who could have moved.

Because demand was low, most districts (20 cities) were able to accommodate all or most of the students requesting transfers. Miami-Dade County, for instance, had only 321 requests and could accommodate all of them. Hillsborough County (Tampa) had 106 requests and accommodated all. Clark County (Las Vegas) had 205 requests and handled all of them. Greenville, South Carolina, had 200 requests, all of which were accommodated. New York City had 8,000 requests and permitted all to transfer.

A number of these districts were able to accommodate as many students as they did because they had open seats, underused buildings, or a relatively small number of schools tagged for improvement. New York City allowed a number of its middle schools to grow beyond capacity, and Miami made extensive use of portable units that it already owned.

The cities that are having the most difficulty, on the other hand, are districts that lack the physical capacity, have large numbers of schools identified for improvement, and have small numbers of schools eligible to receive students.

Philadelphia is a case in point. The district itself is in improvement status. It has 261 schools, 34 of which are in Level I school improvement and 160 of which are in corrective action; together these schools enroll some one hundred thousand eligible students. The district was able to locate only 1,240 open seats in 20 higher-performing schools eligible to receive students. All of the surrounding districts rejected Philadelphia's request for seats, a situation that was mirrored in all 44 cities required to offer choice.

As it turned out, there were only a thousand requests for transfers. But if the number of requests grows substantially in the coming years, the district may have little room for them. Philadelphia is discussing whether to send students to parochial schools, but these schools also appear to have limited space, some private school parents are balking, and legal barriers remain.

Twenty-four cities responding to the survey were in the same situation as Philadelphia and potentially unable to accommodate all the students requesting a transfer. By and large, it appears that when cities cannot accommodate all the transfer requests, they are prioritizing students by income and achievement as the law requires. Districts are using free and reduced-price lunch data to define poverty levels and test scores and/or grades to define achievement.

It appears that the choice provisions are causing some problems for the receiving schools, as well. Much of the difficulty appears to relate to overcrowding and increased class sizes. Twenty-one of the cities reported that one of the negative side effects of the choice provision for receiving schools was larger class sizes. (The survey did not ask for specific data on how large the classes were becoming.) And several cities reported increased disciplinary incidents on buses used to transport students.

Districts like Denver, moreover, are trying to boost capacity by increasing their numbers of classrooms. Denver opened up teacher lounges and resource rooms in the two schools that parents chose the most in order to get seven additional classrooms.

We have seen little evidence to date that strategies proposed by the U.S. Department of Education, including schools-within-schools, virtual schools, and mobile classroom units, are creating enough space to overcome the larger capacity problems. These strategies are often too small scale (virtual schools) or too expensive (mobile classrooms) to absorb the large numbers of students who are eligible to transfer.

The numbers of students eligible to transfer from one school to another are likely to grow in the next several years, even if schools make substantial progress in boosting student achievement. And the ability of the schools to accommodate demand may increase somewhat as more seats are found within the system. But there is a physical limit, rapidly approaching, beyond which schools may not be able to handle large numbers of new transfers.

Supplemental Education Services

The law also requires districts to offer tutorial services to students enrolled in schools that have failed to make adequate yearly progress for at least three years. These services are to be delivered by a public or private provider selected by parents from a list of state-approved providers. School districts are then required to contract with the providers to deliver services. This requirement seems straightforward, but is quickly emerging as a major challenge to implement for many urban school systems.

Participation rates. So far, the school systems in the Great City Schools are providing Title I supplemental services to considerably more students than are taking advantage of the choice option, but the number is still relatively small. Thirty-four cities of the 50 on which we have data have at least one school that is required to offer supplemental services under NCLB. These districts (excluding Detroit and St. Louis), which have 1,196 schools in school improvement (Level II or above), indicated that they expected to serve 133,707 students in a supplemental service program this school year—a rate of about 112 students per eligible school (see table 9.3).

The 16 districts that were not required to provide supplemental services in 2003–2004 were Anchorage, Austin, Broward County, Charlotte-Mecklenburg, Dallas, Des Moines, Duval County, Guilford County, Hillsborough County, Houston, Miami-Dade County, Norfolk, Orange County, Palm Beach County, Pittsburgh, and Salt Lake City.

Many urban school systems are providing supplemental services under NCLB for the first time in 2003–2004. There are two key reasons for this.

Table 9.3. Number of students receiving supplemental education services (SES) in 2003–2004*

Number of students in SES	Number of SES requests	Number of schools with SES	Number of SES students per school
133,707	NA	1,196	111.8

* Detroit expected to serve 6,000 students and St. Louis expected to serve 750 students in 2003–2004 but neither city knew the numbers of schools in school improvement, so their data are not included in this table.

One, supplemental services are not required until after the third year of
failing to make adequate yearly progress, a status that not all schools have
reached. Two, most states had not finalized their lists of approved providers
until well into the 2002–2003 school year or summer 2003.

The delay in naming providers meant that large numbers of urban
students who might have been eligible for supplemental services did not
receive them. The holdup also meant that large amounts of Title I funds that
had been reserved for supplemental services went unspent in 2002–2003.
There have been delays in 2003–2004 as well, but most are due to the late
dates by which districts receive spring testing data from the states. The districts then began the process of verifying results, notifying parents, waiting
for a response, contracting with vendors, enrolling children, and beginning
services. Very little of this work was actually completed by September 2003.

Methods for notifying parents. The majority of districts used the same methods to inform parents about the availability of supplemental services as to
inform them about school choice, including letters, flyers, phone calls, websites, advertisements, community forums, and media announcements. Some
districts notified parents of both opportunities in the same correspondence,
but other districts did separate mailings. And several cities conducted "vendor fairs" at which potential providers disseminated information to parents
about their services.

A spot check of the correspondence sent to parents indicates that school districts did provide the required information. Some districts, however, were more
aggressive than others in encouraging parents to select the services offered by the
school rather than those offered by an outside provider. Some districts appeared
to steer parents to specific providers with whom they had long-standing relations. And some districts did not provide parents with much information, other
than the list of providers sent by the state. Sometimes the names of the providers
were simply listed in checklist fashion with no other information that would
inform parents about what to look for. Providers with high name recognition,
like Sylvan (now known as Catapult Learning) or Princeton Review, probably
have an advantage in these cases over other providers and perhaps over the
schools themselves.

New York City provided parents with a comprehensive directory of
approved supplemental service providers. It included information on the
kind of services provided by each company, when and where the services were
to be provided, the experience and staff qualifications of the providers, their
demonstrated effectiveness, and contact information. Parents wanting more

specific information could contact each provider on their own and fill out a form requesting service.

Other districts required parents to sign up for services at specific locations or centers. It is clear at this early stage in the process that applications are sometimes cumbersome and will require streamlining in the future.

Numbers and types of providers. States have finally issued their approved provider lists, which often consist of national tutoring services and varying numbers of regional or local providers. The number of approved providers in any one city ranges from as few as six in Greenville to as many as 59 in New York City. Only four cities—Albuquerque, Boston, Greenville, and Portland—have 10 or fewer state-approved providers. Eight cities have 31 or more providers; 11 cities have between 20 and 30 providers; and another 11 cities have between 11 and 19 providers. The average city has approximately 23 state-approved providers—or about one provider for every 1.5 urban schools in Level II school improvement, corrective action, or restructuring.

This ratio suggests that there may be a glut of providers in some locales, at least in 2003–2004. Cleveland has 38 approved providers but only 15 schools in Level II school improvement or corrective action. Jackson has 28 providers but no schools that are required to offer supplemental services in 2003–2004. Buffalo has 43 providers but just 22 schools required to offer their services. The apparent oversupply of providers in some sites may spur competition, but it may also be contributing to the frustration the providers feel about the small numbers of students in their programs.

The types of providers vary widely from city to city. Cleveland, for instance, has a list parents can select from that includes such large national tutorial services as Huntington Learning Centers, Kaplan K12 Learning Services, Catapult Learning (formerly Sylvan Learning), and the Princeton Review. A number of small to midsize out-of-town providers are also on the list, including Brainfuse Online, Academia.net, JRL Enterprises, Kumon Reading and Math Centers, Club Z, and Elluminate. And the list contains such smaller local providers as Village One Concepts, Wims Enterprises, Learning for All, the Boys and Girls Clubs of Cleveland, and Geraldine Tucker.

Some companies and providers are specializing in a single content area, like reading, and others concentrate on particular grades or grade spans. Few colleges or universities or faith-based groups appear on any of the state lists. And only a few private school-management firms, such as Edison, are evident. We also saw little evidence to suggest that the cities had any role in selecting, screening, approving, or suggesting any of the supplemental service providers at the state level.

Some city school systems that were not in district improvement were also approved to provide their own supplemental services. Nineteen cities were on their states' provider lists; 15 were not approved providers; and 16 had not reached this stage in the sanctions process. The inclusion of districts on the state lists allowed some sites to begin services earlier than they otherwise would have because of the delays in naming outside providers, signing contracts, making selections, and putting services into place.

Period to choose providers. The survey also asked when the districts informed parents that their children were eligible for supplemental services and how long they had to make a selection. The results suggest that the process is taking longer to implement than the choice provisions. This is probably because arranging for supplemental services requires additional steps, such as the states' naming of approved providers and local districts' contracting with them. This process, like the choice process, is also affected by how quickly data are returned to the districts informing them about which schools are in what level of sanction.

Only one of the districts was able to give parents any options for supplemental services before the end of the last school year (2002–2003). This was likely because most states had not issued their lists of approved providers until well into the school year. Only two districts were able to notify parents by the end of July 2003.

Seven districts were able to notify parents in August about their supplemental service options, and 24 districts informed parents after the beginning of the 2003–2004 school year. By contrast, 20 districts were able to inform parents about their transfer options by the end of July, and only 16 had to wait until after the school year started.

City school districts appear to be compensating for the delays by leaving the selection window open for longer periods than they allowed for transfer requests. Parents were given a month or more to choose a provider in 21 cities rather than three weeks or so in the case of NCLB transfers. Ten cities gave parents three weeks to a month, and three others gave parents one or two weeks.

Cleveland, for instance, gave parents from September 8 to October 31 to choose a supplemental service provider, but three weeks to select another school. Buffalo gave parents from August 15 to November 30, 2003. And Tucson's window was open from November 3 to December 2. Several other districts are providing two opportunities or leaving the window open for extended periods. Toledo and Louisville, for instance, present parents with two rounds of choices. Toledo's first round ran September 15–26, and its second round will go from November 25 to December 19. The D.C. and Greenville schools, on the other hand, have a rolling admissions process.

Contracts. Local school districts are now in the process of negotiating contracts with supplemental service providers. Twenty-four cities had signed at least some contracts by November 7, 2003, and 10 cities were still negotiating them. The law is clear about the responsibility of school districts to inform parents about the nature of the services and enter into contracts with providers. But the law is largely silent about the mechanics. School districts and potential providers have found themselves tussling over the length of the contracts, pupil fees, billing and payment procedures, staff qualifications, union rules, and the like.

For instance, supplemental service providers and urban school districts often disagree about the logistics and conditions of delivering services. Many providers would like to receive a portion of their fees before work begins, but the districts often prefer to pay as the work proceeds. The providers would like to charge the districts a flat fee for the number of students enrolled in the tutorial sessions. The districts think they should be charged only for the number of students who actually attend the instructional sessions. The providers would like to build transportation fees into their overhead charges, but the districts generally disallow these expenses because the law does not authorize them. Some providers would like to provide their services on school grounds, while the districts want the option to charge for use of their space.

Conflicts have also arisen about educational aspects of the supplemental services. The providers would like to provide their services as they were packaged, but the districts want services aligned with their curricula. The providers want the right to reject students with disabilities or limited proficiency in English on the grounds that they require resources and expertise that they do not have. The districts would like the providers to serve all who are eligible.

A scan of sample contracts in cities that have finalized them shows that they contain standard clauses, including a description of services to be provided, educational goals, payment schedules and methods, standard indemnification protections, insurance, access to and confidentiality of student information, criminal background checks, assurances against discrimination and drug use, audits and inspections, subcontracting limits, deliverables, workers compensation, non-performance and termination clauses, and other provisions. Some of the contracts are as short as three pages, while others cover 50 or more pages.

In addition, 22 city school districts allow external providers to deliver their services on school grounds. Others do not. There are advantages for both the provider and the school when services are on school property, but schools are sometimes leery about the practice, particularly when there are large numbers of providers to accommodate. Often it is not feasible to have dozens of providers on school grounds at the same time, and districts generally do not want to be in the position of having to select which providers will be allowed on school grounds and which will not.

Situations like these, involving sometimes complicated contractual and financial arrangements, illustrate why offering supplemental services has taken longer than outside observers would expect. There should be less need in the future to renegotiate contracts from scratch, speeding the process as a result.

Program services. Students are receiving a range of services from private-sector companies and from school programs that have been approved by the state. Minneapolis, lacking a state-approved provider list until November 2003, retained Catapult Learning to provide the district's after-school supplemental services in one-hour blocks, twice a week, for 22 weeks. Long Beach is setting up its own reading and math services, which will run three hours during the school week, three to four hours on Saturday, and six weeks during the summer. The sessions consist of small group and individual tutorials using the district's own intervention materials and those available commercially.

Philadelphia has a mandatory after-school tutorial program operated by Princeton Review and Voyager followed by supplemental services mandated by NCLB. Boston's tutorial program provides 100 hours of reading and math instruction before and after school using "Reading Explorers," "Investigations," and "Connected Math." The Los Angeles school district has set up 20 Beyond the Bell Learning Centers, operating on 10 Saturday mornings between 8 and 11:30 A.M. to provide reading and math tutoring to students in groups of no more than five.

Districts that provide their own supplemental services do so using either their own personnel and materials or those from some of the same private-sector companies that the states have approved as service providers. Some districts use a mixture of their own programs and those from outside vendors.

The next major tasks that both the districts and providers must address involve the alignment of supplemental services with district curriculum and the evaluation of providers' effectiveness. To date, most districts and providers have been busy focusing on logistical, legal, and financial issues, with little time to worry about anything else. But alignment and evaluation issues are beginning to emerge, and the alignment problem is the more complicated of the two.

NCLB states clearly that supplemental service providers are to ensure that their services are consistent with the instruction provided by the schools and aligned with state academic standards. Alignment issues are most acute when providers come with prepackaged curricula or ready-to-use materials. It seems unlikely that so many approved providers are aligned to state standards to the same degree. The extent of alignment undoubtedly varies from state to state and from provider to provider within the same state.

Many urban school districts are discovering that they make the greatest academic gains when they use a more cohesive, less splintered, and sometimes more prescriptive instructional program. Often, these curricula come with quarterly assessments that are used by teachers to gauge the specific skills of individual students. Districts with the best instructional results often have very specific requirements or specific materials for their after-school interventions that may or may not be consistent with what individual service providers are prepared to use. The problem is compounded as the number of providers increases.

The challenge is further complicated when a district uses a detailed pacing guide that specifies when particular skills are taught. These pacing guides are usually aligned with state tests in a way that ensures that teachers teach the skills measured on the state test before the test is given, rather than after. The ability of districts and providers to get this process right will determine in large measure whether the supplemental services provision of the law spurs student achievement, dampens it, or is irrelevant.

The districts also face evaluation and assessment challenges. The law requires that services be evaluated, providers be assessed, and approval of providers be withdrawn if success is not evident for two consecutive years. The law is ambiguous, however, about who assesses the providers, how the evaluations are conducted, and what success means. For districts and schools, success means making adequate yearly progress, but it may mean something else to outside providers. Most service providers like using their own evaluation tools to assess the effectiveness of their own services. These tools may or may not be aligned with the state assessments, however, and may or may not have the requisite technical strength to measure academic gains reliably. The problem will eventually beg the question, how does one tell what is working?

This issue of effectiveness will also be affected by delays in the return of data, if the delays continue. There are significant numbers of cases in 2002–2003 and 2003–2004 where students will not be provided a full school year's worth of services, as the law intended, before they are assessed on a full year's worth of material and their schools are pushed into the next level of sanctions. The problem will be compounded if more states begin administering their accountability tests in January and February in order to get results back to the schools by early summer. Ironically, supplemental services provided under these shortened time constraints may spur achievement less than the law's sponsors envisioned. And the effectiveness of the providers—and the law—could be harder to demonstrate.

Expenditures. It does not appear that NCLB is having any effect on districts' general fund expenditures, since the vast majority of cities (35 districts) use only Title I funds to pay for supplemental services and school transfers, but the law is having an effect on how districts use their Title I funds.

The costs of supplemental services and choice are absorbing much of the sizable increases that cities received in Title I funds over the last two years. Denver, with 22 of its 141 schools in Level II school improvement in 2003–2004 and three other schools in corrective action, is spending approximately $2.5 million on choice and $1.7 million on supplemental services—the equivalent of 18.8 percent of its Title I allocation. The total expenditure of about $4.2 million absorbed most of the district's $5.5 million Title I increase in the first year of NCLB, leaving about $1.3 million, about $29.15 per student, for overall program improvement.

About half of the cities (24 districts) were told by their respective states in 2002–2003 to reserve 20 percent of their Title I allocations for supplemental services and choice. But much of this money went unspent in 2002–2003 because so many states had not issued their approved provider lists and the U.S. Department of Education would not allow districts to provide supplemental services on their own. There were three results. One, money that could have been used for after-school instructional programs was frozen. Two, the U.S. Department of Education had to issue waivers to districts allowing them to exceed the 15 percent caps on the amount of Title I money they could carry over for supplemental services and choice. Three, it muted the effects of the large increase in Title I funds, particularly in districts whose Title I increases were below 20 percent. The problem was exacerbated by sizable cuts in local and state funding that resulted from the poor economy.

The Buffalo school district, for instance, cut about $37.5 million, or 7.4 percent, from its general budget in 2002–2003—an amount that dwarfed the increase of $10.5 million that the district received in Title I funding between fiscal years 2001 and 2003. On top of the cuts, the district had to reserve 20 percent of its Title I funds for the NCLB provisions.

Discussion

It is still early in the implementation of No Child Left Behind, especially when one considers the scope of the act and the magnitude of the changes it envisions. Many states and school districts, including those in the major cities, are just getting started. Although implementation has been somewhat uneven, the programs and policies of NCLB are starting to take shape in the nation's urban schools.

More students are taking advantage of the act's choice and supplemental service options in 2003–2004 than occurred in 2002–2003. This increase can be attributed to several factors, including the larger number of schools now required to offer supplemental services, the growing experience of school districts in running student transfer programs, and more aggressive marketing. School districts are securing signed contracts from private providers and are putting in place more effective systems for communicating with parents and the community. Districts are budgeting the Title I funds required to operate the new requirements. And leaders of the urban systems are working to implement NCLB programs in ways they never had to do when Title I could be relegated to the compensatory education office and forgotten.

The law is experiencing growing pains, however, even among urban school leaders, who as a group support it. The act is thick with requirements that no amount of rhetoric about flexibility can simplify. It has tied up millions of dollars for transportation and supplemental services that otherwise could have been spent on improving instructional programs. And it has created logistical and operational difficulties that people who don't actually run programs of this magnitude can little appreciate or understand.

At this point, one has to conclude that the internal gears of this massive piece of legislative and its regulatory machinery are poorly calibrated for smooth operations. It is taking time for federal, state, and local agencies to work out all the bugs, especially in systems as large as the school districts that are members of the Great City Schools.

In the meantime, frustrations are mounting. The U.S. Department of Education is writing angry letters to state officials about bad faith and accusing local administrators of resistance. State officials blame the department for not giving them enough flexibility. Local administrators fault the states for not providing enough technical assistance. Teachers unions and school systems grouse that the administration hasn't appropriated enough money. Parents claim that no one told them about the free tutoring. And vendors complain about the bureaucracy.

Unfortunately, the finger-pointing is starting to take its toll on Capitol Hill, in the press, and in opinion polls. The public appears more confused than ever before about the quality of its schools. Some schools are tagged as needing improvement under NCLB at the same time they are being recognized for gains under separate state accountability systems.

The administration's passion for choice and supplemental services is warming the hearts of enthusiasts of these provisions, but the provisions are causing enormous frustration among urban school leaders who back NCLB. One hears very little carping among urban leaders about those NCLB components that are more directly linked, in their view, to student performance and accountability. But the link between student achievement and choice or supplemental services is less obvious—in part because the provisions were set up as elements of the sanctions process, not the instructional process, and are rather poorly sequenced.

Choice and supplemental services may eventually prove to be useful tools in raising student achievement, but at this early stage of implementation, carrying out these requirements is absorbing substantial amounts of time, expertise, and resources without a clear connection to what NCLB purports to be about—student performance. Conversely, many leaders of large urban districts and schools see less energy being devoted at the federal and state levels to raising achievement than to implementing the law's choice and supplemental service provisions.

It is still too early to tell whether the act will result in higher test scores or greater student achievement. And it is also not clear what role the NCLB provisions for choice and supplemental services will ultimately play in that improvement. But it is clear from NAEP data and state test results that performance is already advancing in the nation's urban schools.[2]

One cannot draw a solid line yet between NCLB and this improving performance. But anecdotal evidence suggests that the nation's urban schools have become increasingly focused on student achievement and subgroup gaps, and that NCLB is part of the reason.

Eventually, No Child Left Behind and the paradigm shift it represents are likely to give the nation exactly what it wants urban public schools to deliver—more options and higher achievement. As that happens, urban schools will have succeeded in meeting an educational challenge as ambitious as any in history. And their support of the act will have proved to be worth the effort.

Notes

1. Responding districts were: Albuquerque, Anchorage, Austin, Baltimore, Boston, Buffalo, Broward County (Fort Lauderdale), Charlotte-Mecklenburg, Chicago, Clark County (Las Vegas), Cleveland, Columbus, Dallas, Dayton, Denver, Detroit, Des Moines, Duval County (Jacksonville), Fresno, Greenville, Guilford

County (Greensboro), Hillsborough County (Tampa), Houston, Indianapolis, Jackson, Jefferson County (Louisville), Long Beach, Los Angeles, Miami-Dade County, Minneapolis, Nashville, Newark, New York City, Norfolk, Oklahoma City, Orange County (Orlando), Palm Beach County, Philadelphia, Pittsburgh, Portland, Richmond, Rochester, Salt Lake City, San Diego, San Francisco, Seattle, St. Louis, Toledo, Tucson, and Washington, D.C.

2. National Center for Education Statistics, *Results of the NAEP 2003 Trial Urban District Assessment* (Washington, D.C.: U.S. Department of Education, 2003) and Michael Casserly, Sharon Lewis, and Janice Ceperich, *Beating the Odds: A City-by-City Analysis of Student Performance and Achievement Gaps on State Assessments, Results from the 2002–2003 School Year* (Washington, D.C.: Council of the Great City Schools, 2004).

10

San Diego: Do Too Many Cooks Spoil the Broth?

Julian R. Betts and Anne Danenberg

Introduction

Since January 2002, when President Bush signed the No Child Left Behind Act (NCLB) of 2001 into law, school districts around the country have scrambled to understand the law, how it affects their district, and how to implement its public school choice and supplemental service provisions.[1] San Diego City Schools is no exception. This essay explores that process as it unfolded in San Diego through descriptive statistics and qualitative interviews with key district and school personnel and private-sector supplemental service providers, as well as through the impressions of a focus group organized for us by a community-based organization.[2] In all we conducted interviews with 21 key informants between August 2003 and February 2004. Eleven of these were external to the district.

In general, districts in California received little guidance on implementing the law. In February 2003, California's state superintendent of schools, Jack O'Connell, issued a memorandum to all district superintendents, county superintendents, and categorical program directors in the state announcing that school districts would have to submit five-year local educational agency plans by June 1, 2003, to receive federal funding under NCLB.[3] It is evident from this and other documents on the state education department website that interpretation of federal requirements was left mainly to local districts— which conforms to the law's intention to allow more local control and flexibility.[4] San Diego's submission was fully approved in the first round of plan approvals in July 2003.[5]

Ranking San Diego

Before examining San Diego's implementation of NCLB's public school choice and supplemental service provisions, it is useful to rank the district on a number of dimensions. San Diego City Schools is the second-largest district in California and one of the largest districts in the United States—in 2001–2002 it ranked eighth in enrollment nationally among large city districts.[6] The district shares characteristics common to many urban districts: compared to California as a whole, it has relatively high shares of non-white students, students with limited English proficiency (LEP), and students who are economically disadvantaged—approximately 74 percent, 29 percent, and 57 percent, respectively.[7]

Table 10.1 shows selected district and student characteristics in San Diego compared with the other four districts in California that have historically been the largest urban districts in the state: Los Angeles Unified (no. 1 in size), Long Beach Unified (3), Fresno Unified (4), and San Francisco Unified (5). In the 2001–2002 academic year, San Diego ranked first among the five districts in per-pupil expenditures—at more than $7,500—and was substantially higher than the state's district average of $6,719 per pupil.[8] In terms of student demographics, San Diego has the lowest percentages of non-white students and economically disadvantaged students when compared to the other four districts in the table, each of which has more than 80 percent non-white and more than 58 percent economically disadvantaged students. The percentage of LEP students, while not the lowest of the five districts, is close to San Francisco's low of approximately 28 percent. Still, each of the five districts has considerably higher percentages of non-white, LEP, and economically disadvantaged students than California as a whole. Although there is some variation among the districts, each of them exhibits student characteristics common in large urban districts. Most of these districts also have a substantial number of schools that have been identified as "improvement" schools in which students are eligible to transfer to better-performing schools under NCLB.

As the table shows, the number and percentage of schools tagged as needing improvement and the number and approximate percentage of students in each district who attend such schools also varies across districts.[9] Of the five large districts, only Long Beach has fewer than 10 percent of its schools and students in improvement status as of fall 2003. San Diego falls on the

Table 10.1. Selected summary statistics for San Diego, other large urban districts, and California, 2002–2003

	San Diego	Los Angeles	Long Beach	Fresno	San Francisco	California
Total K-12 enrollment, 2002–2003	140,753	746,852	97,212	81,222	58,216	6,244,403
Number of schools	185	677	89	101	114	9,087
District expenditures per pupil (2001–2002)*	$7,501	$7,353	$6,796	$6,967	$7,313	$6,719
Student Characteristics (%) 2002–2003:						
Non-White Students	73.8	90.6	82.8	81.7	87.9	65.7
Limited English Proficient:						
Total LEP	28.7	42.9	32.8	32.3	27.9	25.6
LEP who speak Spanish	80.5	93.3	84.0	62.1	38.0	84.3
Socioeconomic indicator:						
Free or Reduced-Price Meals	56.8	75.4	65.2	76.4	58.9	48.7
PI schools and students (Fall 2003):						
Schools:						
Number of PI schools**	33	109	7	40	30	1,205
Percentage of PI schools***	18	16	8	40	26	13
Enrollment:						
Approximate number of students	38,588	255,213	7,095	38,588	11,106	1,198,462
Approximate percentage of students	27	34	7	48	19	19

Sources: Authors' calculations from California Department of Education CBEDS and AYP datasets.
* District financial statements can be found at www.ed-data.k12.ca.us
** "Program Improvement" (PI) is the designation that California gives to schools needing improvement under NCLB rules.
*** Denominator includes all schools in district.

median, with 18 percent of schools attended by 27 percent of students in the district. Fresno has the dubious distinction of having the largest percentages of schools and students in failing schools—40 percent of its schools have been identified as needing improvement, and almost half of the district's students attend these schools.

Because San Diego's position is quite similar to the other large urban districts in the state, both in terms of student demographics and the large numbers of students attending failing schools, the district is likely to encounter NCLB implementation challenges that are similar to theirs. The ensuing analysis focuses attention on how these new opportunities were implemented, how much participation the program drew, and the tensions between the NCLB public school choice and supplemental service programs and existing programs.

Implementation and Emerging Issues

Organization

In San Diego the implementation of NCLB has been overseen by the superintendent's office. Leaders in that office are coordinating the process through a team that includes people from the legal, communications, legislative services, instructional support, human resources, and other departments. Under this committee are subcommittees (including supplemental service and public school choice committees) that provide feedback from their own departments, which are relayed back to the upper levels of management.

The school board has not been actively involved but has voted on some of the implementation provisions. The board approved reservation of the *maximum* required by law—20 percent of Title I funds for the school choice and supplemental service provisions—and chose to allocate 5 percent for supplemental services and 15 percent for busing related to the district's array of public school choice programs—including NCLB school choice. The 2003–2004 allocations are $7 million for all school choice programs and close to $2.4 million for supplemental services.[10] These amounts appear to further confirm the district's commitment to supporting choice and supplemental service provisions.

Our overall impression of the response to NCLB is that there is a clear consensus among district administrators that the intent of the legislation is laudable, but that implementation issues abound. Overall, support from the district seems quite clear. Alan Bersin, the district's superintendent, attended the NCLB bill signing. As one administrator remarked, "You can't go to the bill signing and then not implement."

When asked to characterize the implementation process, one administrator suggested that the district could have proceeded more quickly if the federal regulations accompanying the legislation had come out more quickly: "The legislation was signed in early 2002, but there were no regulations to go with it, so it hasn't been uppermost in people's minds until now." However, the same administrator opined that because of the cross-functional process described above, the district had a better structure in place than the many districts that relied entirely upon their Title I office to handle implementation. Other administrators pointed to delays in receiving the state's initial interpretation of how to implement details of the program.

Partly counterbalancing concerns about the rush to implement NCLB, several administrators acknowledged that the U.S. Department of Education had previously granted a waiver to the district to use much of its Title I allocation to fund its Blueprint for Student Success, which beginning in 2000 implemented a variety of interventions for students who lag behind academically. (The waiver was required because these interventions do not target students in Title I schools. Rather, any student in any school who lags behind is eligible for these services.) Like NCLB, the district's program, which was implemented in 2000, provides tutoring to students in need.

The district also implemented NCLB's public school choice and supplemental service provisions largely without help from local non-governmental organizations. A district advisory council, which is a non-district stakeholder involved in Title I schools, has provided some advice, as has the local chapter of the Association of Community Organizations for Reform Now.[11] One administrator acknowledged assistance from the Council of Great City Schools, which he characterized as the best source on (financial) set-asides under the law, and more generally of assistance in interpreting the federal regulations to accompany the law.

Identification of Improvement Schools

The first link in the chain of implementation is identifying which schools are failing to meet the federal definitions of academic progress. Timing has already emerged as a crucial issue. Because the state test takes place in the spring, the state department of education does not announce which schools have not made AYP—and thus have been newly designated as failing—until late August each year. District observers suggested that it is quite difficult for parents to make decisions about switching their children to higher-performing schools and for the district to update its web of bus routes in the few weeks between the announcement and the start of school. There is less uncertainty for schools that were designated in 2002, because the district decided that for the sake of continuity such schools would be designated as failing for a second year, and parents were notified in March of their options for the 2003–2004 school year.

Information Provided to Schools and Parents

The second key link in implementation is to inform parents with students in low-performing schools of the options available. The district sends out a series of letters to all parents of students at schools that have been designated as needing improvement.[12] In 2002, the district mailed more than one hundred thousand letters in multiple mailings to families in affected schools. Our interpretation of these letters is that they are, for the most part, quite neutral. Although the letter that informs parents about public school choice does state that supplemental services available at a low-performing school may not be available at a higher-performing school, we do not interpret this as a direct attempt by the district to discourage parents from moving their children. Rather, it points to a flaw in the legislation itself—that services are linked to the school and do not follow the student if s/he moves to a better school. However, we also acknowledge that the letters may not be targeted to the average parent at a failing school, in that they do not highlight parents' options early in the letters, clearly identify supplemental services as free tutoring, or use large, easy-to-read fonts. On the other hand, the letters are accurate and concise.

Communication with non-English-speaking parents creates further challenges for the district, as just less than 30 percent of students are LEP. Given the large numbers of immigrant families in San Diego, this probably understates the percentage of parents who lack proficiency in English. Letters mailed to parents are routinely translated into Spanish, but language translation services for five languages are available through the district. In some cases, groups of parent volunteers translate for parents who speak other languages. However, focus group participants told us that sometimes ethnic-misidentification is also a problem—for example the translation may go out in Vietnamese, but the family is Laotian. Furthermore, district and focus group respondents universally agree that written translation does little to inform parents who are not literate in their native language.

The district held a number of parent meetings to explain NCLB's provisions. At the district's "focus schools," which are the elementary schools in the lowest decile of the state's test-score system, "parent academic liaisons" (PALs) are in place to help parents with NCLB and other issues.[13] No comparable resource exists at other schools, however, and a principal at one of the schools tagged as failing said that although teachers do discuss the NCLB options in parent–teacher conferences, the lack of a PAL in that school severely limited the school's ability to help parents understand their options. Several district administrators acknowledged that the complexity of the NCLB public school choice and supplemental service provisions coupled with language barriers made it quite difficult to get all the information that they would like parents to know into their hands.

Choice Implementation: Patterns in Place

In some ways, San Diego has a head start in its ability to implement public school choice provisions of NCLB: its history over the last 25 years is one rooted in various school choice options for students in the district, in large part because of court orders in the late 1970s to desegregate the district.[14] San Diego's board of education adopted a policy of voluntary integration through several programs over the years, including the Voluntary Ethnic Enrollment Program (VEEP) and magnet programs.[15] The key characteristic common to all of these programs is the opportunity for a student to attend a school other than the neighborhood school to which he or she might otherwise be assigned. Of these programs, VEEP and the magnet programs, both of which provide busing, are by far the most extensive.[16] There are two other important options in the district: open enrollment through the state's School Choice program and a network of charter schools.[17] In 2001–2002, 6 percent of the district's students participated in busing through VEEP, 6 percent were bused into magnet schools, 7 percent participated in the state's School Choice program, and 6 percent attended charter schools—a total of 25 percent of the district's students in some type of choice program.[18] The district does not provide busing for the pre-NCLB School Choice program or, in general, for the charter school program.

As a result of its integration programs, San Diego has established an extensive busing system. Moreover, many of the VEEP sending schools are also improvement schools under the terms of NCLB, meaning that the district already has busing patterns in place to accommodate student transfers easily. On the other hand the new NCLB choice program has the potential to clash with the existing choice programs in several ways, ranging from financial to the planning of bus routes.

ARRANGEMENT OF BUS ROUTES AND PROCESSING OF STUDENT
BUSING APPLICATIONS

The VEEP program allows students to apply for busing between schools within each of several allied patterns. (Allied patterns were designed to promote racial integration. However, now that the district is no longer under active court supervision, students of any race within a VEEP allied pattern can apply to attend a receiving school.) As noted above, busing is also provided for students in the district's magnet program.

One of the logistical challenges that districts face in implementing NCLB's choice provisions is designing bus routes. Not surprisingly, the district has piggybacked its NCLB busing program on top of its VEEP program. Students at a given improvement school thus are offered a menu of school options that lie within that school's VEEP allied pattern. There are other cases in which a school newly designated as needing improvement has not already been part of an allied pattern, or has been in an allied pattern as a receiving rather than a sending school. For these schools, new busing options were created. As a result, some schools in the district that receive students as VEEP receiving schools also send students to higher-performing schools under NCLB.

The district had two reasons for piggybacking on top of existing VEEP busing patterns. The first was simply a desire to serve as many students as possible in a cost-effective manner. The second reason was that administrators were concerned that if the NCLB designations of schools in VEEP patterns change over time, so that, for instance, a traditionally VEEP-sending school is no longer pegged as low-performing, students who wished to remain at their choice school could do so by reapplying through the VEEP program. More to the point, many administrators expect the number of failing schools to grow over time, so that students who had chosen to attend a VEEP receiving school would have the option of continuing to be bused to that school should it become designated as needing improvement. In other words, administrators have sought to provide consistency to students in the face of expected fluctuations in *which* schools are designated as low-performing. Given that the district appears to be in a relatively strong position to implement NCLB public school choice provisions, a natural question arises: How many students who were eligible for a change of school have requested such a change?

Though participation rates in NCLB-mandated busing have been low, the second year has seen a marked increase over the first year. In the first year, 72 students filed 90 applications for busing under NCLB, and 24 (one-third) actually enrolled. In the second year, 480 students (about 1 percent) of eligible students filed 600 applications for a transfer by August 2003. As of late October 2003, approximately 300 of these students had accepted the district's offer of bus service to a higher-performing school.

Figure 10.1 illustrates the percentage of students for grades K to 5, 6 to 8, and 9 to 12. Overall, very few students who were eligible applied to another school—just 39 elementary, 225 middle school, and 216 high school students. As the figure shows, the applications as a percentage of 2002–2003 enrollment in low-performing schools ranged from half a percent in grades

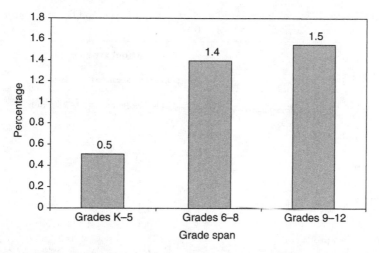

Figure 10.1. Choice applicants as a percentage of studens in San Diego program improvement schools for 2003–2004 academic year, by Grade Span, August 2003.
Source: SDCS enrolment options office and CBEDS.

K to 5, to 1.5 percent in grades 9 to 12. Although the absolute number of students applying to change schools in grades 6 to 8 is slightly higher than in grades 9 to 12, the percentage is slightly lower.

In any case, as of late December 2003, only 692 students—53 in elementary schools, 324 in middle schools, and 315 in high schools—had applied to change schools in the 2003–2004 school year, and the district did not have a final transfer count.[19]

The main reason for the low uptake rate in fall 2002 was timing. The district did not know which schools were designated as low-performing until late summer, and parents in effect were offered a chance to submit applications in many cases around the time that their children had already started or were about to start their school year at their local school. Applications for fall 2003 proceeded in a much more timely fashion, partly because all schools that had been designated as low-performing in 2002 were automatically designated as such for the 2003–2004 school year. This allowed the district to mail letters to the parents of all students eligible to enroll in the NCLB choice program in March 2003.

Improvement and Choice Schools

A comparison of selected school and student characteristics at sending and receiving schools in table 10.2 suggests that the two types of schools are significantly different in some key ways. Low-performing schools have higher

Table 10.2. Selected school, student, and teacher characteristics in San Diego. Comparison of program improvement and choice schools, 2002–2003

	School type		
	Program improvement	**Choice**	**T-tests**
Percentage of each characteristic:	(31 schools)	(41 schools)	
Students:			
American Indian	0.4	0.7	***
Asian	8.3	11.3	*
Pacific Islander	1.2	0.9	*
Filipino	7.9	8.5	
Hispanic	52.3	22.4	***
African American	19.7	8.0	***
White	10.4	48.4	***
Limited english proficient	38.2	10.8	***
Free or reduced-price meals	71.7	25.3	***
Did not attend same school continuously between fall 2002 and spring 2003	8.1	4.0	***
Academic performance:			
School's API rank, 2002–2003	609.1	773.6	***
Teachers:			
% Lacking full credentials	0.8	0.2	*

Note: T-test that the enrollment-weighted means are significantly different in the two types of schools: Probability> |T| * = 0.10, ** = 0.05, *** = 0.01.
Student ethnicity percentages may not add to 100 because of rounding.
Sources: SDCS Enrollment Options Office, CBEDS, API, and AYP datasets.

proportions of non-white students, LEP students, and economically disadvantaged students. Close to half of the students in choice schools are white, whereas only about 10 percent of students in low-performing schools are white. Close to 40 percent of students in low-performing schools are LEP, whereas approximately 11 percent in choice schools are LEP. Almost 72 percent of students in low-performing schools receive free or reduced-price meal assistance, but only a quarter of students in choice schools receive such assistance. The latter of these factors is closely associated with low academic performance.[20] Students in low-performing schools are also significantly less likely to be enrolled in the same school for the entire school year—more than twice as many of these students change schools (8.1 percent) than do students at choice schools (4 percent).

Of course, the academic performance of the schools tagged as needing improvement is lower, and this can be measured by the Academic Performance Index (API), a weighted average of test scores of students at each school. Choice schools score, on average, approximately 165 index points above the lower-performing schools—scores that are much closer to the target of 800 that the state has set for all schools. Finally, the proportion of teachers who lack full credentials is higher in low-performing schools. Most teachers in San Diego have full credentials, so the absolute numbers are small in either case. Still, the contrast is stark—four times more teachers at low-performing schools lack full certification.[21] Clearly, the choice schools are quite distinct from schools tagged for improvement on a number of dimensions, and this translates into a sizable gap in test scores.

Why, if given the option of attending better schools, are so few students in failing schools electing this option so far? Previous research, as well as our own recent interviews suggest a few possibilities. First, immigrant parents may not understand their rights and the rights of their children, and may have expectations that the school system knows what's best for their children.[22] Thus, they may hesitate to exercise options that are available to them. Second, economically disadvantaged parents may not want to send their children by bus to a school far from home, where, if the student became ill, for example, the parent or a caregiver would not be able to pick the child up from school early. Third, some students might have to make as many as five bus transfers on public transportation if they missed the school bus, according to a high school principal. Other factors behind the low application rates may include late notification of parents and letters that do not clearly highlight options. However, district personnel insist that the district is making every effort to inform parents of their options. It may also be that parents think that supplemental services offered at the neighborhood school will help their children more than sending them to other schools.

Supplemental Service Providers

In 2002 the state released a list of potential supplemental service providers to districts and the general public. By the end of 2003, this list consisted of 102 providers other than the district itself, 51 of which are listed as *potential* providers in the district.[23] However, for a variety of reasons, the district did not allow parents in improvement schools to choose freely from this state list. Rather, the district created a subsample of the state list and then allowed parents/guardians of eligible students to choose a provider from this reduced list.

There were four reasons for paring down the state list. First, the service provider had to be able to provide services locally. Second, simply because a provider had put his name on the state list did not guarantee that the provider really was interested in participating in the local program. A prominent example was Sylvan Education Solutions (now known as Catapult Learning)—when San Diego City Schools contacted the company's local office, it was told that Sylvan did not plan to provide supplemental services in San Diego County. A third issue was providers' lack of capacity to serve a variety of students. For instance, one administrator told us: "(Private providers) often are not equipped to deal with a range of students. Some have told us they have no capacity for English learners." Because the state's list does not include information regarding a company's capacity to serve diverse student populations, the responsibility for confirming capacity lies with each district.

A fourth reason for paring down the state list is the legislation's requirement that districts be responsible for ensuring that providers are living up to their promises. The district's legal department took this responsibility quite seriously. For example, if a student was injured by an employee of a supplemental service provider or by any other person on the premises of that provider, the district could be liable. As one administrator put it to us: "We routinely fingerprint teachers for background checks." All staff working with students, including supplemental service providers (on site or Internet), must undergo these checks.

An important wrinkle in the provision of supplemental services has emerged in San Diego: the district itself has become the dominant provider of these services. Several administrators mentioned to us that they believed that the district's own Blueprint for Student Success, implemented in 2000, in many ways captures the spirit of NCLB's supplemental service, school choice, and professional development requirements. For example, the district has used test scores since 2000 to identify students who lag behind, and then steers these students into a series of interventions, including the Extended Day Reading Program in which students receive teacher-supervised reading time at the start or end of the school day, and the similar Extended Day Math Program. As one administrator put it: "We're an ideal provider because we can provide this as part of a coherent system. The district already has in place a set of preventive measures and interventions for students who lag behind. A student can now spend another 90 minutes with her same teacher who knows what she needs. Coherence is everything."

However, an external provider opined that giving students "more of the same" in an underperforming school may do little to improve student performance, and the principal of a low-performing school told us that it is extremely difficult to convince the best teachers to serve as supplemental service instructors in the extended-day programs. Given our finding that sanctioned schools have four times more uncertified teachers than choice schools, it seems likely that students in the district-run programs are not always getting the quality of instruction that they need—during the regular school day or through the district's supplemental service program.

The number and nature of the supplemental service providers has changed considerably between the 2002–2003 and 2003–2004 school years. In the first year, only one non-district provider met the district's criteria. This company provided secondary school students with help over the Internet. Because so few students opted for these services, the provider decided not to continue for a second year. In contrast, five state-approved providers worked for the district in the 2003–2004 school year. Two providers work at school sites rented from the district, and the other three providers work with students online. Notably, there are no providers that are working with students at off-campus locations. A district official told us that one potential provider did not sign a contract because it could not find a suitable off-site location in time for the 2003–2004 school year.

Getting the supplemental service providers lined up is only half the work, however. The district still must actively recruit students into the program. In both years, the district has done an initial mailing to parents, and then had schools give students letters to take home to parents. In addition, teachers remind parents in parent–teacher conferences that as part of the "learning contract" that students have, they need to enroll in after-school academic programs, according to one principal. Although only 25 percent of students in that principal's school were receiving supplemental services in early 2004, that percentage represented virtually all of the students performing at "far below basic" proficiency. Ultimately, all who applied for supplemental services in the district received it.

In any case, by far the largest provider has been the district itself. In 2002–2003, only three students enrolled in the online program, and 4,370 students received supplemental services directly from the district—which represents 86 percent of students who were eligible to receive the free tutoring.[24] In 2003–2004, 4,227 students enrolled in the program. About 26 percent of these students chose non-district providers, up from only 0.1 percent in 2002–2003. This growth suggests that the district is opening up opportunities for outside providers. However, one supplemental service provider told us that it only had 10 students enrolled as of February 2004, and that the district had limited this company's enrollment to 100.

It is worth pointing out that the district is competing with external providers for meaningful amounts of federal money. For instance, Internet-based providers are typically paid a maximum of $900 per student. Onsite providers receive about the same per student, and they charge $50–$60 per hour per student. In theory, any district that set itself up to compete with outside service providers would have a large incentive to direct "customers" its way. One external supplemental service provider who works for the district told us, however, that the district was not "aggressively discouraging" students from enrolling in the external provider's program and, when asked how easy it was to work with the district, ranked the district "8 on a scale of 1 to 10." But another external provider ranked the district "3 on a scale of 1 to 10," and suggested that the district was making it difficult to do business because the "massive amount of paperwork" that reduces providers' profits. The principal of one of the sanctioned schools told us that external services would be welcome at that school—as long as the principal knew that the external staff was qualified and had a good rapport with students.

Early Challenges and Emerging Long-Term Problems

Initial Barriers to Implementation

This section itemizes transitory problems related to implementation. One administrator summed up the 2002 implementation as follows: "Globally, the concern has been the fast pace of implementation." The deadlines for implementation by fall 2002 caused a rush to implement. This was compounded by the late release of the regulations to accompany the federal law. These regulations were issued by both the U.S. Department of Education and the state Department of Education to provide more detailed instructions to districts. The latter regulations arrived just 10 weeks before classes began. These delays made it difficult for the district to implement fully the school choice and supplemental service provisions of NCLB in time for classes in fall 2002. A senior administrator summarized some of the difficulties the district experienced in 2002 as it attempted to implement the state's regulations: "Materials from the state were overly general. The materials had to cater to all sorts of districts. They were not sufficient to convey details to a local audience. We had to make a lot of phone calls to the state to understand implementation. It was a typical case of flying the airplane while you are building it."

The same administrator stated that one of the biggest problems was that all decisions about which students would enter the VEEP and magnet systems and related decisions about bus routes had been made by April 2002, two months before state regulations arrived. Another administrator amplified these concerns:

The timing has been very poorly managed. July is a difficult time of year, especially for notification to principals and staff, who are on vacation at that time unless it's a year-round school. Turnaround between July and August 15 was very difficult turnaround time—it was just thrust upon the district and wasn't very well explained. Usually with the STAR [state test score system] release there's a package of information, but the AYP didn't have one. It would have helped to have a media kit or more information with the timing. Sacramento folks aren't talking about how complex a measure this is.

Implementation of NCLB apparently proceeded more smoothly for the 2003–2004 school year. But some additional hiccups occurred. For example, the state introduced a new definition of AYP that was not available until June 2003. This made even preliminary analyses of which schools might qualify as low-performing schools impossible until summer 2003. And some school administrators and community members alike voiced concerns that parents did not have a ready information source about NCLB and the relations between its two key elements (AYP and improvement schools) and the state's preexisting accountability system. The nine community-based organization members we interviewed told us that they had received virtually no questions from parents about any aspect of NCLB. They found this striking because they interact with thousands of parents each year. Some stated that the district could have done more to interact with parents, especially those who do not speak English, but that the overarching issue was the sheer complexity of the new federal law.

Several administrators also suggested that the state could have provided better information on the qualifications and offerings of the supplemental service providers on the state's official list. The state made the list available on the Internet and directly to districts, but according to San Diego district officials the state did not provide much information beyond that list. Given the district's concerns about providers' curricula and health and safety standards, this presented a major obstacle that limited the number of external providers that would be chosen to work with the district.

For the most part, the district sees these initial challenges as temporary. Indeed, the numbers of choice applications, supplemental service providers in the district, and students receiving supplemental services, are all increasing with time.

Potential Flaws in the Law Itself

Unlike the apparently temporary issues above, the problems we outline below are best considered as systemic long-term impediments to the success of NCLB.

SYSTEMIC PROBLEM #1: TIMING

We cannot dismiss all timing problems as temporary glitches. Because students are tested toward the end of the school year, and because it takes several months to grade the millions of tests, the California Department of Education does not designate schools as low performing until late August each year, about two weeks before school starts. This gives the school district two weeks to devise new bus routes and to inform parents of their choices. This schedule is, in the words of one administrator, "completely unworkable."

One administrator gave a detailed picture of the pandemonium that has taken place in the last two weeks of August. Once the list of sanctioned schools is released to the district, the bus routes must be overhauled. This is time consuming because a fixed number of buses must be stretched to meet the needs of new NCLB choice requirements while continuing to serve the VEEP students, magnet students, and the students who started NCLB busing in a prior year. Contracting out for additional buses on very short notice is apparently not a realistic possibility, in part because it is hard to obtain private sector bids at the rates the district is willing to pay. This administrator next mentioned the challenge of communicating options to parents, in some cases in late summer after a school has newly been identified as needing improvement:

> This year we mailed out 105,000 letters overall to parents. . . . For each letter, a draft must be reviewed by legal, communications, and the departments that deal with teachers, supplemental services, and busing. Then we need to print and deliver all of these letters just at the time when our business services department is already fully booked [with other items that are distributed at the beginning of the school year]. So we have to put the contract out to bid and wait the required number of days before choosing a contractor.

The district also prints this letter in six languages. The total number of letters referred to by the administrator includes a general mailing that is followed up by more specific and more highly targeted letters indicating whether choice or both choice and supplemental services are available to given students. The administrator continued with the next steps:

> After that, the next challenge is to handle requests from parents. . . . In comparison, setting up busing for students (in low-performing schools) who apply in spring is quite easy. But when we make further additions to busing in fall it is very difficult to change teacher allocations at schools in response. I believe that it is state law that teacher allocations are locked in by the fourth Friday in September.
> . . . Another problem is re-confirming student addresses over the summer. We wait until September to re-confirm student addresses because we get a much better response.

. . . Overall, I can't see how this is viable long term unless we get real-time test score data.

A respondent from a community-based organization said that "at the very time when the increased requirements are appearing regarding communicating with parents, the school district has reduced its parent involvement and translation units." District administrators confirmed that this has occurred because of tight budgets. But one administrator told us that the cuts were too small to have affected NCLB communications greatly.

Systemic Problem #2: Inconsistencies in AYP Definitions and Improvement School Selection

Administrators criticized the formula for calculating AYP on a number of grounds. This matters because schools can be incorrectly labeled as low-performing due to flawed statistical assumptions embedded in the definition of AYP.

Thomas Kane and Douglas Staiger analyze NCLB eligibility criteria and argue that small random errors in school outcomes on each of the criteria can lead to a school being deemed to have failed to meet AYP.[25] If a school fails to make AYP for two consecutive years it is designated a school needing improvement, and its low-scoring students now qualify to be bused to another school at district expense. District officials seemed keenly aware of the probability that for random reasons many schools will be labeled as needing improvement. One administrator put it most simply: "Almost all schools will occasionally fail (to meet AYP)." A second also voiced this concern, combined with a related concern that it is unrealistic for the NCLB legislation to expect 100 percent of students to meet Proficient standards by 2014: "Without legislative changes, NCLB twenty years from now will be viewed as a disaster. Every school in the state will be PI [a 'program improvement' school]." Unless California lowers its rather high standards, or the reauthorization of NCLB allows some flexibility, this San Diego administrator's prediction may well be borne out.

A second problem identified by several administrators is that under NCLB the only thing that matters for AYP is the percentage of students who meet the test score defined by the state as evidence of proficiency. Many argued that a single absolute cutpoint does not provide a complete measure of school quality.

A third weakness in the definition of AYP is that there is no longitudinal component, meaning that the calculations in two consecutive years can be based on quite different student populations.

SYSTEMIC PROBLEM #3: INCONSISTENCIES ON CAPACITY
CONSTRAINTS IN BUSING

A third common criticism we heard is that the law and the accompanying
federal and state regulations are highly contradictory on how districts should
deal with capacity constraints in the busing system as demand for school
choice grows, especially if the supply of higher proficiency schools falls—a
distinct possibility if the definition of AYP is not amended. In San Diego this
problem already seems to be severe: roughly half of the comprehensive high
schools have been denoted as failing schools. For every additional high school
that comes under federal sanctions, the number of students eligible to apply
for busing to non-failing schools increases, and the number of those high
schools that could potentially accept bused students falls.

District officials were careful to point out that the district's own allocation
of the 20 percent Title I set-aside between busing and supplemental services
determined the maximum number of dollars that the district would be
required to spend on NCLB-related busing. Nonetheless, certain popular
receiving schools could become swamped well before the district reaches its
spending cap for NCLB busing. A receiving school principal told us that
already in fall 2003 the school had to turn away ninth-grade applicants.

Unintended Consequences

We now concentrate on six unintended consequences of the NCLB's choice
and supplemental service provisions. Typically, it is too early to tell whether
these consequences will impinge in a major and negative way on students.

A first unintended consequence that several administrators predicted is
that the school choice provision could lead to some perverse mislabeling of
schools as failing. Based on the first two years of NCLB choice, one administrator told us, "One prediction we have is that all schools' test scores will
fall because better students appear to be leaving PI [Program Improvement]
schools." One upshot of this non-random selection of students is that schools
that are tagged as low performing will find it hard to escape that designation
because their test scores will, quite mechanically, decline. Similarly, at higher-
performing receiving schools, the arrival of NCLB choice students will lower
average test scores. As a receiving school principal said, "We aren't *afraid* that
our scores will fall—we *know* they will." *In other words, large movements of
NCLB choice students could condemn both low-performing (sending) and
higher-performing (receiving) schools to failing status.*

A second unintended consequence of NCLB could be that choice will create what one administrator called "us–them tensions" at receiving schools. Unlike existing programs like VEEP, the new busing program explicitly targets low-scoring students. One administrator suggested that this will stigmatize the NCLB students at their new schools. A second administrator worried that students who switch schools under NCLB will be blamed for any decline in test scores at the receiving school. Neither administrator had evidence that these tensions had already arisen, but both worried that they will occur as the choice program grows.

Indeed, students who opt to attend a school far from home are clearly crossing much more than the 25 miles between home and school, as a principal described:

> Imagine plunking down students who are unfamiliar with the culture of the school, the culture of the community. . . . There are discipline issues [that the new kids bring with them] and the incoming kids get the blame for fights even when they are not involved. We have more at-risk kids without extra support [in the form of counselors and bilingual staff]. Almost 30% of my incoming students are LEP, and I have no bilingual staff.

A third unintended consequence stems from the assumption implicit in NCLB that districts have not already taken steps to boost learning at their lowest-performing schools. In San Diego, the district implemented the Blueprint for Student Success in 2000, which has devoted considerable resources to students and schools that have lagged behind. Several district administrators worried that students who leave the bottom-performing schools under NCLB will often go to schools that currently have fewer supports in place for students who are behind.

Compounding the irony, the time students spend on the bus may aggravate this problem: a school principal in a choice high school told us that although students being bused in from sanctioned schools are eligible to take advantage of the district's extended day tutoring programs in the new school, few of these students enroll. The principal told us that the programs take place after school but the students "don't take advantage of the services because they [would] get home at 6:30 to 7:00 at night. So, it's kind of undermining the whole purpose."

A fourth side effect of NCLB again stems from the assumption in the federal legislation that districts have not already implemented similar actions. Many administrators spoke to us about the potential negative consequences of NCLB choice on the long-standing school choice programs in San Diego, principally VEEP and magnet programs. We detected two strands of argument here. First, because the district is taking NCLB choice so seriously, it is raising questions about the long-term viability of existing busing programs like VEEP and magnets. Second, families who have applied to the VEEP, magnet, and the open enrollment (School Choice) programs have reacted quite negatively to the district's decision to give top priority to the NCLB choice applications, thus delaying decisions about applications to the pre-existing choice programs.

A fifth side effect of NCLB that several district officials mentioned is that NCLB has the potential to confuse the public as it attempts to grasp the differences between the state and federal accountability systems. One administrator told us that it will take some time for parents to learn what it means for a school to be in "improvement." Indeed, some principals did not seem to understand the concept well, in spite of central office attempts to offer training sessions for principals. One administrator implied that if the understanding among principals were so low, the public would fare even worse. The principals with whom we spoke do not seem to distinguish between NCLB students and other students who may be in choice programs or in need of additional instructional services. Moreover, our conversation with staff from community-based organizations confirmed that school personnel appear to know little about what the legislation means in practice.

Another administrator worried that the NCLB concept of adequate yearly progress is likely to confuse parents:

> It took a number of years for people to understand the state accountability system. In California people are just now getting the idea. NCLB adds a new layer on top of that. . . . Unintended consequences are most likely to crop up in public relations. AYP is very hard to explain to any audience. I worry that some schools are about to be blindsided even though they are genuinely improving. We could also be overly reactive. Parents may flee [schools] based on very incomplete information. A single number doesn't tell all. Conversely, a pretty mediocre school could meet AYP even though all subgroups just barely met targets.

A final side effect of NCLB suggested by one administrator is detrimental to charter schools. Almost all charters in San Diego are Title I schools and so are subject to the NCLB choice and supplemental service provisions. The administrator predicted trouble for charter schools regardless of whether they were tagged as low performing. If a charter becomes an NCLB improvement school, "it cannot charter buses on its own" and so would become dependent on the district. Conversely, a non-improvement charter school that opted to accept NCLB choice students would then become subject to NCLB regulations for receiving schools. In 2002–2003 no charter schools in San Diego acted as receiving schools, but five are doing so in 2003–2004.

Possible Remedies for Problems Encountered to Date

Our findings suggest some fine-tuning to NCLB that could improve the long-term prospects for the NCLB choice and supplemental service programs.

(i) The Timing Problem

One of the biggest problems with NCLB implementation in San Diego is the two-week period in which the district must arrange busing options for newly identified improvement schools each August. A simple remedy is to reverse the current NCLB policy that offers students busing in the first year that their school is under that designation and both busing and supplemental services in the second year. Instead, supplemental services would be available immediately, and busing, the provision that is more difficult to implement, would be offered the second year. All students at the low-performing school would receive a letter by the start of the school year listing a menu of alternative sources of supplemental services, and during that academic year any student who wished could also apply to be bused to a higher-performing school the following year.

(ii) Mitigating Definitional Problems

One administrator suggested to us that the base-year API used to determine whether the school has met its growth target should use only those students who were also in the school the prior year. This innovation would prevent schools being mislabeled as having failed to make AYP, or mislabeled as low-performing schools, simply because the student population had changed in a way that reduced average achievement. It would also eliminate the possibility that NCLB busing causes test scores at both sending and receiving schools to fall, increasing further the number of schools mislabeled as low performing.

(iii) Simplifying and Aligning Accountability between District, State, and Federal Levels

Strikingly, three separate entities have endeavored to create accountability systems in San Diego. The district adopted its Blueprint for Student Success in 2000, which incorporates district-specific testing and district-designed interventions. On top of this system is the state's accountability and testing system and the new federal requirements.

There is a sense of "too many cooks spoil the broth" in all this. It might behoove Congress to consider a far less prescriptive system of testing and rules for designating low-performing schools. If Congress afforded each state the opportunity to qualify with the U.S. Department of Education its own system of testing and identification of lagging schools, players at all levels could benefit.

(iv) Improving Information Dissemination

Our meeting with several representatives of community-based organizations yielded many ideas for how San Diego City Schools could disseminate better and more timely information to parents. Suggestions included a mandatory parent–teacher conference to discuss enrollment options, district-sponsored training on NCLB for both district and community-based organization staff, and the hiring of parent liaisons at each school. Of course, all of these sensible reforms are costly.

Conclusion

Implementation of NCLB's choice and supplemental service provisions appears to be proceeding fairly well in San Diego. Participation in supplemental services is quite high, with 86 percent of eligible low-scoring students applying for and receiving services. So far, the district itself has been the dominant provider of supplementary services. It uses the Title I funds it earns from these tutorials to enhance its preexisting interventions for low-performing students. However, non-district providers served fully 26 percent of these students in 2003–2004, up from less than 0.1 percent in 2002–2003. The two external providers we interviewed had divergent opinions on doing business with the district. One bemoaned the paperwork required by the district, while the other praised the district as being very open to working with outside providers.

Participation in NCLB choice is small, at around 1 percent of eligible students, but growing. Given that about one quarter of SDCS students were already participating in other public school choice programs, the low participation is not surprising. Furthermore, the NCLB requirement that newly identified improvement schools immediately offer school choice has clearly hampered participation, because the district has had only about two weeks before classes start to design new bus routes and to inform parents at those schools.

Although district administrators repeatedly told us that they support the intent of NCLB, they are tangibly frustrated with many of the details of NCLB implementation. The previous section suggests some possible remedies. Perhaps the most important of these suggestions is to switch the order in which supplemental services and choice are rolled out at schools newly identified as low performing. In this way, choice would become available only in year two for students at these schools, instead of year one. This would mitigate the severe timing difficulty that the district faces in organizing school choice options after the state identifies new improvement schools late each summer.

In light of the many press and media accounts of districts actively opposed to the NCLB, the greatest puzzle in our account of NCLB implementation in San Diego may be that the district administration appears to support the broad goals of the new law. One explanation is that before NCLB the district had itself implemented reforms that facilitated school choice and supplemental services for students who lag behind. These reforms in San Diego are very much in the spirit of the NCLB. In the end, the degree of alignment of goals and strategies—at least in broad terms—between the district and the federal government may prove crucial to the successful implementation of NCLB.

But underlying this similarity in broad goals between San Diego and federal legislators simmers a very real tension between three systems of accountability that have been imposed at the local, state, and federal levels. The provisions of these accountability systems overlap and in some cases are quite inconsistent with each other. Perhaps the key question for the next five years is simply this: In districts like San Diego that have already implemented similar reforms, will the NCLB provisions for school choice and supplemental services simply become a case of too many cooks spoiling the broth?

Notes

1. We are indebted to the many people we interviewed in San Diego City Schools district, including private-sector supplemental service providers and members of several community-based organizations for sharing their insights. In particular, we are grateful to Karen Bachofer and Ellen Yaffa for facilitating many of these conversations. We thank Chester Finn, Rick Hess, and conference attendees for valuable suggestions.

2. We are grateful to Ellen Yaffa, a staff member of Social Advocates for Youth (SAY-San Diego) for organizing a meeting with this group.

3. Jack O'Connell, "Local Educational Agency Plan Memorandum," Sacramento, California Department of Education, February 26, 2003. See this and several other state documents at http://www.cde.ca.gov/pr/ leap (available December 2003).

4. The state documentation appears to confirm interview respondents' experience that they had received little guidance from the state in how to interpret the new provisions.

5. See San Diego City Schools, "Local Education Agency Plan, June 10, 2003," San Diego, 2003, at http://www.sdcs.k12.ca.us/nclb/ draftLEAplan.pdf (available December 2003).

6. Although Sable and Aronstamm Young (table 10.1, p. 12) rank the district as 17th, when districts that encompass more than a city-unified district (such as Puerto Rico, which includes the whole island) are removed, San Diego district is 8th. Jennifer Sable and Beth Aronstamm Young, *Characteristics of the 100 Largest Public Elementary and Secondary School Districts in the United States: 2001–02* (Washington, D.C.: U.S. Department of Education, National Center for Education Statistics, 2003).

7. LEP students are known as "English learners" in California. We maintain the acronym LEP for consistency with other studies across the nation. Economic disadvantage is measured as free or reduced-price meal assistance under the Federal Title I definition. These two measures are highly correlated nationwide and stand at 0.74 in California.

8. Education Data Partnership, "District Financial Statement," in *Fiscal, Demographic, and Performance Data on California's K-12 Schools,* Sacramento, 2003. Can be found at http://www.ed-data.k12.ca.us (available December 2003).

9. Improvement school status is based on spring 2003 test data, and enrollment is collected in the fall of 2002 for the 2002–2003 academic year.

10. Christiane McPhee, San Diego City Schools, personal correspondence, February 17, 2004.

11. Non-district stakeholders could include individuals or representatives of community-based organizations, the business community, and private-sector tutoring providers who either serve the district in a formal or informal advisory capacity or who act as an external lobby.

12. See Alan D. Bersin, "Year 1 Letter," San Diego City Schools, 2003, at http://www.sdcs.k12.ca.us/nclb/yr1_ltr.pdf (available December 2003). Also, see the letter regarding supplemental services at http://www.sdcs. k12.ca.us/ nclb/yr2_ltr.pdf (available December 2003).

13. PALs are certificated resource teachers who work directly with parents of children in focus schools. For more information on PALs, see http://www.sdcs.k12.ca.us/ comm/factsheets/pals.pdf (available December 2003).

14. The main cases are *Crawford v. Board of Education* (1976) and *Carlin v. Board of Education* (1977). In the first, the California Supreme Court ruled that the

effects of segregation are more important than the reasons why segregation occurred, and in the latter, the California Superior Court in San Diego County ruled that the district must take measures "to alleviate minority racial isolation—whatever its cause" (p. 1). A third case, *NAACP v. San Bernardino* (1976) allowed a broad range of strategies to integrate districts. San Diego City Schools, Office of Instructional Support, *Report on Voluntary Ethnic Enrollment Program (VEEP) Schools,* at http://prod031.sandi.net/saa/programstudies/reports/VEEP 2003.pdf (available November 2003).

15. According to the district's report on VEEP schools (ibid.), other programs that existed over the years included Already Balanced Community (ABC) program and Learning Centers/Exchanges. The programs that exist in 2002–2003 are VEEP, magnet, Academic Enrichment Academy (AEA), Off Campus Integrated Learning Experience (OCILE), Academic Academies, and Race/Human Relations.

16. For a full discussion of VEEP, see San Diego City Schools, Office of Instructional Support, *Report on Voluntary Ethnic Enrollment Program (VEEP) Schools.*

17. San Diego City Schools includes 21 charter schools to date. These schools were listed separately from the district in the 2002–2003 Title V, Part A, entitlement list. However, only 18 of them received funding. California Department of Education, School Fiscal Services Division, "Entitlements for NCLB Title V—Part A Innovative Programs Fiscal Year 2002–2003," Sacramento, 2003.

18. Lorien A. Rice and Julian R. Betts, "Who Leaves and Why? An Analysis of School Choice Options in a Large Urban District," manuscript, Department of Economics, University of California—San Diego, 2003.

19. These numbers represent an increase of fewer than one per 100 students between August and December 2003 across the schools that were eligible.

20. Julian R. Betts, Andrew C. Zau, and Lorien A. Rice, *Determinants of Student Achievement: New Evidence from San Diego* (San Francisco: Public Policy Institute of California, 2003); and Julian R. Betts, Kim S. Rueben, and Anne Danenberg, *Equal Resources, Equal Outcomes? The Distribution of School Resources and Student Achievement in California* (San Francisco: Public Policy Institute of California, 2000).

21. See Betts, Zau, and Rice, *Determinants of Student Achievement: New Evidence from San Diego.*

22. Alec Ian Gershberg, Anne Danenberg, and Patricia Sánchez, *Beyond "Bilingual" Education: New Immigrants and Public School Policies in California* (Washington, D.C.: Urban Institute Press, 2004).

23. California Department of Education, "Approved Providers, Supplemental Educational Services" (Sacramento: 2003). Can be found at http://www.cde.ca.gov/iasa/titleone/pi/ssp_search.asp (available December 2003).

24. This represents only about 11 percent of students at improvement schools in part because many such schools were in their first year of that status, and so the

students at these schools are not eligible for supplemental services. Further, because NCLB authorizes districts to direct supplemental services to the lowest-scoring students in each school, the district in 2002–2003 aimed supplemental services at approximately 5,000 of 24,957 students in eligible schools.

25. Thomas J. Kane and Douglas O. Staiger, "Volatility in School Test Scores: Implications for Test-Based Accountability Systems," in *Brookings Papers on Education Policy 2002*, ed. Diane Ravitch (Washington, D.C.: Brookings Institution Press, 2002).

11

Worcester: Thunderous Clouds, No Rain

William Howell

James Caradonio is furious. Indeed, he can hardly contain his odium for the federal government's latest efforts at education reform. It takes little prodding to get him going. Just mention No Child Left Behind (NCLB), stand back, and watch: "*Reductio ad absurdum,* you know. But this is what we're dealing with in terms of this insanity. Oh, it's numbers and it looks great. We've got numbers. Simple. And it all looks great and it's just killing, killing teachers and killing principals."[1] He should know. As the superintendent of public schools in the third-largest school district in Massachusetts, and the only superintendent to serve on the inaugural statewide NCLB Implementation Team, Caradonio possesses intimate knowledge of, and influence over, the act's local successes and failures.

When asked whether NCLB was right to set basic achievement objectives and hold schools accountable for realizing them, Caradonio shoots back, "That cockamamie approach is based on the insanity that you're saying we want to get all kids to 100 percent [proficiency], but you're not tracking the trajectory of individual kids towards proficiency." Instead, Caradonio notes, the accountability system considers the test scores of successive cohorts of students, without adjusting for the fact that the pool of students being tested within a school changes markedly from year to year. The result? "Well intentions gone awry. Absolutely insane . . . [This law] violates a lot of just simple things about testing and statistics and sampling and all that. [But] people [in Washington] just kind of get that wild cowboy look in their eye, they just don't give a God-damned."

Caradonio has plenty more to say about the law's additional stipulation that schools demonstrate adequate yearly progress (AYP) not just for students as a whole, but also for subgroups of students defined by ethnicity, English proficiency, and special needs. "There is a lot of fallacy [in this accountability system], a lot of *ex unus disce omnes,* from one learn all. And that is in operation here in the state of Massachusetts for NCLB. From one, learn all. From one, condemn all. Hang the scarlet letter over the entire school because one group" doesn't make AYP.

NCLB, which Caradonio refers to as the No Teacher Left Standing Act, was supposed to introduce choice and accountability into public education. By demanding that schools demonstrate proficiency not just for students as a whole, but for different subgroups as well, the act was supposed to ensure that districts attend to the interests and needs of all students. Moreover, it was supposed to provide meaningful educational alternatives for kids trapped in failing schools. And its effect was supposed to have been greatest in urban centers with large minority and socially disadvantaged populations—places, frankly, just like Worcester, Massachusetts.

Instead, during its first two years, NCLB ran into a buzz saw.

As of June 2003, 12 of Worcester's 46 public schools had been deemed in need of improvement for two consecutive years, as had five schools for three years in a row.[2] Under the new federal law, a total of 4,689 students in the 2002–2003 school year were entitled to switch out of underperforming public schools and into higher performing schools elsewhere in the district. Among these students, 1,769 had the option of using Title I funds to obtain supplemental services from qualified private providers.

Thus far, one child has taken advantage of NCLB's choice provisions to switch schools. One other child has jumped at the opportunity to obtain supplemental services from a provider outside of the public school system. Though billed as the most important federal education legislation since the original authorization of the 1965 Elementary and Secondary Education Act, NCLB has hardly affected the ways in which Worcester's children are educated. As John Monfredo, principal of Belmont Elementary School, notes: "We're not doing much different now than what we were doing before."[3] Though Belmont Elementary has made AYP, Monfredo's sentiments appear common stock throughout the Worcester district. Indeed, local officials generally have taken the fact that so few parents have switched schools or demanded free supplemental services from a private provider as confirmation of the district's educational excellence. Reflecting on the apparent lack of interest in NCLB's choice provisions, Worcester mayor and school committee chair Timothy Murray suggested that "generally speaking, the public schools in Worcester compared to cities with the same demographics and roughly the same size, I think you would see that over time we've enjoyed a high level of support [and] of confidence among the population of parents and families and the business community. And that, I would suggest, probably doesn't exist in other communities."[4]

Why aren't more parents jumping at the opportunity to switch out of underperforming public schools or obtain free supplemental services from a private provider for their children? And why aren't Worcester public schools scrambling to retain their students, and the federal monies attached to them? This chapter highlights five contributing factors:

1. Worcester public schools already face alarming student mobility rates, and hence have good cause to restrict additional enrollment changes.
2. The district oversees a state-mandated desegregation plan that has objectives that can conflict with NCLB's.
3. The district, which stands to lose students and monies, has few incentives to aggressively promote NCLB's choice and supplemental services provisions.
4. Parents know very little about NCLB's new educational opportunities, and the information they do have is often erroneous.
5. Private providers of supplemental services have few means by which to communicate directly with potential customers.

Obviously, the implementation of any major law proceeds in fits and starts, making it much too early to proclaim NCLB an unmitigated success or failure. Still, for reasons inherent in the writing of the law, the district's disincentives to implement it, and parents' minimal awareness of its provisions, NCLB is not likely to revolutionize public education in Worcester any time soon. Indeed, if anything, the act may only encourage bureaucratic entrenchment and reinforce local opposition against federal regulations of the city's public schools.[5]

Preexisting School Mobility

Worcester serves roughly 25,000 students in 46 public schools (36 elementary, 4 middle, 5 high, and one preschool–12 schools).[6] Per-pupil funding has increased rather dramatically in the past decade, from approximately $5,900 per child in the 1992–1993 school year to almost $8,000 in 2002–2003. The federal government provides just 10 percent of the district's $265 million annual budget, with state appropriations, local contributions, grants, and revolving funds covering the balance.

According to a wide variety of indicators, Worcester public schools accommodate an increasingly diverse and disadvantaged population of students. During the past 20 years, the percentage of non-white students in the Worcester public schools has more than doubled, from roughly 20 percent in 1980 to just over 50 percent in 2002. The district supplies English as a Second Language (ESL) tutorial programs to 7 percent of its students who represent no less than 60 different language groups. More than 50 percent of students qualify for free or reduced-price lunch. On the Massachusetts Comprehensive Assessment System (MCAS)—the state's standardized test, first administered in the spring of 1998—Worcester public school students in different grade levels were 8 to 20 percentage points less likely to score at or above proficiency than were students statewide.[7]

The roughly 175,000 residents of Worcester are no more advantaged than the students who fill the public schools. As of 1999, roughly 57 percent of housing units were renter occupied, with a median monthly rent of $580. The median value of owner-occupied housing units, meanwhile, was $118,400.[8] Among renters, the median household income was $25,500; among owners, it was $52,100. Approximately 15 percent of families and 17 percent of households had incomes at or below the federal poverty level.[9] Almost 65 percent of women, and 75 percent of men, had no more than a high school education.[10]

Worcester public schools serve extremely mobile families. During the 1999–2000, 2000–2001, and 2001–2002 school years, the average mobility rates in Worcester elementary schools ranged from 22.7 to 37.4 percent; among middle schools, mobility rates ranged from 24.4 to 32.4 percent; and for high schools, they ranged from 24.0 to 28.1 percent. During any given academic year, roughly one-quarter to one-third of Worcester students transferred schools. And much of this turnover occurred across district lines. In 2001–2002 academic year, for instance, within-district mobility rates among elementary schools averaged 12.2 percent, as compared to 21.0 percent across districts. That such a high proportion of Worcester families are transitioning in and out of the district as a whole only exacerbates the problems of tracking students and delivering a consistent, coherent educational program.[11]

Worcester schools that failed to make AYP serve some of the most mobile student populations. For those elementary schools that were deemed in need of improvement between 1999 and 2001, mobility rates reached as high as 50.9 percent. Rates rose even higher when further restricting the sample to schools with high proportions of minority students and students who qualify for free or reduced-price lunch. When determining whether a school has made AYP, the state does not account for these mobility rates—a fact that almost every public official in the district is quick to point out. Mayor Murray explains: "You really can only determine whether you're making progress or not if you're testing the same kids, year after year. And that's something that is not lost, I think, on parents or the school committee."

The causes of mobility vary widely, though by all accounts, few have much to do with parents seeking better schools. As Brian O'Connell, vice chair of the school committee, notes: "Parents are moving from one apartment to another or husband and wife separate, mother and boyfriend separate, evictions take place, friends go off, parents move, parents are homeless, parents leave in November to go back to Puerto Rico and come back in the spring and come back to a different school."[12] Rather than contribute to student mobility by encouraging families to take advantage of new choice opportunities under NCLB, principals and teachers, for the most part, are trying to contain it. And for good reason. Every time a parent moves across town, at least two classrooms and two school administrations must adjust, further disrupting possibilities for student learning.

With such a mobile population, it may make little sense to conceive of individual students being trapped in failing public schools—a condition that the public school choice provisions of NCLB intend to correct. Schools may be failing. And students may well benefit from switching schools. But wholly divorced from NCLB, a tremendous amount of moving is already going on—so much, in fact, that schools struggle just to keep track of who passes in and out of their doors each year.

Preexisting Choice

More than one-third of students move in and out of Worcester's public schools during any given academic year, and more still exploit educational options outside their immediate neighborhoods. During the 2002–2003 school year, only 61.3 percent of students attended their neighborhood public school. The rest attended one of two charter schools or six citywide magnet schools, participated in the interdistrict choice program,[13] or joined in the district's desegregation plan. As Robert Vartanian, the school choice coordinator at the Parent Information Center, notes: "We're already giving parents choice, regardless of test scores."[14] (The Parent Information Center assigns new students to schools and processes all transfer requests.)

The district's most concerted relocation efforts revolve around its "deisolation" plan. The race-based program—one of 22 in the state of

Massachusetts[15]—relies entirely on the voluntary participation of parents
who are interested in sending their child to a school outside of their immediate neighborhood. Instituted in January 1990, the Worcester program
requires that every school maintain a minority population within 15 percentage points of the district mean. For the better part of a decade, the state
offered districts financial inducements for achieving these objectives. Though
monies are no longer available, the mayor, superintendent, and school committee all continue to support the program.

To apply, parents submit their school preferences to the Parent
Information Center, which then matches students with schools in ways that
advance its desegregation mandate. In three ways, though, choice under this
program is highly constrained. First, parents can select among only those
public schools located within one of four residential attendance zones:
North, South, Burncoat, and Doherty. Second, because each of the residential attendance zones offers just one middle school and one high school, as a
practical matter choice is restricted to elementary schools. And finally, not all
parental requests are honored. Though grievance procedures exist, the Parent
Information Center ultimately can assign students when and where it pleases.

At first blush, NCLB and de-isolation plans appear to complement one
another—both expand the array of school choices that parents can pursue.
Deeper tensions, however, underlie the state and federal laws, for each offers
choice in service of a different objective. NCLB intends to free students stuck
in failing public schools; the de-isolation plan intends to improve the racial
balance of student bodies. What happens when a white child attending a predominantly minority, underperforming public school demands a transfer?
Should the student's right to attend a higher-performing school supercede
the district's interest in desegregation? Put differently, should the district obey
the state before the federal government, or the federal before the state
government?

The choice provisions of NCLB are not implemented in isolation. In every
school district, they play against a different backdrop of previously established state regulations and mandates, some of which conflict with those laid
out in the federal law. Until the federal government demonstrates that it
takes noncompliance seriously and cuts Title I funding when districts skirt
NCLB's provisions—an eventuality about which local school officials in
Worcester remain quite skeptical—the federal government's is just one of
many voices trying to influence how students are taught.

How does this play out at the local level? In the short term, of course, conflicts between state and federal laws can create headaches, as administrators
scramble to try and figure out what is required of them. In the longer term,

though, the regulations can be liberating. Rather than being tied to the mandates of any single state or federal law, superintendents and school board members can simply choose among them. With his usual flair, Superintendent Caradonio explains,

> What happens when the state and the federal government give you conflicting [laws]? . . . You figure as an administrator, well, you [the state] are going to set the cattle prod at 50 volts and you [the federal government] are going to set it at 150 and you [the state] are going to put it in this part of my anatomy and you [the federal government] are going to put it in this part of my anatomy. So, I think I'll go with you [the state]. I like where you're going to put it and it's a lower voltage. And that's what you do. And we've been doing that for . . . . Here we are again, you know.

Ironically, as state and federal education mandates accumulate, control may resort back to local school boards and administrators. For as the menu of local, state, and federal regulations expands, so rises the probability that a district can find a prescribed course of action that suits its own independent interests and complies with the wishes of at least one higher authority. State and federal governments, as such, suffocate under the weight of their own largesse; their zeal to regulate may ultimately undermine their influence.

Districts Defining Options

The job of introducing and advertising NCLB's public school choice provisions ultimately falls on public schools—the very schools, in fact, that stand to lose students and money if parents pursue the act's new educational opportunities, and the very schools that already are struggling with astronomical school mobility rates. Plainly, such schools have every incentive to present the act as muddled and misinformed, to highlight new and innovative programs being initiated within the public school system, and to make the process of switching schools and securing supplemental services from private providers as cumbersome as possible. At least in the short term, the strength of NCLB's accountability system depends on the willingness and ability of parents to exercise choice. To undercut the act, districts need only explain to parents (again and again) why it is such a bad idea to change schools or to entrust private companies with their children's educational welfare.

In the late spring of 2003, the Worcester district notified families at underperforming schools of their rights to NCLB's choice provisions.[16] The designation "in need of improvement," the letter explained, "means that although these schools are succeeding in some areas, there is still room for growth."[17]

After highlighting limitations of the NCLB grading system, the letter underscored unattractive features of the act's choice provisions. For example, "In most instances, because of space limitations, we may not be able to transfer every child in a family to the same school." Further, the letter noted, NCLB stipulates that families with children at underperforming schools who switch schools forfeit their rights to supplemental services. But not to worry, the letter intoned, because exciting things are happening in Worcester public schools. "We believe that your child's school is on its way towards achieving the NCLB goals. The principal and teachers at your child's school have implemented new programs and services during the school day as well as after school. These include: a proven literacy approach designed to meet the individual needs of the students; the Everyday Mathematics program for students in grades K–6; an after-school program to help students improve MCAS scores; and other special programs."

The district then set up a multistage procedure for parents to exercise their rights under NCLB. The first step involves a meeting between a parent and her child's principal, wherein the parent has an opportunity to explain why she is unhappy with her child's school, and the principal can clarify the problems with NCLB and the reasons why the family ought to stay put. According to principals and district officials, parents are informed about public school improvements, new programs that are being introduced, and problems and misperceptions of NCLB—all themes of the original letter notifying parents that their school was underperforming. Principals also explain why students are best served by receiving supplemental services within their schools. (The district offers an academically based after-school program for Title I students that qualifies as supplemental services under NCLB. Currently, over 800 students are enrolled in the program.) They highlight the importance of maintaining continuity between the teaching that occurs during the school day and the tutoring that occurs in an after-school program—continuity that can only be preserved when parents turn to their child's public school for supplemental services. In addition to reviewing the academic strengths of the district's after-school program, principals can advertise their own programs' special amenities. When presenting parents with options for supplemental services, principals "cannot tell them which one would be best for their child because that's against the law," notes Joan Fitton, who is in charge of overseeing the district's Title I funding. "So what we said is, 'You can suggest a program. You can tell parents what you are offering.' And, again, these are going to sound like little petty things but, in most instances, we do provide snacks for the kids. That's not offered in other places for the kids."[18]

Very few parents requested to meet with their principal. According to Elaine de Araujo, principal of Harlow Street Elementary School, "Nobody has wanted to change. Not one parent has come forward. If you were here, you would see why. You would see what a nurturing, wonderful place this is."[19] Ruthann Melancon, the principal of Elm Park Elementary School, notes that "a couple of parents came to me thinking that the school was going to close. I sat down with these sets of parents and reassured them. They've been here since preschool and they have liked what they've seen."[20]

It is not difficult to ascertain why so few parents are requesting meetings with their principals. Notes Roberta Schaefer, a member of the state board of education and executive director of the Worcester Regional Research Bureau,

> If you told me I had to go to the principal [if I wanted to switch school], that's the first issue. Because if you [as a parent] think there's a problem, that's the source of the problem. Why would you go there? You have to have some kind of independent agency, a third party you can speak to. Why would I go to the principal? I'm in effect saying, principal, you're not serving my kid well. You set up a confrontation right there. So I can imagine, if that's the first step, how many parents are going to go? . . . It's designed to fail, right away. Nobody is going to do that.[21]

The process of switching out of underperforming schools, however, extends beyond this initial meeting. If after consulting with the school principal parents still want to change schools, they must schedule yet another meeting at the Parent Information Center. Robert Vartanian claims that he has met with just two families interested in NCLB choice, and only one of the families ended up switching their child to a different school. Each time, Vartanian takes the opportunity to reiterate many of the points that principals made during their meetings with parents. He notes that parents who switch schools forfeit their rights to free supplemental services; that their neighborhood public school is implementing any number of reforms to improve itself; and that additional disruptions to students' educational lives may not be in their best interests. Perhaps most importantly, though, Vartanian informs parents that the district may not be able to accommodate their request to attend any specific school. Indeed, as the district is obligated only to offer parents a choice of two schools that made AYP, that is all they can expect to receive. Further, there are no guarantees that either of these schools will be near the family's home or that transportation will be provided over the longer term of a child's education. As Fitton explains, "The feds told us we had to offer a choice—not the parent's choice, but a choice."

What Parents Know and Want

Because the district controls much of the information flow, and because the law is still relatively new, many parents in Worcester simply do not know about NCLB's choice and supplemental services provisions. Here, I draw upon the results from a telephone survey administered during the summer of 2003 to a stratified random sample of a thousand public school parents in the ten largest Massachusetts districts.[22] Chapter 8 explains in greater detail how these data were collected; because it considers observations collected across the state, chapter 8 presents findings from analyses that are not possible to conduct for the subsample of 250 Worcester respondents.[23] Nonetheless, some simple descriptive statistics reveal additional reasons why NCLB has not caught on in Worcester. Specifically, those parents who were most likely to qualify for NCLB's choice and supplemental services provisions were least likely to know the status of their child's school; and parents generally expressed ambivalence about the new schooling options that the law provides.

At first blush, parents in Worcester appear to know a fair amount about NCLB. Consider the results presented in table 11.1. Among those surveyed, 68 percent claimed to have heard of the act; 50 percent claimed to know about the option of switching from an underperforming school to one that

Table 11.1. Knowledge of NCLB in Worcester

	Percent responding affirmatively	
Parents claimed to have heard of:		
No Child Left Behind act	68.0	[250]
Act's choice provisions	50.0	[250]
Act's supplemental services provisions	38.8	[250]
Source of information about act (in order asked):		
Friend/family	2.9	
PTA/other parents	5.3	
School district	26.5	
Newspaper/television/radio	54.1	
Internet	1.2	
Work	4.7	
Community organization	1.8	
Church	0.6	
Other	3.0	
Total	100.0	[170]

Number of observations reported in brackets. Source question asked only of those parents who claimed to have heard of NCLB.

made AYP; and 39 percent claimed to have heard about the availability of supplemental services. Of those who claimed to have heard about NCLB, 54 percent received their information from the media, 26 percent from the school district, 5 percent from other parents, 5 percent from their place of employment, and the rest from other assorted sources.

Overall, 25 percent of parents surveyed in Worcester had children who attended underperforming schools. When asked whether their child's school was on the list of underperforming schools, however, only 6 percent of parents responded affirmatively; 54 percent claimed that their school made AYP, and 41 percent said that they did not know. Among those who claimed to know whether their child's school was on the list of underperforming schools, 32 percent received their information from the newspaper or television news, 21 percent directly from the school, 9 percent from the district, 5 percent from other parents, 2 percent from the internet, 1 percent from a friend, and the rest did not know the source of the information.

Considerable confusion persists about some basic points of fact. Because the survey asked for the name of the school that each child attended, I was able to check parents' responses. The results are alarming. Only 49 percent of surveyed parents in Worcester correctly identified whether their child's school made AYP. Among those who claimed to know, 18 percent of parents incorrectly identified the status of their school. Curiously, parents who received their information directly from the school district were 9 percentage points less likely to identify the status of their school correctly than were parents who received their information from other outlets.

Though parents of children at performing and underperforming schools were equally likely to claim that they knew about the choice and supplemental services provisions of NCLB, they were not equally likely to know whether in fact they qualified for them. Indeed, as table 11.2 shows, 62 percent of parents with children in schools that made AYP correctly identified their school's status, as compared with just 7 percent of parents with children in schools deemed in need of improvement. *Fully 93 percent of parents of children in Worcester public schools that failed to make AYP either did not know that their school was deemed in need of improvement, or incorrectly thought that their child in fact attended a school that made AYP.* Plainly, when hazarding a guess, many parents probably presumed that their child's school was not on the list of underperforming schools; as such, parents in schools that made AYP may have been more likely to guess correctly than parents in schools that did not.[24] Still, the sheer magnitude of the observed differences raises serious concerns about the quality of the information disseminated to parents in underperforming schools.[25]

Table 11.2. Parents who correctly identified whether their child's school made AYP

	Percent Correct
School status	
Parents of child attending performing school	62.0 [179]
Parents of child attending underperforming school	7.3 [55]
Ethnicity	
Whites	53.6 [196]
African Americans + Hispanics	28.0 [25]
Place of Birth	
Born U.S.	52.4 [206]
Foreign born	25.9 [27]
English	
Primary language	50.9 [222]
Secondary language	16.7 [12]
Education	
Graduated from 4-year college	58.5 [106]
Some college or less	41.4 [128]
Home ownership	
Home owner	54.4 [182]
Renter	30.4 [46]
Marital status	
Married	51.3 [187]
Single	41.5 [41]

Number of observations reported in brackets.

As one might expect, informational disparities often broke down along socio-demographic lines. Again, look at table 11.2. Whereas 54 percent of whites knew whether their child attended an underperforming school, just 28 percent of African Americans and Hispanics did. Only 26 percent of parents born outside of the United States and 17 percent of parents of children who receive instruction in English as a second language knew whether their school was underperforming. Just 41 percent of parents who did not graduate from a four-year college correctly identified their schools' status, as compared with 58 percent of parents who had. Startlingly, only 30 percent of renters correctly identified their school's status under NCLB, as compared with 54 percent of homeowners. For single and married adults, the figures were 41 and 51 percent respectively.

If NCLB is to liberate students trapped in failing schools, it is not enough for parents simply to know about the options available to them. Parents also must want them. Relative to parents in Worcester's performing schools, parents in underperforming schools express slightly more interest in leaving. But in absolute terms, both populations appear fairly content in their current schools. Table 11.3 presents the relevant survey findings. When asked whether there was another public school in the district that they would rather their child attend, 8 percent of parents with children in schools that made AYP responded affirmatively, as compared with 13 percent of students in underperforming schools. Eleven percent of both groups claimed that they would prefer to send their child to a public school in another district; and 6 and 4 percent claimed that they would rather send their child to a charter school in the district. Consistent with these responses, parents generally appear to be satisfied with their public schools. Eighty-seven percent of parents with children in schools that made AYP gave their school an "A" or a "B," as did 80 percent of parents with children in underperforming schools.

Interest in alternative educational settings, however, spikes when the conversation turns to private schools, a schooling option NCLB does not afford. Fully 58 percent of parents with children in underperforming schools claim that they would rather send their child to a private school, as compared with 39 percent of parents with children in schools that made AYP. When asked "if costs were not an obstacle, which type of school would you most like your child to attend," 49 percent of parents with children in underperforming schools picked a private school, 44 percent a public school in their district, 4 percent a public school outside of the district, and just 2 percent a charter school. By comparison, 37 percent of parents with children in schools

Table 11.3. Parental interest in alternative schooling options

	Parent with child currently attending . . .			
	an underperforming school		a performing school	
Would prefer that child attends:	(percent)		(percent)	
Different public school in same district	12.7	[55]	7.8	[179]
Different public school in different district	10.9	[55]	11.2	[179]
Charter school	4.0	[50]	6.1	[163]
Private school	58.2	[55]	38.6	[179]
Most preferred type of school for child:				
Public school in same district	43.6		50.3	
Public school in different district	3.6		5.0	
Charter school	1.8		2.2	
Private school	49.1		37.4	
Don't know	1.8		5.0	
Total	100.0	[55]	100.0	[179]
Give current school an "A" or a "B"	80.0	[55]	87.2	[179]

Number of observations reported in brackets.

that made AYP preferred to send their child to a private school, 50 percent a public school in their district, 5 percent a public school in another district, and just 2 percent a charter school.

The clause "if costs were not an obstacle" apparently freed up some parents' imaginations to consider elite (read expensive) private schools. When asked to name a preferred private school, roughly half named independent private schools (the most popular being Worcester Academy and Milton Academy) with tuitions that eclipse the monetary values of even the most generous school vouchers offered in public and private programs around the country. The rest identified a Catholic or Protestant day school, most of which were located within the city of Worcester.

Misalignments of information with eligible families and interests with schooling options have effectively limited NCLB's influence in Worcester. Those parents who qualify for public school choice and supplemental services are least likely to know it—unbelievably, less than one in ten parents with children in schools that failed to make AYP could correctly identify their school's status. Meanwhile, Worcester parents are most interested in pursuing schooling alternatives that NCLB does not furnish. Though parents with children in underperforming schools are slightly more likely to want to switch to another public school in the district than parents with children in performing schools, the vast majority would much prefer an area private school.

Private Providers Standing on the Sidelines

The state government in Massachusetts generates lists of approved supplemental service providers for each district and monitors the quality of services they render. As of November 2003, the state had contracted with nine for-profit companies and three not-for-profit organizations; nine of these operate in Worcester.[26] In addition, the state has also authorized six districts, including Worcester, to compete with these private providers; because the relevant portion of Title I funding flows through the district, and not the school, supplemental services can be provided at the same underperforming schools that qualifying students attend.

The job of placing students in individual programs, meanwhile, falls on districts. Though the state approves providers and maintains information about each on its website, districts retain the responsibility of notifying parents at least once a year of the available services. If requested by parents, districts must also assist them in choosing a provider and "apply fair and equitable procedures if requests exceed provider spaces or funding requirements."[27] Though the state does collect some basic information about the progress of students receiving supplemental services, it has not instituted a formal review process to ensure that districts are cooperating with private providers and relaying information about their services to parents.

Given minimal state oversight, districts hold captive their clientele. They can wax eloquent about the benefits of their own programs directly (and repeatedly) to parents while giving short shrift to private providers, who have few opportunities to interject. As Seppy Basili, the vice president of Kaplan K12 Learning Services, notes: "The school district is the owner of the relationship between provider and the parent. And I can't get in."[28] Private providers do not even know who in the public school population receives Title I funding. Companies, as such, must rely on the district and its representatives to present their services to parents in a favorable light, which is akin to asking a BMW dealer to extol the benefits of buying a Volvo.

Curiously, though, private providers are not complaining. At least not publicly, and at least not yet. For some companies that provide private tutoring, the money involved ($1,238 per year per student in Worcester) simply is not sufficient to warrant serious investment. Huntington Learning Centers, which has the distinct honor of serving the only Worcester student to receive supplemental education services outside the public school system,[29] typically contracts with families for 100 to 150 hours of individual tutoring. The Title I money allotted by the state for supplemental services, however, covers only 30 to 40 hours of tutoring, which would require either an abbreviated or an entirely restructured program. Notes Mark Shobin, the owner of three Huntington franchises in Massachusetts:

> "From a financial perspective, it doesn't make sense for us to try to corral these students into our program. We are happy to work with and develop programs for those students who seek us out. But I am not going to seek them out . . . Also, ethically, this isn't something I'm very comfortable with. In 30 hours, I can help a student improve his reading by one full grade level, but at Huntington we are committed to doing much more than that. I feel uncomfortable putting together a program that doesn't meet our usual standards."[30]

With few vacancies in their existing programs, other private providers do not appear bothered by the district's efforts to cordon off Title I students at underperforming schools. For the most part, providers lack the staff and building facilities required to accommodate a major influx of new students. Without assurances that the law will be strengthened so that providers can communicate directly with parents, few appear willing to devote the resources required to lure students away from their public school programs. Says Basili: "Right now,

I can't handle more than a couple thousand students nationwide. If a district did not get back to us, then I didn't follow up. Cambridge, Somerville, they got back to us early, and we are there as a result. If we can't find a way to get in easy, we're just not going to bother. It's not because we're a bad provider, it's just an awfully big boulder to roll uphill." Providers' short-term strategy, as such, is to work with those families and districts that come forward, and to ignore the rest.

As previously indicated, the state government in Massachusetts oversees the approval process of private providers. While this procedure obviously alleviates some of the related hassles of negotiating separate contracts with separate districts, it also inhibits local market penetration. Having not chosen them, school committee members, superintendents, and principals are unlikely to promote private providers' services enthusiastically. As NCLB's choice provisions are currently constituted, the best chances for private providers to make inroads are via cooperative endeavors with districts—wherein, in exchange for Title I funding, companies boost student test scores so as to ward off more draconian penalties (corrective action and restructuring) that await schools that fail to reach AYP for four and five years. As long as state governments retain sole discretion to determine who can, and who cannot, offer supplemental services that satisfy NCLB, private providers will lose much of the flexibility required to forge relationships with districts and develop strategies for addressing the particular needs of a public school's population.

Two final problems are worth recognizing. First, private providers are paid only for those sessions that a student attends. Unlike many dentists and doctors, private providers are not remunerated when a client skips an appointment. To acquire the full sum of the Title I funds, therefore, providers typically must schedule more hours than the contract stipulates. Many also rely upon bribes. Kaplan, for instance, gives its students in New York City two movie tickets after they attend 15 hours of after-school services; two more after 20 hours; and a gift certificate to a record store after 25 hours. Plainly, such enticements eat away at profit margins, discouraging providers from aggressively pursuing students at underperforming schools who qualify for supplemental services. But without offering incentives that boost attendance, providers cannot be sure that the state will pay them the full amount of a student's Title I funding.

Transportation problems further inhibit parental interest in private providers. Those students who receive supplemental services from the Worcester public school district remain at their home institution throughout the entire school day; students who receive supplemental services from private providers, meanwhile, must find a way to travel across town. "We don't provide transportation for supplemental services," explains Joan Fitton. "And neither do the supplemental service providers provide transportation. So, there, right away, is a big glitch in the whole program. We're not required to provide transportation. And, to be honest, to send money out of the district, I'm not sure that we would even offer to do that." As long as a child continues with her own school's program, the parent does not need to worry about transporting her across town to receive services, just as the district does not need to worry about losing the money attached to her.

Over time, of course, much can change. The state has recommended, but not mandated, that districts offer mailing services to those private providers that wish to contact parents whose children are eligible for supplemental services, a move that might enhance the range of educational possibilities that are presented to children attending schools deemed in need of improvement.[31] As has already occurred in a few Massachusetts districts, local public school officials may enlist the aid of select private providers in an effort to boost student test scores. (In Boston and Springfield, for instance, 771 and 723 students receive supplemental services from such private providers as Catapult (formerly Sylvan), Kaplan, Citizens Schools, and the Bell Foundation.) And in time, capacity and transportation difficulties may ease, as private providers make the investments required to hire new staff and bus children after school to their sessions. Up until now, though, each of these factors has discouraged providers from entering Worcester and deterred public school parents from pursuing after-school educational programs outside of their public schools.

The Road Ahead

Thus far, high mobility rates, local political opposition, and lack of information have all conspired to mute the effects of NCLB's choice provisions in Worcester. Assuredly, some of these problems will work themselves out in time. As private providers advertise their services and as media outlets continue to report on school performance rankings, information about and interest in NCLB's choice options may spread. Eventually, parents may even conceive of new rights to select schools, a development that should accelerate the process of change. But a basic challenge confronts the federal government and will continue to do so as long as demands for state oversight and accountability butt up against the realities of local school control. Districts, in short, have few incentives to fully implement and faithfully execute

NCLB—and absent wholesale changes in the federal government's involvement in public education, little can be done about it.

In our system of separated and federated powers, as scholars have long recognized, few laws are self-executing. Congress and the president may mandate change, but ultimately both depend on others to implement the law, to interpret its meanings, and to redirect the doings of government. Unfortunately, rarely do the intentions of those who write laws perfectly match the interests of those who implement them. To ensure compliance among departments and agencies within the executive branch, therefore, Congress and the president must occasionally fire officials, slash budgets, relocate operations to others parts of the federal government, and restructure lines of authority. The challenges of ensuring that the Environmental Protection Agency or the State Department stays on track, however, pale in comparison to those that arise when 50 states, and almost fifteen thousand school districts, are charged with implementing NCLB. For here, the law plainly offends many of those charged with implementation, and the only leverage the federal government has to demand change comes with the modest education funds it willingly distributes.

It is sheer folly to expect districts to implement vigorously an accountability scheme that disrupts their school assignment procedures, draws money away from their coffers, and threatens to eradicate schools' administrative autonomy. Facing penalties, schools, like all bureaucratic entities, will resist. Many will do the absolute minimum that the law requires of them. If NCLB requires that parents at underperforming schools be offered at least two options, two is all they will get. When communicating with parents, districts will downplay the new education options created under the law, just as they celebrate every positive development within their own schools. And though they may introduce new policies and personnel that create impressions of reform, districts reliably will fight on behalf of their fundamental interests, foremost among them being the preservation of their financial resources and their institutional autonomy.

In Worcester, distrust of NCLB runs rampant. Though many principals freely extol the benefits of using student achievement data as diagnostic tools, officials downtown remain deeply suspicious of the longer-term consequences that accompany repeated failures to make AYP. Notes Caradonio: "We're screwed. This whole thing has been set up to make sure it looks bad so we can bring in the miracle drugs, the vouchers, and all this is very clear." School committee member Kathleen Toomey expressed much the same sentiment to the city newspaper, though she saw a different cavalry of education reformers on the horizon. "[NCLB] is one way to promote flight out of city schools. Proponents of charter schools will be able to say, 'Look, see, those public schools are not working.' "[32] Many local officials have assumed a defensive posture, poised to circumvent a law that they perceive as designed to set them up for failure.

Given such widespread distrust, it is hardly surprising that Worcester offers the minimally required number of options to parents, sets tight deadlines for parents applying to switch schools, creates onerous procedures for interested parents to follow, and offers few (if any) guarantees that students will attend a preferred public school. Moreover, none of these actions violate state or federal NCLB requirements. So far as I can tell, the district has done nothing that explicitly violates the law. Indeed, to hold on to its students and the money that is attached to them, the district has not had to. There remain ample opportunities for blunting NCLB's local effects while still operating well within the letter of the law.

The future, meanwhile, does not look especially bright. As increasing numbers of schools are deemed in need of improvement (as inevitably will occur, given that schools in 2003 will be held accountable for the performance not just of students as a whole, but also all qualifying subgroups of students), and as penalties become stiffer (which will occur as well, given that some schools are approaching their fourth year of failing to reach AYP), efforts to deflect the law will only intensify. James Peyser, former Massachusetts board of education chair, anticipates that "districts may redefine the meaning of a school, making failing schools 'off campuses' of successful schools. They may start to create schools within schools, substituting intraschool choice for district choice. . . . And if we really have volume issues, where demand far exceeds physical capacity, then you can expect real avoidance strategies. Schools might close temporarily and then reopen under a new name, giving them a clean slate to work off of."[33] The detail and care put into NCLB, which currently runs in excess of a thousand pages, may only be matched by the creativity with which districts try to disassemble it.

Some short-term solutions may reduce shirking. For starters, it is nonsensical to make the district the messenger of NCLB's choice provisions. Without an independent organization disseminating information and assisting public school parents in matching the needs of their children with available educational opportunities, parents are not likely to leave failing schools in droves. Notes Roberta Schaefer: "I don't know of a parent advisory committee that is providing information about underperforming schools and the options that parents have. The Parent Information Center is supposed to provide information to parents, but based on incidents on which I'm familiar, it seems that it advocates on behalf of the district."[34] Until an independent organization is established that disseminates information about which schools are underperforming, which students qualify for choice and supplemental services, and which providers are available, there is little reason to expect that NCLB will induce an exodus of students from underperforming schools and an outpouring of demand for private supplemental services.

In addition, the state department of education needs to do a better job of meeting federal guidelines for identifying underperforming public schools. Up until now, the state has released its lists of underperforming public schools during the middle of an academic calendar, precisely the time when parents are least likely to pull their child out of her current school, and schools are least equipped to accommodate student transfers. Unless lists are released during the summer months, transfer rates, which currently are less than one percent among the statewide eligible population, will remain extremely low.

Even if an independent agency assumes the responsibilities of disseminating information to Worcester parents, and even if lists of underperforming schools are released during the summer months, we are not likely to witness a massive reallocation of students and resources. The district will continue to pursue its strategies of blame avoidance. If the survey results are any indication, few qualifying families appear likely to switch to a different public school. And as the number of schools that fail to make AYP rises, so in direct proportion will the number of remaining educational options that families can choose among dwindle. Ironically, attempts to erect strict standards and to protect the interests of various ethnic minorities and students with special needs may undermine their opportunities for genuine school choice. There is little reason to expect this round of education reform to look much different from past efforts: namely, considerable fuss and funds in the service of marginal change.

Having begun with Superintendent Caradonio, it only seems appropriate that we end with him. Reflecting on what lies ahead for NCLB, he wondered:

> "Will there be a learning curve? Will there be a feedback loop? Will we learn? Implementation is a learning experience. So, will we learn? We didn't learn before. We just legislated. Shot an arrow in the air. 'Well, I think it should be blue. Well I think it should be white. I think it should be black. Well, we'll make it gray.' Now we found out that the real thing, it should have been purple. Will we make it purple? I don't know."

If they are to make more headway in the next two years than they have in the last, proponents of NCLB will either have to convince the likes of Caradonio that they have remade the law purple, or they will need to restructure its implementation so that his views on the matter become less influential.

Notes

1. Personal interview with Joseph Caradonio, August 19, 2003.
2. Massachusetts evaluates schools in two-year cycles, under an accountability system that predates NCLB. Hence, students attending schools identified in Cycle I have the option of switching to a different public school in the district, and students who qualify for federal Title I funding and who attend schools identified in Cycle II have access to supplemental services. Statewide, 209 out of 1,571 rated schools failed to make AYP for two years, 194 of which have a sufficiently high proportion of low income students to qualify as Title I schools. Four of the 12 public schools that failed to make AYP in Worcester—Forest Grove Middle School, Worcester East Middle School, Burncoat Middle, and Sullivan Middle—were not Title I schools.
3. Telephone interview with John Monfredo, September 18, 2003.
4. Personal interview with Timothy Murray, August 19, 2003.
5. Mindy Spencer provided invaluable research and administrative assistance on this project. The American Enterprise Institute provided financial assistance. Joseph Caradonio, Rachelle Engler, Joan Fitton, Judith Reardon, and Roberta Schaefer stand out among the many cooperative public officials who were consulted. Standard disclaimers apply.
6. By comparison, 26,594 students were enrolled in Springfield public schools in the 2002–2003 school year, and 61,522 were enrolled in Boston's. Because of budget constraints, three elementary schools—Greendale, Granite Street, and Adams Street—were closed in Worcester for the 2003–2004 school year.
7. All demographic data supplied by the Massachusetts Department of Education.
8. Since 1999, the cost of housing in Worcester has increased markedly. By some accounts, as of 2003 median single-family home sales jumped to $180,000. See www.thewarrengroup.com.
9. Twenty-one percent of families with children under 18 years of age are below the poverty level, as are 24 percent of families with children under age 5.
10. Sources: National Center for Education Statistics, U.S. Department of Education, Bureau of the Census, and U.S. Department of Commerce.
11. All data on mobility rates provided by the Worcester public school district.
12. Personal interview with Bryan O'Connell, August 26, 2003.
13. During the 2001–2002 academic year, Worcester sent 154 of its students to surrounding school districts; Worcester does not currently receive students from these districts. See "Mapping School Choice in Massachusetts: Data and Findings 2003," Center for Education Research and Policy at MassINC, The Boston Foundation, Boston, Massachusetts.
14. Personal interview with Robert Vartanian, July 30, 2003.
15. Other districts with "deisolation" plans include Boston, Brockton, Cambridge, Chelsea, Fall River, Fitchburg, Framingham, Holyoke, Lawrence, Lowell, Lynn, Malden, Medford, Methuen, New Bedford, Northampton, Revere, Salem,

Somerville, Springfield, and Waltham. See http://list.terc.edu/pipermail/masspip/2000-March/000017.html.

16. The last several years, the state of Massachusetts announced the list of underperforming school in the winter or early spring, forcing students to either forestall choice until the summer or to pick up and move in the middle of the school year.

17. Letter to parents/guardians of students in Worcester public schools in need of improvement, dated June 2003, from Dr. Stephen E. Mills, deputy superintendent for teaching accountability and learning.

18. Personal interview with Joan Fitton, August 19, 2003.

19. Telephone interview with Elaine de Araujo, September 15, 2003.

20. Telephone interview with Ruthann Melancon, September 15, 2003. Under NCLB, both Harlow Street and Elm Park have failed to reach AYP every single year that the schools have been evaluated.

21. Telephone interview with Robert Schafer, May 12, 2003.

22. The author gratefully recognizes the financial and administrative support of the Pioneer Institute in Boston, Massachusetts, for making it possible to conduct the survey. Stephen Adams, Kathryn Ciffolillo, Elena Llaudet, and Kit Nichols provided especially helpful feedback and support. Opinion Dynamics in Cambridge, Massachusetts, administered the survey.

23. Some of the findings presented in this section rest upon relatively small numbers of observations. Except where noted, however, all are consistent with those found for the larger Massachusetts population.

24. See chapter 8 for a longer discussion of this and related issues.

25. Differences in information levels of parents in Worcester's performing and underperforming schools extend beyond their knowledge of their child's school's status under NCLB. Whereas 63 percent of parents at public schools that made AYP were able to correctly name their child's principal, only 45 percent of parents with children at underperforming schools could do so. Similarly, when asked about the size of their child's school, 43 percent of parents of children at performing schools picked the right population range, compared with 34 percent of parents of children in underperforming schools. (Again, to determine whether parents answered these questions correctly, survey responses were compared with administrative records.) And as they did with knowledge about whether a school made AYP, differences tended to break down along the lines of ethnicity, education, home ownership, and involvement in a child's school. The one exception concerns gender. Whereas men and women were about equally likely to know if their child's school was underperforming and the size of their child's school, women were fully 20 percentage points more likely to know the name of their child's principal.

26. Brainfuse (The Trustforte Corporation), EdSolutions, Kaplan K12 Learning Services, Knowledge Connection, Kumon North America, Platform Learning, Princeton Review, and the Summit Educational Group are available to serve Worcester public school students.

27. See http://www.doe.mass.edu/ses/.

28. Telephone Interview with Seppi Basili, September 15, 2003.

29. This child received supplemental services from Huntington Learning Centers during the summer of 2003. Because Huntington is not an approved provider in Worcester, however, the district has notified this child's family that he must select an alternative provider.

30. Personal interview with Mark Shobin, August 19, 2003.

31. Thus far, no private providers have requested this assistance in Worcester.

32. As quoted in Clive McFarlane, "New Statute May Swell School-Transfer Ranks." *Worcester Telegram and Gazette,* December 22, 2002, p. A1.

33. Personal interview with James Peyser, May 15, 2003.

34. Telephone interview with Roberta Schaefer, April 7, 2004.

12

Montgomery County: A Tale of School Choice

Douglas S. Reed[1]

Introduction

This is a story of a national school reform unfolding in a single school district, Montgomery County Public Schools in Maryland. It is a story of school choice as formulated by Congress, as understood by district officials, and as exercised by parents. Telling this story requires that we understand several dimensions of educational decision making: the decisions of district officials confronted with a perhaps unwanted, but important and serious, task; the decisions of parents (and children) at the schools where choice is now available, who must decide whether to leave or to stay; and finally the actions and decisions of children and parents at the receiving schools, whose own characteristics and demographics affect both the policymakers' decisions and the decisions of the parents and students offered school choice. It is a story told here through the re-creation of the decision-making processes of these individuals, as informed by the information they had at their disposal. The story does not pretend to depict any individual's actual conduct but is drawn from an in-depth quantitative and geographic analysis of the effects of their decisions over the past two years. The reconstruction of their logic is drawn exclusively from the aggregate data produced by the completion of those tasks and their decisions about schooling choices.

This local story of NCLB school choice consists of four acts. "In Fair Montgomery" provides important scene and plot information about Montgomery County Public Schools and school choice, as implemented in No Child Left Behind. "The Receivers' Tale" attempts to identify the relevant criteria used by district officials to select the "sending" and "receiving" schools under this new scheme of federally mandated school choice. "The Travelers' Tales" seeks to document the characteristics of those who (a) decided to take up the offer of choice, (b) declined to do so, and (c) exercised choice, but decided not to pursue it after one year. This section also offers a few comments on the provision of supplemental education services to Title I students in the school system. "Lessons Learned" provides the moral of our story, thus far. This section examines how the challenges that the Montgomery County school district confronted intersect with the individual preferences of those inclined to exercise choice to produce outcomes that, at this juncture in the story, are sharply at odds with the goals of No Child Left Behind.

In the course of this analysis, I draw heavily on a geographic information system analysis of the demographics of school attendance zones in this district and demographic data for real schoolchildren, sometimes aggregated up to the school level. These two tools help tell a story of both the bureaucratic considerations in the implementation of that choice and the characteristics of individual preferences in the exercise of school choice. Because the actual story is still unfolding, and this is only one chapter of the broader narrative of No Child Left Behind, it is premature to write the final act. Nonetheless, there are still lessons to be learned from the drama thus far.

In Fair Montgomery: The Contexts of NCLB School Choice

Among the nation's school districts, Montgomery County's is atypical. With more than 139,000 students, it is larger than 95 percent of the nation's school districts. Fifty-five percent of its students are non-white, and no racial or ethnic group is in the majority. Its per-pupil spending levels are comparatively high; $10,577 in 1999–2000, some 53 percent higher than the national average of $6,911 that same year. Finally, its test scores are consistently higher than national averages. The 2003 results on the norm-referenced California Test of Basic Skills put the district's fourth-graders at the 74th percentile nationally for language skills and the 78th percentile for mathematics. In sum, the Montgomery district is larger, less white, more affluent, and higher-performing than the majority of the nation's schools districts.

At first glance, these characteristics suggest that the No Child Left Behind Act of 2001 would have a substantial effect on the district. Because of the attention that NCLB pays to the test-score gap among white and minority students, as well as the required disaggregation of test-score results by limited English proficiency (LEP) and poverty status (students eligible for free and reduced-price lunch), Montgomery County's story could be one of the educational haves being confronted by the underperformance of the educational have-nots. The accountability mechanisms of No Child Left Behind open the possibility that any sizeable test-score gap could bring significant federally mandated changes to what is generally regarded as a well-run, highly performing, and generously resourced district. This chapter will explore the likelihood of those changes by examining the ways that the choice mechanism has been implemented in this district and whether the operation of the NCLB choice mechanism has produced substantial change in school attendance patterns or district policies. In a nutshell, my findings are that choice has not substantially changed the attendance patterns in Montgomery County Public Schools and has not induced significant policy change. In fact, the operation of NCLB choice at Title I schools may exacerbate disparities in racial and economic attendance patterns in the district.

In 2003–2004, the district had 18 Title I schools, all of them elementary schools (out of a total of 125 elementary schools, four of which are special-education schools). Ten of those 18 were identified previously by the state as needing improvement. The 18 Title I schools enrolled a little more than nine thousand students in 2001–2002, or roughly 7 percent of all students in the district. The 10 designated as in need of improvement enrolled approximately sixty-two hundred students for the same year. For the 2003–2004 school year, the district received $14.6 million in Title I funds, which amounts to less than 1 percent of its $1.5 billon dollar operating budget. Despite this relatively minor role that Title I funds and schools play in the school system, NCLB has sought to exert a disproportionate influence over district policies.

After the enactment of NCLB, the district embarked on an effort in the spring of 2002 to identify both the participants in school choice and the schools to which they would transfer. The rollout for the choice plan began in April 2002 when district officials met with the principals of both the sending schools (identified by the state as Title I schools with failing test scores for two consecutive years) and receiving schools. At that meeting, district officials provided an overview of the enrollment options for Title I students, distributed a sample letter of invitation to sending-school parents, provided sample agendas for informational meetings to be held at both sending and receiving schools, and even provided a sample school newsletter item about the program. The letter of invitation was, according to the superintendent's office, translated into seven different languages.

Accompanying the letter of invitation sent home to parents at all ten Title I schools designated as in need of improvement was a brochure titled "Answers to Questions about My School and the Title I Enrollment Option." That document describes "special efforts under way" in the sending schools to improve school performance and details the process of applying for school choice. It also states that some students will have priority over others (students who are identified as low performing and low income) and lists which schools the students would be eligible to attend. The brochure also states that transportation will be provided to the receiving school, but warns that "the distance between sending and receiving schools may be lengthy since students will no longer be attending their neighborhood school. The number of students participating also will affect the length of the ride."[2] In response to the question "Will transportation always be provided?" the document further states: "Not necessarily. Transportation service to the receiving school is provided only as long as your current home school remains involved in the Title I Enrollment Option program."[3] In effect, if a student's home school improved enough to meet AYP, the district would no longer bus that child to his or her choice school. The child could, however, continue to attend the choice school—she would just have to find her own way to school.

The enrollment period for parents at Title I schools in the first year, ran for a month from May 10 to June 10. Between May 16 and May 29, each sending school held an evening informational session for parents, with translators available for non–English speakers. High-level district officials described the plan and answered parents' questions. At those meetings, officials described the offerings that were available at the neighborhood Title I school and those at the designated receiving schools. For example, the Title I schools have a full-day kindergarten, but the rest of kindergartens are only half-day programs. Similarly, the Title I schools have extensive summer programs that are unavailable at the receiving schools. Informational sessions were also held at each of the receiving schools between May 30 and June 11. Parents had a full month to complete the applications, with the applications due in mid-June as the school year drew to a close. The district also allowed new students, just moving into the school attendance zone to apply late to the NCLB choice program. Parents were notified of the results of the application in July. As one district official put it, "We wanted the transportation piece of all this settled [by August] so that when kids started school they knew exactly where to catch the bus and where to go." At first, district officials worried that they would have to rank applicants (per U.S. Department of Education guidelines) by poverty and achievement levels, if too many applied for the spaces available. But because fewer than anticipated students applied, such a ranking was not necessary.

Indeed, on June 17, 2002, Superintendent Jerry D. Weast sent a memo to the members of the Montgomery County Board of Education indicating that requests for student transfers were not sweeping the Title I schools. The memo detailed the results of the application process, noting that a total of 118 students had applied prior to the June 10 deadline. A week later, Weast wrote another memo to the Board of Education, indicating that 16 requests had been withdrawn by parents. Wrote Weast, "Altogether, there are now just 102 students from more than 6,000 students enrolled in the 10 participating schools who have applied for the option, reflecting less than 2 percent of the students in these schools." He adds a few lines later, "Further reductions are anticipated when parents are asked later this summer to confirm their child's placement at the receiving schools."[4]

In the second year, 2003–2004, students at the same ten Title I schools were again eligible for choice. This was the result of a decision by Maryland State Department of Education officials to not add any new schools to the "needs improvement" list because of NCLB-required changes in the testing instrument. This shift from a school-level to an individual-level assessment meant there was no basis for comparing 2002 and 2003 test results. Consequently, no new schools will be added to the "needs improvement" list in Maryland until the 2004 test results are known. In Montgomery County, the choice enrollment process looked very much the same in the second year as in the first, the only significant change being that the cycle began a month earlier, with parents at Title I schools mailed an information packet in early April. The application period ran from April 21 to May 21, with informational sessions held in late April and early May. Overall, district officials thought the choice recruitment process went well. "We probably did more than we had to," said one official. "And I'm pretty sure we did more than most other districts." She indicated that the process of setting up the choice mechanisms took extensive planning, but, "once it's up, it's a straightforward process of implementation."

In general, the county's actions can probably best be read as reluctant but significant compliance with the requirements of NCLB's choice provisions. In the public announcement of the Title I choice program, district officials indicated that "the immediate school system goal is to improve the academic progress of the 10 schools so that they no longer qualify for the enrollment option." While the goal of improving academic progress is undoubtedly laudable, the district's language seems to indicate that the elimination of choice is as great a priority. Other indications that the district would rather not engage the choice option can be found in the warnings to parents at Title I schools that enrichment programs, such as after-school programs, summer programs and accelerated instructional programs, are limited to Title I schools: "Most of these special services," reads a press release from April 2003, "were not available at the designated receiving schools."[5]

Part of the district's reluctance to embrace choice may have stemmed from concerns over public reactions to the system of sending and receiving schools. The designation of receiving schools was, on its face, the result of a neutral calculus of space and educational performance. Indeed, the official language of the brochures released to parents indicates that receiving schools were selected according to several objective criteria. To be considered for receiving-school status, a school's performance index needed to be above the state average, based on attendance and test scores, and its current enrollment could be no more than 95 percent of its official capacity. In addition, the district considered transportation time, but excluded potential receiving schools if they were "involved in, or considered for, boundary changes."[6] These official objective criteria, however, do not necessarily indicate why any *particular* receiving school was chosen, among all the schools that met the selection criteria. Nor do we know if these stated criteria overlap with other significant demographic or testing criteria. To answer those questions, we have to engage in a kind of "reverse engineering" of the selection process by mapping out how particular school attendance zones fare against others in an iterative process of receiving-school selection. This identification of other schools that meet the formal criteria but were not chosen as receiving schools can help us illuminate some of the obstacles to the implementation of NCLB school choice.

The Receivers' Tale

Consider the task of the school official or officials who were responsible for implementing the federal requirement of school choice in Montgomery County's Title I schools. (For simplicity's sake, let us assume that this task was the responsibility of one person—clearly an erroneous assumption in a district as large and complex as Montgomery County Public Schools.) A number of issues had to be confronted. First, the formal requirements of NCLB placed restrictions on the implementation of the choice mechanism. Those requirements meant that any Title I school currently designated as "in need of improvement" under existing state assessments had to offer school choice to its students. Based on prior years' test results, ten Title I schools in the district had previously been designated by the state as in need of improvement and were therefore immediately required to offer options to their students. In short, the sending school designation was very simple. These ten sending schools are concentrated into two clusters. The first, in the southeastern portion of the county, relatively close to the District of Columbia, centers on the Silver Spring and Wheaton areas. Silver Spring is home to a long-standing African American community, and Wheaton houses many new immigrants, many from Central and Latin America. Both areas have relatively high concentrations of students who are learning English and students who are poor. The other cluster lies farther north, centered on Gaithersburg in the middle portion of the county. The identification of these schools was not difficult. The more challenging demands of NCLB choice forced school officials to ask: "Where could students at these schools go?"

Again, the formal requirements of the federal law placed restrictions on the answer. None of the designated receiving schools could be deemed "failing" under NCLB or, more precisely, designated as "in need of improvement." This meant that all of the selected receiving schools had to be reasonably assured of making adequate yearly progress in future years under the state's accountability and testing programs. The goal of this requirement was to ensure that Title I choice students would be able to attend schools that were, by some demonstrable evidence, succeeding. While state officials, in conjunction with the U.S. Department of Education, were still working out the AYP requirements in the spring of 2002, it was reasonable for district officials to assume that, in the short run, the county mean score was a reasonable target at which to aim.

Another concern of district officials was the capacity of potential receiving schools. Crowded schools, with students spilling into hallways or placed in portable classrooms, would not make good candidates for receiving more students. Because of growing enrollments in Montgomery County, the number of portable classrooms has increased in recent years. Though many elementary campuses have none, some have several, and a few have more than ten. Cresthaven Elementary has 17 portable units. Forcing principals to accept an unknown number of transfer students onto campuses already bursting at the seams would certainly produce principal and parent complaints and would worsen classroom situations that were already less than ideal. Thus, for both pedagogic and political reasons, the district needed to take into account the degree of crowding before selecting the receiving schools.

Finally, though not an expressed concern, the effects of concentrated poverty may well have been considered. An extensive research literature shows a strong relationship between concentrations of poverty in schools and lowered expectations and performance. Since all of these students were coming from Title I schools, it made sense to assume that they were most likely students at-risk because of low household income. It certainly would make no sense to offer to these students an option that did not afford any real difference in the learning environment they faced at their home schools. Moreover, to further concentrate poor students in other schools where poverty already existed would only exacerbate any problems extant in the receiving schools. As a result, let's assume that the officials looked for schools that enrolled roughly the county mean of students eligible for free or reduced-price lunch.

Examining all of these criteria together, some expressed in district policy, others reasonable assumptions, let's look at the school attendance zones (and their demographic characteristics) that qualify on test scores, and at available space and poverty levels. These criteria mean that the receiving-school candidates are those schools that were at or above the county mean on the 2002 Maryland School Performance Assessment Program (MSPAP) school score (45.3 percent of students passing), below the county average number of portables on campus (4 per campus), and below the county average percentage of students at a school eligible for free or reduced price lunch (25.5 percent). The important question now is simple: How well do these criteria align with the schools actually chosen by district officials in the late spring of 2002? In short, how well do they explain which schools were chosen? These three criteria successfully identify seven out of the ten schools chosen in Year I of NCLB choice as receiving schools, but they overidentify schools. In fact, 41 of the district's elementary schools meet these criteria. So, although this selection method yields seven out of ten of actual receiving schools, it fails to account for those schools above the county means on these scores that were *not* chosen. If we are to accurately re-create the logic of district officials, we need to find some criteria that both successfully incorporate the three omitted receiving schools and exclude those schools that were not chosen.

One way to do this is to relax some of our initial assumptions and select schools that are a little bit poorer and a little lower scoring. (We'll leave the capacity issue as is for now.) Moreover, it makes sense to consider further the demographics of both the sending schools and the schools that were not chosen as receiving schools. It is a blunt fact of life in Montgomery County that a racial line divides the eastern and western portions of the county. Though not a hard-and-fast division, those portions generally west of Silver Spring are predominantly white, while those to the east and north have larger minority populations, both Hispanic and African American. It is conceivable that district officials took into account the racial characteristics of the sending schools and estimated both the comfort level of students exercising choice at virtually all-white schools and the reception those students would receive.

This logic of taking racial populations into account might have run two ways: First, largely minority students attending Title I schools arguably may be more inclined to exercise choice if a critical mass of racial peers attends the receiving school. Second, at the receiving schools, students, parents, and administrators may be less inclined to attach any stigma to arriving minority students if the school already has a significant minority population. Indeed, taking race into account at the receiving school selection stage may prevent receiving schools from viewing the NCLB choice mechanism as an exercise in school desegregation rather than an exercise of individual choice. This is not to say that district officials actually engaged in this logic, but it may be useful to explore the selection process through the lens of race.

Let's consider what happens when we incorporate both the relaxed testing and poverty assumptions with a requirement that minority students make up at least one-third of the students at the receiving school. Figure 12.1 maps out both these relaxed assumptions as well as the racial dimension. The shaded areas are those schools that meet the following criteria: The school is below the county mean for the number of portables, it scored at or above one-half standard deviation below the county mean on the 2002 Maryland

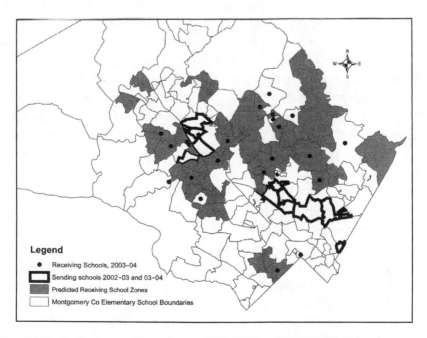

Figure 12.1. Predicting receiving schools, 2002–2003 and 2003–2004 Relaxed test score, space and poverty assumptions, plus race (at least 1/3 minority enrollment)

School Performance Assessment Program test, it has no more than one-half a standard deviation above the county mean of students in poverty, and it has a minority student enrollment of at least 33 percent. The thick-bordered school zones are the sending schools, and the actual receiving school zones for the two years of NCLB transfers are represented by dots. Figure 12.1 shows that, by relaxing the poverty and test score assumptions and including race as a criterion, we can accurately predict 75 percent of all the receiving school zones (12 out of 16) through just these four criteria. Moreover, our selections are far less overinclusive than the district's own expressed criteria.

How should we interpret this? What does mapping the characteristics of receiving schools tell us? First, test scores and poverty alone are poor predictors of receiving school status. Across the district, test scores and poverty levels map rather poorly onto the receiving schools. Race alone is far too overinclusive (91 of Montgomery County's 121 regular elementary schools have minority enrollments of at least 33 percent). Of course, selection by race alone would also be unconstitutional. But a combination of space, race, test score and poverty gives us a fairly consistent rubric by which we can predict whether a school is chosen to be a receiving school.

District officials also sought to take into account distance from home school. As we can see from figure 12.1, a number of the gray-bordered school zones are some distance from the black-bordered ones. In order to make the pairings work, the school district had to at least minimize those distances. Nonetheless, when we look at the distances elementary school children had to travel, along highly congested roads at peak travel times, it becomes clear that distance was not a very high priority for district officials. In the first year of NCLB school choice, the farthest separation between pairings was 8.5 miles (between Wheaton Woods Elementary in Rockville and Belmont Elementary in Olney), and the closest was the 2.7 miles between Summit Hall Elementary and Diamond Elementary. The school pairings averaged 5.5 miles apart. To put these distances in perspective, the two most distant schools in the county (Burtonsville Elementary in far eastern Montgomery County and Poolesville Elementary in the westernmost reaches of the county) are 36.7 miles apart. The two most distant schools along a north-south axis are Bannockburn Elementary in Bethesda and Damascus Elementary in Damascus, at 26.3 miles apart. Thus, the bus ride for the most distant choice pairing (Wheaton Woods to Belmont) requires elementary students to travel anywhere between one-third and one-quarter of the way across the county. And these are simply the calculated distances between *schools*; actual distances traveled depend on how far the student's home is from the receiving school.

Nonetheless, district officials appear to have done a commendable job when one examines the characteristics of the sending and receiving schools. Table 12.1 lists the ten school pairings, along with key demographic information for each school, based on 2001–2002 data. In the sending schools, for example, the percentage of children qualifying for free or reduced-price meals averaged 62.4 percent. Not surprisingly, given that level of poverty, the average percentage of students within each sending school to pass the 2002 MSPAP test was under 30 percent. In addition, these schools appear to be overcrowded, with an average of more than ten portable classrooms installed on each campus.

Table 12.1. Poverty, test score, and overcrowding characteristics of sending and receiving schools, 2002–2003

Name	Partner	% FARMS*	MSPAP 2002 score**	Number of portables
Sending schools				
Broad Acres	Stonegate	88.0	0.198	11
Burnt Mills	Cloverly	52.7	0.241	11
Gaithersburg	Candlewood	66.0	0.327	15
Harmony Hills	Olney	72.0	0.296	9
Highland	Flower Valley	63.6	0.198	10
Kemp Mill	Westover	57.4	0.298	8
Rosemont	Cold Spring	53.9	0.257	10
Summit Hall	Diamond	59.3	0.263	4
Weller Road	Lucy V. Barnsley	56.5	0.375	14
Wheaton Woods	Belmont	54.2	0.286	11
Sending Avg.	—	62.4	0.274	10.3
Receiving schools				
Stonegate	Broad Acres	8.1	0.511	2
Cloverly	Burnt Mills	9.9	0.443	0
Candlewood	Gaithersburg	17.3	0.511	0
Olney	Harmony Hills	13.5	0.483	0
Flower Valley	Highland	14.0	0.513	0
Westover	Kemp Mill	16.2	0.444	0
Cold Spring	Rosemont	2.1	0.774	0
Diamond	Summit Hall	10.7	0.551	0
Lucy V. Barnsley	Weller Road	16.7	0.452	0
Belmont	Wheaton Woods	5.1	0.563	1
Receiving Avg.	—	11.4	0.525	0.3
County Averages		25.5	0.453	4.0

* Indicates percentage of students receiving free and reduced-price meals.
** Maryland School Performance Assessment Program.

In contrast, the receiving schools are demonstrably better learning spaces: fewer children in poverty, higher test scores, and significantly less crowding. In the receiving schools, only 11.4 percent of students are poor and the schools averaged a 52.5 percent pass rate on the 2002 MSPAP. The receiving schools also have far fewer portable classrooms on school grounds, averaging only 0.3 per receiving school (indeed, only two receiving schools had *any* portable classrooms). In sum, table 12.1 indicates that each of the receiving schools appears to be a better alternative than the sending schools (based on test scores and poverty levels of students, and overcrowding). But we should remember that looking at the receiving schools in isolation is somewhat misleading. Yes, they may be better schools (even significantly better) than the sending schools, but there were other schools not chosen that had measurably higher test scores and were closer to the sending schools. Given these differences, and the significant distances that students had to travel to attend these receiving schools, the next chapter in the story of No Child Left Behind school choice in Montgomery County focuses on how many students at Title I elementary schools accepted this offer of choice, and whether those students have any common characteristics. We learn those things from listening to the Travelers' Tales.

The Travelers' Tales

Each student has a unique relationship to both the sending and receiving schools. But our present focus must be on the aggregate patterns that emerge from these individual exercises in choice. Each family has its own reasons for departing a neighborhood school for a choice school and it is exceptionally difficult to identify motivations, especially when those motivations are complex and perhaps conflicted. But to the extent that we can see any patterns in the racial and economic distribution of children taking the advantage of the choice option, there is an aggregate story to be told. This section will focus on three elements: (1) where the students went, (2) who went, and (3) whether any divergences among sending and receiving schools can best explain the pull of particular receiving schools.

First, we need to remember that accounting for student enrollments can be somewhat messy and, in a two-year analysis of choice attendance patterns, we need to make some distinctions among students and where they go to school. In general, I will speak of four segments of the Title I choice population in Montgomery County Public Schools: (1) choice students who entered in year 1 of the program, (2) the continuers in the choice program from year 1 to year 2 (i.e., those who did not select out of the program or did not graduate from grade 5), (3) year 2 entrants to the program those who opted for choice beginning in year 2 of the program, and, (4) all students participating in the program in year 2 (continuers plus new entrants). It's important to account for each student as he or she moves in and out of the program because patterns in each group may tell us something about how the program has evolved or will evolve.

First, let's look at the numbers, by school, of those who have participated in NCLB choice over the past two years. Table 12.2 provides a school-level breakdown of the major categories of participants in the program. Most striking is the fact that only 88 students participated in the program in its first year, out of a total choice-eligible enrollment of 6,191 students in 2002. That figure is worth repeating: Of roughly 6,200 students attending Title I choice schools in 2001–2002, only 88—1.4 percent—took advantage of the choice option in its first year. Of those, 66 continued on in the second year, 10 students graduated from the fifth grade (and thus were ineligible to continue in the choice program), and 12 students left the program (either returning to their home school or moving outside the sending-school attendance zone). In the second year of the choice program, academic year 2003–2004, 115 students joined the program, and, together with the 66 continuers, represent a participation rate of 2.9 percent of all Title I eligible students. Clearly, the district has not seen a rush to the exits of the Title I schools and the receiving schools have not been flooded with new choice participants.

Table 12.2. NCLB choice participation, 2002–2003 and 2003–2004

	Year I entrants	5th Grade Grads. in Year II	Continuers in Year II	Non-continuers	Year II entrants	Year II participants
Broad Acres	0	0	0	0	0	0
Burnt Mills	9	1	8	0	15	23
Gaithersburg	4	2	2	0	5	7
Harmony Hills	4	0	3	1	11	14
Highland	4	0	4	0	13	17
Kemp Mill	8	0	7	1	9	16
Rosemont	23	3	18	2	24	42
Summit Hall	6	1	5	0	14	19
Weller Road	10	2	7	1	12	19
Wheaton Woods	20	1	12	7	12	24
Total	88	10	66	12	115	181

When we look at these figures by school, we see that both the original 88 and the current 181 participants are not evenly distributed. In the first year of the program, two sending schools, Rosemont and Wheaton Woods, accounted for nearly half of all participants, and the top five schools accounted for four-fifths of all participants. In the second year, the program has broadened somewhat, but the top two schools (again Rosemont and Wheaton Woods) still account for more than 36 percent of all participants, and the top five schools still account for 70 percent. One sending school, Broad Acres, has yet to see its first student leave.

When we look at the percentages leaving within schools, the exodus is not huge by that measure either. The school that has seen the largest percentage of its students leave under the NCLB choice mechanism is Rosemont, which currently has 7.9 percent of its 2001–2002 enrollment in the choice program; the next two largest participants (by percentage of students) are Burnt Mills Elementary and Wheaton Woods Elementary, both at 3.7 percent. The overall picture, though, is that relatively few Title I students are choosing to leave their neighborhood schools, and those who are leaving are coming predominantly from two or three schools. The trend may be toward broader participation across all Title I schools, but thus far the modal experience has been a student leaving either Rosemont Elementary or Wheaton Woods Elementary and attending Cold Spring Elementary and Belmont Elementary, respectively.

So we know, generally, where the travelers are coming from. But who are they, and where are they going? Are the leaving students demonstrably different from those who stay? Do the schools that attract the highest number of students appear to be different in any systematic way from those that attract comparatively few students? Let's consider the characteristics of the leavers, then explore the places to which they are going.

As we observe the entry of Title I students into the choice system, it is important to make a distinction between first-year movers and second-year movers, as the two groups seem to be composed of different members. Table 12.3 shows the racial and poverty breakdown of Title I choice participants by year of participation. If we look at the first-year entrants, half are white (44 out of 88), and less than a quarter are African American or Hispanic (13 and 7 out of 88, respectively). More than a quarter are Asian American (24 of 88). The district did not collect information on the poverty status of the first-year entrants. In contrast, the second-year entrants are significantly more African American and Hispanic, with 51 of 115 entrants falling into those two groups (35 African Americans and 16 Hispanics). Asian American participation is still high, approaching the rate of African Americans, but

Table 12.3. Racial and poverty characteristics of NCLB choice participants, by year

	County average	Sending school average	Year I entrants	Continuers	Year II entrants	Year II participants
% FARMS	25.5	62.4	NA	NA	29.6	NA
% African American	20.1	25.2	14.8	12.1	30.4	23.8
% Hispanic	17.9	49.3	8.0	6.1	13.9	11.0
% Asian	13.6	11.7	27.3	30.3	28.7	29.3
% White	48.0	13.5	50.0	51.5	23.5	29.3
Total N			88	66	115	181

white participation dropped from 50 percent in year 1 to roughly 25 percent in year 2. In year 2, students receiving free or reduced-price lunches represent less than a third of all entrants, and the numbers of boys and girls are roughly equal in both years. In sum, it appears that whites and Asian Americans were substantially overrepresented in the choice group in year 1 (especially given the racial characteristics of the sending schools), and that African Americans increased substantially in year 2. It also appears that the first group of those exercising choice out of Title I schools were substantially more white and Asian American than the student body as a whole at the sending schools. In contrast, the second group of travelers had an African American participation rate that was roughly comparable to the sending school average, with white and Asian participation still running roughly two to three times the size of their enrollment at the Title I sending schools. In both groups of travelers, Hispanics were far and away the most underrepresented in both years.

When we consider what is perhaps the target group of this policy—poor black and/or Hispanic students—the lack of minority participation is rather staggering. Among year 2 entrants only—the more racially diverse of the two years—poor African American students constituted only 13.4 percent of the entering students, and poor Hispanics made up just 6.1 percent. These participation rates are emerging from schools that *average* more than 62 percent students who receive free or reduced-price lunches, more than 25 percent African American, and more than 49 percent Hispanic. The Title I choice program, as it operates in Montgomery County, does not appear to reach the average students at these schools. In fact, even when we look only at year 2, after the program had broadened and participation rates had increased among minorities, more than 80 percent of the transfer students fall outside of the group that advocates argued would be the prime beneficiary of the policy. Even if we assume that all of the African American or Hispanic continuers from year 1 received free or reduced-price lunches (a generous assumption), the grand total for poor African American or Hispanic participation in MCPS Title I choice in the second year is just 18.8 percent of all participants. The conclusion that needs to be drawn, then, is that the Title I school choice policy, as it operates in Montgomery County Public Schools, is not reaching its target audience.

So the travelers are, in general, significantly different from their fellow students who stay behind. And yet as we saw in table 12.2, participation was not even across the sending and receiving pairs. The next question is whether the receiving schools with high choice enrollments have specific characteristics that account for their comparatively high participation rates. What is it about schools like Cold Spring Elementary and Belmont Elementary that explains the numbers of NCLB transfer students enrolled there? Before we tackle that question, it's important to make a few more distinctions. First, the data are limited and cannot fully answer this question with complete confidence. Because of the small number of receiving schools (10 in the first year, 16 in the second), exploring Title I participation rates through multivariate regression analysis is not practical. Instead, we will have to rely on less sophisticated tests of statistical significance. Second, it is important, again, to distinguish first-year from second-year movers; in the analysis below, they demonstrate different relationships to particular demographic characteristics of the receiving schools. As such, it appears that the parents of year 1 movers were looking for different things for their children than the parents of year 2 movers were looking for.

Table 12.4 lists the simple correlations between the number of participants attending each receiving school in years 1 and 2 and several demographic categories. What table 12.4 suggests is that those who entered into the choice program in its first year went to schools with substantially different demographics than those who participated in the second year. For example, the correlation between test scores at the receiving schools and the number of participants at those receiving schools is quite high, at 0.716. In general, the higher the score of the receiving school, the more participants it received in the first year. In the second year, by contrast, that bivariate relationship is not only smaller, it is not even statistically significant. Other demographic characteristics for which there are strong negative correlations are the percentage of students at receiving schools who are African American and the percentage of students at receiving schools who qualify for free or reduced-price lunch. In year 1, fewer students participated in the choice program if the receiving school had comparatively higher percentages of African American students. Similarly, fewer students participated in year 1 as the percentage of

Table 12.4. Pearson correlation between number of participants at receiving schools and receiving school demographics

	MSPAP 2002 test score	Pct white students	Pct black students	Pct FARMS students	Distance
Number of Year I Participants	0.716*	0.602	−0.779**	−0.646*	0.245
Number of Year II Participants	0.282	0.262	−0.301	−0.531*	NA

* p < 0.05, ** p < 0.01.

students in the receiving school who qualify for free or reduced-price lunch rose. In year 2, however, the relationship between the number of choice students and the percentage of African American students at the receiving school is so small as not to be statistically significant. In contrast, the percentage of students at the receiving school who qualify for free or reduced-price lunch is still robustly linked to the number of participants in the choice program, indicating that this is consistent signal across all participant groups. Fewer students join the choice program if they are offered the choice of a receiving school with significant numbers of students in poverty.

Surprisingly, the physical distance between sending and receiving schools shows little significant relationship to the number of choice students moving between them.[7] This means that distance does not correlate well with the difference in the participation rates among the receiving schools. It may, however, effectively reduce the number of applications for a choice transfer. That is, if the receiving school is distant, that may discourage students and families from even signing up for the program.

In sum, those who are participating in the NCLB choice system in Montgomery County Public Schools are, especially in the first year, significantly whiter than the enrollments at the Title I sending schools, and they are significantly less poor than the average student at the Title I sending schools. In addition, they are willing to travel relatively long distances to avoid students in poverty. In the first year of the choice program, they looked for higher test and lower attendance of African American students than they looked for in the second year. Hispanics are, by far, the racial or ethnic group most underrepresented in the districts NCLB choice program. These findings lead us to some important policy recommendations, which will be advanced in the conclusion. Before making those recommendations, however, another facet of NCLB remains to be explored in MCPS: supplemental services offered at the Title I sending schools.

Supplemental Services: The Yet-to-Be-Told Story

The story of supplemental services in MCPS is, in many ways, still unable to be told. Although NCLB requires districts to offer supplemental services to students in Title I schools that are designated as "in need of improvement" for three consecutive years, more than half of the 2003–2004 school year had elapsed before in-school providers were working with students.[8] Some of these complications can be attributed to initial start-up problems, but the problem may also be more structural. In districts like Montgomery County where the total market for supplemental services is relatively small and where labor costs are relatively high, it may be difficult for for-profit enterprises to enter into and sustain the long-term relationship needed to provide a true benefit to students. Moreover, as the difficulty of meeting districtwide adequate yearly progress benchmarks increases, school districts themselves could be barred from providing supplemental services, since districts that do not meet districtwide AYP cannot be supplemental service providers. (In 2002–2003, *all* Maryland school districts failed to meet districtwide AYP.) The result could be a statutory requirement to provide supplemental services but an institutional incapacity to do so. In short, supplemental services in MCPS are posing more significant problems than district officials expected, partly because of logistical problems and partly because providers themselves often lack the capacity to undertake the provision of these services on multiple fronts simultaneously.

The selection of supplemental service providers in Montgomery County began in the late spring of 2003, when Maryland released its list of approved providers. Those providers had responded to the states' earlier request for proposal and had passed muster in Maryland's screening. Although Maryland did not set forth its criteria for approval, six vendors were initially approved by the state and indicated that they would be interested in working in Montgomery County Public Schools (that figure later grew to seven). In the early summer of 2003, district officials began contacting those providers to determine the seriousness of their interest and to begin working out in-school leasing arrangements and the details of the providers' participation.

Because MCPS officials did not know which schools would be required to offer supplemental services until the state released the Maryland School Assessment test results in August 2003, it was initially unclear how many students would be eligible for the program. That, in turn, made for-profit enterprises hesitate or seek guarantees that they would have a minimum number of enrollees. Because of these complications, and other considerations (such as leasing agreements, liability issues, compliance with federal and state regulations, and seemingly minor but important issues such as the use of closets and storage space in already overcrowded classrooms), the district was not able to send out draft contracts until late November.

At that point, the capacity questions of the supplemental service providers significantly slowed progress. One provider failed to respond to the district's contract offer and eventually withdrew from the process. The provider, a franchise-based operation, cited difficulty in finding a local franchisee to implement the contract being negotiated. (Communications problems also plagued this particular provider as its computer firewall repeatedly blocked the email attachment that contained the draft contract sent out by MCPS.) All the other providers also reported that they were having difficulty hiring staff to run the tutoring programs, despite their desire to hire teachers within the school system and despite strong efforts by the district to assist in their recruitment efforts. The district contacted teachers on behalf of the providers, publicized openings in newsletters and memos to schools, and even made available to providers a list of retired teachers. With the providers paying $21 to $30 an hour for actual tutorial time, with no compensation for preparation, the inducement to existing teachers in the school system is relatively small. For teachers with children, an administrator with the district noted, that wage is eaten up by day care, and all teachers must weigh whether the combined effects of taxes and an increased burden of adding two hours' work to one's workday makes the task worthwhile. In any event, few district teachers rushed to fill the tutoring jobs. Indeed, staffing difficulties presented the biggest cause of delay for the providers, once contracts were in place.

By January 2004, the district had completed agreements with five providers who were to operate in four schools (one was an exclusively in-home provider). No school was scheduled to have more than three providers on site, and some had only one. One national provider dropped out when it was unable to secure an agreement that would guarantee 125 students per site. Other providers, however, praised the district for its efforts to create a workable and sustainable program. One negotiator for a national provider stated that Montgomery County Public Schools "was the best we've dealt with." "They did a wonderful job and gave [the providers] ample opportunity" to recruit students, he said. "I would do it again, in a minute."

Though the experience of securing agreements with providers proved more difficult than anticipated, the sign-up of children, in contrast, was, by all accounts, a success, even though that success created other administrative difficulties. The recruitment process began with mailings in October 2003 announcing the program. Those materials were translated into several lan-guages and were followed up by community meetings at local schools. In addition, district officials attended PTA meetings at each of the schools that was required to provide supplemental services. Schools also held supplemental service "provider fairs" at which representatives from potential providers set up booths and offered promotional materials. According to one provider, district officials "went the extra mile" to ensure that materials would be widely available in multiple languages. Finally, district officials were physically in place at schools on the countywide parent–teacher conference days in November 2003. According to one district official, staff "sat in the hallways from dawn to dusk" with forms at the ready, as parents arrived to meet with their children's teachers. The recruitment paid off: out of roughly eighteen hundred eligible, six hundred signed up for supplemental services.

The student applications, however, proved to be only the first of the administrative hurdles to get children into tutoring sessions. After the initial sign-up, on which parents ranked their preferences for providers, the district sent out a confirming letter and asked parents to reply with a permission form allowing the district to share confidential education information about their children with the provider. As the provider options changed—as providers dropped in or out of the program—the district had to track those changes for each school and for each child enrolled in the program, making sure that each provider had permission to examine the child's confidential educational information. Though setting up those database systems was complicated by the uncertain status of the provider contracts, now that the system is in place district officials express confidence that it will become easier to enroll and track future cohorts of supplemental services students. Still, the Title I coordinator for MCPS, Chris Richardson stated, "I don't think anyone could have imagined the amount of staff time it has taken to get this program under way." Virtually every department, she indicated, from procurement to curricular support to legal affairs, has been involved in the process.

The final complicating factor is the district's own status as a supplemental service provider. In December 2003, the district submitted an application to the Maryland Department of Education to provide supplemental services to its own students, and district officials are confident that the state will approve the application. But federal requirements bar any district that fails to meet its own AYP objectives in the preceding year to provide supplemental services. In the 2003 MSA test administration, no district in Maryland met districtwide AYP, typically because of insufficient numbers of proficient students in the special education and limited English proficiency subgroupings. The district's apprehensions about meeting the 2004 AYP benchmark extend not only to the sanctions that fall on schools and districts, but also to the district's ability to provide supplemental services under No Child Left Behind.

As I said at the beginning of this section, the story of supplemental services is only beginning to be told. Initial logistical difficulties will, most likely, be ironed out, and Montgomery County has demonstrated to providers and students alike its capacity to mount and implement a significant new program in a relatively short period of time. Two larger structural questions nonetheless loom: whether the for-profit providers can profitably operate in a district with comparatively high labor costs servicing relatively few students (one provider was tutoring only nine children in the district) and, second, whether the failure of school districts in Maryland to meet districtwide AYP will prevent them from acting as their own supplemental service providers if for-profit enterprises cannot efficiently meet the demand.

Conclusion: Lessons Learned

Evaluating the effects of a new policy only two years after its initial implementation is something like evaluating the college prospects of a kindergartner. While it may be somewhat unfair, even misleading, to draw definitive conclusions, there are some clear indications of both successes and failures in Montgomery County Public School's NCLB choice program in its early stages. Some may be unique to the district, while others may be generalizable.

Student poverty limits entrance into the choice system. It is clear from the data that the pool of students transferring out of failing schools is significantly less poor than is typical for students in their home (sending) schools. With an average of more than 62 percent of students in sending schools receiving free or reduced-price lunch, and only, at best, 30 percent of the students exercising choice at the same level of poverty, it is clear that a low-income limits either the inclination or ability to exercise choice. But the poverty limitation is a two-way street: Receiving schools with higher levels of student poverty are generally seen as less desirable options. So to the extent that options are constrained, students are less likely to engage in school choice if the proposed receiving school has higher levels of poverty than other receiving schools. The lesson for school administrators is that, if choice is to be viable for students at Title I schools, additional outreach and counseling need to be undertaken specifically for students in poverty. Moreover, administrators should look carefully at all options before designating a school with significant percentages of children in poverty as a receiving school.

Widening the receiving school options available under choice helps make choice more inclusive. In the first year of NCLB school choice in the district, half of the students exercising choice were either white children moving from a predominantly African American and Hispanic school to a predominantly white school (from Rosemont to Cold Spring) or white or Asian American students moving from a predominantly Hispanic and African American school to a school in which whites make up nearly 80 percent of the students (Wheaton Woods to Belmont). If this structure of school choice were left in place, and rates of white and Asian American flight continued, NCLB would have a significantly segregative effect. However, in the second year of operation, with the addition of further choice options for each sending school, the participation rates for African Americans, in particular, increased substantially. Though the increased choice options will not diminish the increasing racial and poverty isolation felt at Wheaton Woods and Rosemont, it may reduce the segregative effects of NCLB *throughout* the school system. The lesson to be drawn here is that more numerous options need to be made available in order to prevent NCLB choice from acting as a mechanism for white and Asian American families to leave behind African American and Hispanic students.

Greater attention needs to be paid to the choice calculus of Hispanic students. The participation rates of Montgomery County Hispanic students in the NCLB choice program are substantially below—by a factor of five—their enrollment rates at Title I schools. This level of underparticipation needs to be better understood and, if necessary, addressed. The possible causes for this underparticipation are numerous and range from language barriers to poverty levels to greater geographic identity with neighborhood schools in immigrant communities. The policy recommendations that might follow from these causes are equally numerous: greater outreach to specific students and families; better access to Spanish-language orientations, materials, and forms. Or the policy response may simply be a better effort to understand the value of and commitment to neighborhood schools within predominantly Hispanic and/or new immigrant communities. Whatever the response, administrators, and community leaders need to ensure that there is not a systematic deprivation of choice opportunities to Hispanic students.

School administrators need to be wary of contributing to NCLB's potential for segregationist effects by allowing portions of school districts to opt out of receiving school designation. What is perhaps most striking about the maps of sending and receiving schools in MCPS is the extent to which the southwest region of the county, an area with a local reputation as having excellent schools, is mostly free of receiving schools. Though classroom capacity and transportation issues are important factors in the designation process, the northeastern portion of the county clearly bears a far greater share of receiving school duty than do the Bethesda and Potomac schools. If the demand in MCPS for school choice increases, receiving schools need to be more widely distributed across the county. Doing so may incur short-run political costs, but it may also minimize the segregative effects of NCLB in the district. There is also a more prudent reason for expanding the choice options across the county: MCPS may need backups if any of the current receiving schools fail to meet AYP in the next two testing administrations and thus become ineligible to serve as receiving schools.

Greater attention needs to be paid to the provision of supplemental services. Logistical start-up problems and provider capacity issues have worked against supplemental services in MCPS. A student at a Title I school will be well into the second year of NCLB provision before she sits down with a tutor after school. Moreover, the comparatively few number of students seeking supplemental services plus the prospect of the district providing its own supplemental services may lead some contractors to withdraw from the district. In addition, both the district and state need to ensure that contractors are providing information on contact hours with students and evidence of consistency and quality of services. The state, in addition, needs to play a stronger role in guaranteeing access to quality supplemental services by establishing clear and explicit criteria for approving providers and making more information about provider applications publicly available.

In sum, NCLB choice in Montgomery County Public Schools appears to be a relatively small but possibly growing education option for students at Title I schools. Whether the availability of student choice offers poor and minority children a ticket out of a not-so-wonderful school or simply exacerbates racial and economic isolation in those schools will only be known as NCLB moves forward. As parents explore the costs and opportunities of choice for their children, policymakers and educators need to better understand how different parents weigh those costs and potential advantages. Understanding these dynamics will help us learn whether NCLB's choice mechanisms are truly transformational or simply new ways to preserve old inequities.

Notes

1. My thanks to Rick Hess and Checker Finn for their comments and suggestions. I also gratefully acknowledge support from the Advanced Studies Fellowship Program at Brown University, which is supported by the William and Flora Hewlett Foundation and the Spencer Foundation; neither the Program nor the Foundations are responsible for the content of this chapter.

2. Maryland County Public Schools, "Answers to Questions about My School and the Title I Enrollment Option, 2003–2003." Available online at http://www.mcps.k12.md.us/info/press/Title1QA.pdf.

3. Ibid.

4. Office of the Superintendent, Montgomery County Public Schools, Rockville, Maryland, memorandum, dated June 20, 2002, from Jerry D. Weast, superintendent of schools, to members of board of education. Available online at http://www.mcps.k12.md.us/info/press/Title1ApplicationsUpdate.pdf.

5. Office of Communications, Montgomery County Public Schools, "Title I School Choice Enrollment Option Begins," April 21, 2003. Available online at http://coldfusion.mcps.k12.md.us/press/

6. Maryland County Public Schools, "Answers to Questions about My School," p. 3.

7. In the second year of the program, distance became a less useful indicator of participation because multiple schools are offered to eligible students. Because of that, the second-year distance correlation is not calculated here.

8. On in-home provider was operating as of late January 2003, but none of the other in-school supplemental service providers with whom Montgomery County Public Schools had contracted had begun operations as of mid-February 2004. One provider indicated it would be ready to begin operations on February 28, 2004, but that start date had been moved several times.

13

Conclusion

Frederick M. Hess and Chester E. Finn, Jr.

Two years after passage of the No Child Left Behind Act (NCLB), it's premature to gauge how that epochal statute or the options that it mandates for students in struggling schools are affecting pupil achievement. But it's not too early to ask whether supplemental services and public school choice are being conscientiously and constructively implemented or whether the machinery they established is on track to fulfilling the intent of Congress. If yes, then those provisions of NCLB should be given time to work, albeit closely watched, carefully analyzed, and objectively evaluated. If no, then federal policymakers should consider making midcourse corrections in these elements of the law. Such steps, taken at an early stage when states and districts are still formulating policies, could prove far easier than efforts at a later date to alter ingrained practices and assumptions.

Nothing is gained by avoiding the question of how the law is working or innocently assuming that well-intentioned efforts will suffice. As veteran policy analyst Michael Kirst has noted, it took more than a decade, and multiple legislative and administrative adjustments, before the original (1965) Elementary and Secondary Education Act's (ESEA) Title I program really functioned as its authors intended. That's the norm for ambitious new federal programs: they almost never work smoothly at the outset. They usually bring a raft of unforeseen problems, unintended consequences, unwanted loopholes and unworkable features. Far better to spot these difficulties early and (as with faltering schools) take corrective action than to ignore signs of malfunction or assume that time and experience will set matters right.

In fact, NCLB is vastly more ambitious than the original ESEA of 1965. ESEA's original Title I program sought to spread additional money to established institutions and interests. Though Lyndon Johnson's rhetoric insisted that this would boost the achievement of disadvantaged youngsters and thereby lift them out of poverty, its mechanisms were purely fiscal, and the main implementation challenges were how to get the new money to its intended destinations and ensure that it was spent in permissible ways. Though that entailed complex calculations and intricate procedures, in reality the original Title I program nestled reasonably well into existing arrangements. By contrast, NCLB's goals, mechanisms, and remedies do not fit neatly into the status quo. One may fairly say they ask states and school districts to engage in unfamiliar, even unnatural acts. Hence we ought not be sanguine that its kinks will simply get worked out in due course.

At NCLB's heart is the insistence that public schools annually test all students in grades 3–8 in reading and math and that every state measure whether its public schools are making "adequate yearly progress" (AYP) toward universal pupil proficiency in those two core subjects. Schools must show steady improvement in every grade and for multiple demographic groups. If they do not, various sanctions and interventions are supposed to follow, all of them intended to rectify the problem and set the school on a path toward rising achievement.

Among those sanctions and interventions are twin NCLB provisions designed to offer better education options to students stuck in faltering schools—and also intended, via competitive pressures, to create incentives for those schools to improve. If a Title I school fails to make NCLB-defined AYP for two consecutive years, its students are supposed to be offered "public school choice." The local district is to provide each such child with at least two options of alternative public (and charter) schools that *are* making adequate yearly progress. If a child's school fails to make AYP for three consecutive years, the district is supposed to provide that child with the opportunity to enroll in "supplemental educational services"—which in practice typically amounts to about 30 hours of free after-school tutoring. Various providers, including private vendors, can deliver the tutoring, which is to be paid for with a portion of the school's Title I dollars, federal funds meant to promote learning for poor children.

Education choice programs typically rest on three rationales:

- Families possess a natural right to control their children's education.
- Competition among schools will provide new room for entrepreneurship while prodding troubled schools to find ways to serve students better.
- Society owes it to needy children to provide sound alternatives to the slipshod education afforded them by ineffective schools.

In designing NCLB, Congress opted to focus chiefly on the third justification, pay some attention to the second (which is why the choice provisions are included in the cascade of interventions and sanctions for "schools in need of improvement"), and almost ignore the first. This decision was rooted in legislative preference and political compromise, but it also illumines the nature and limits of this law.

In other words, NCLB's choice provisions were not designed primarily to enhance school options or to foster choice per se but, rather, to (a) give kids in failing schools access to other places and service providers whereby they could learn reading and math and meet NCLB standards and (b) give failing schools an incentive to improve by threatening to reduce their enrollments and budgets.

In examining NCLB's choice provisions, therefore, the proper frame of reference is how well they are apt to help meet NCLB's own goals: how effective these measures will turn out to be at helping participating students to master essential academic content, particularly in reading and math, and whether they spur troubled schools to improve and provide tools (such as tutoring) that help them serve their pupils more effectively.

Nobody should be surprised that such ambitious and largely untested provisions in a sweeping federal law would yield uneven results in the face of diverse local realities, some of which mesh nicely with them but others of which tend to frustrate them; or that it will take fine-tuning and revision to get them working right. Nobody should assume that NCLB's numerous and complex elements would all work perfectly right from the start.

Because it's early in the implementation cycle, no evaluator can yet answer the two big questions posed above. The appropriate question to ask *today* about the choice provisions (and, indeed, about all provisions of NCLB) is whether, as presently constituted, they have a reasonable *chance* of succeeding, given time and practice, or whether they assume things that are extremely unlikely to happen. If the latter, then they need rethinking and reshaping, not just patience, practice, and minor adjusting.

Findings

This preliminary study yields six major conclusions.

First, NCLB's choice provisions currently rely on local school systems to engage in what, for most, are unfamiliar and unnatural actions that clash with what they perceive to be their own interests. Districts (and to some extent states) are instructed to tackle tasks that many of them cannot do, will not do, or won't be able to do with the energy and finesse needed to succeed with bold new policies and unaccustomed practices. This reality will destine NCLB's choice provisions to falter or limp except in rare circumstances where they happen to mesh nicely with preexisting policy preferences and practices.

One dilemma is that effective schools that find room to attract students from troubled schools are likely to suffer in terms of academic results, at least in the short term, and schools that shed these pupils may benefit under NCLB-style accountability. This depends on which students change schools. If relatively high-performing students leave a low-performing school its results may deteriorate, even as those same youngsters also tug downward on test scores in the high-performing schools that they enter. Where, in this picture, is the incentive for either sending or receiving schools to promote choice?

Another paradox: schools that manage to improve enough to meet AYP targets will render their students ineligible for tutoring. This means it is possible for the most effective supplemental services providers to effectively put themselves out of business—a strange way to reward excellence on the part of either school or tutor.

Second, the NCLB supplemental service and public choice provisions are playing out very differently, with supplemental services unexpectedly turning out to be somewhat more acceptable to school districts. Many policy skeptics, ourselves included, assumed when the law was passed that districts would be more comfortable with public school choice, which at least keeps all the federal money inside the public education system, than with tutorial programs, which entail paying some of the money to private providers. That, we supposed, was why Congress treated the provision for supplemental services as the more draconian intervention, to kick in only after three years of school failure, including a year of public school choice. In reality, though, the research presented here suggests that districts are more troubled by the challenges of public school choice than by the supplemental services mandate. Perhaps this is because districts are themselves purveyors of tutorial services and serve as referees and gatekeepers for other supplemental services providers.

Still, we're struck that supplemental services (conceived of by some proponents as "mini-vouchers") are generally viewed by districts as minimally disruptive. Students using them remain in their accustomed schools, which means that identifying eligible pupils (and service providers) relatively late in the school year is not an insuperable problem. With public school choice, on the other hand, districts must find space in schools that are making adequate yearly progress. Because districts don't want to disrupt bus routes and are often restricted by laws, policies, or court orders governing student assignment and ethnic balance, they frequently regard the choice mandate as a huge bother.

Moreover, some principals and district officials seem to view supplemental services as a potentially useful tool that can help boost student performance, improve school outcomes, and increase prospects for making AYP. By contrast, they see choice as a mechanism for shifting children from one school to another, not addressing problems at the sending school and perhaps imposing new burdens on the receiving school.

Third, statutory constraints built into NCLB's public choice provision create such limited options—namely, other public schools within district boundaries—that, in many communities, they'll prevent most children from availing themselves of better education opportunities. Student movement is constricted both by the paucity of existing options and by the lack of incentives to create new ones. Since districts must offer pupils the opportunity to transfer only into schools that are making their AYP targets, youngsters in the most troubled school districts can find few real options. Because students coming from poorly performing schools are unlikely to boost a receiving school's performance, principals at AYP-compliant schools have no incentives to accommodate more children. Most good charter schools already boast waiting lists, and high-performing school districts, often suburban districts, have shown no inclination to accept students from poor schools in adjacent communities. Rural communities may have but a single school and may also lack the population density to attract private providers of supplemental services. The result: just not enough space in high-performing schools to provide attractive alternatives for more than a handful of children.

Meanwhile, NCLB contains few incentives—beyond reliance on the good intentions of educators—for states or districts to create more high-performing schools. Nothing in the law suggests that state or district leaders will benefit by taking such steps, nor does it identify sanctions for failing to do so. Instead, the status quo remains intact, with all its preexisting obstacles and logjams. For instance, in the past two years, charter schools have come under increased political opposition and scrutiny, with more states moving to limit their growth and expansion, curb their funding, and burden them with added regulations. NCLB does nothing to encourage districts or states to create more room in effective public schools, while the law's accountability mechanisms can actually trip AYP-compliant schools that make room for more than a handful of students from failing schools. Some of the perverse consequences of NCLB's choice (and accountability) policies may even deter a school system that was considering its own choice programs. Consider: kids who move may aggravate the AYP prospects of both sending and receiving schools.

NCLB's fiscal considerations may also serve to dissuade districts from enthusiastically promoting the law's choice options. The more of a district's mandatory 20 percent Title I budget set-aside gets spent on public school choice and supplemental services, the less money there is to spend on extant programs—and the more likely that even 20 percent won't be sufficient to pay for the demand. Also, the more supplemental services providers that move into a community, the less control a district has over what its pupils actually learn from their tutors, even though the district's schools will still be judged by how those students do on state tests.

Fourth, the NCLB choice mechanisms, besides yielding few viable options for children, are unlikely to be "felt" by schools in ways that prompt them to improve; hence the law's provisions are unlikely to motivate schools to alter their practices in the achievement-enhancing and customer-satisfying ways that the law's framers envisioned. It's unrealistic to imagine that a school is going to turn itself inside out because it's losing 10 or 20 kids to intradistrict transfers or because 75 students sign up for tutoring through a non-district provider. After all, few tangible consequences flow to individual schools—and, as we discuss below, some of those consequences are rather more attractive than repugnant. Moreover, many troubled schools are in states or districts where sundry forms of school choice, including interdistrict choice, magnet schools, and charter schools, have long been the norm. In communities like Milwaukee, Philadelphia, Washington D.C., Houston, Los Angeles, San Diego, or Boston, schools have operated for five or ten years within a framework of burgeoning choice programs. If that kind of competition has failed to trigger much response by the system's traditional schools, one must ask why NCLB's incremental choice bump will dramatically alter the picture.

Fifth, state school chiefs have been unenthusiastic about using the NCLB choice provisions as levers to drive school improvement. For the most part, state education and political leaders seem to regard themselves as bystanders when it comes to NCLB's choice provisions. They have left these provisions to local districts, and they appear to believe that the burden for ensuring that districts are behaving responsibly is the duty of the federal Department of Education. Although the federal agency has been blessed with uncommonly creative and committed leadership in its Office of Innovation and Improvement, the unit charged with implementing NCLB's choice programs, states have not done their parts. They have been unhurried about identifying failing schools, ensuring that eligible students receive timely, accurate information and appropriate choices, demanding that districts find desirable placements for students who wish to exit from failing schools, or pressing districts to fulfill the spirit of the law. States have taken little initiative to devise options for children in rural communities, whose schools may be every bit as much in "need of improvement" as in the cities but where public school choice and even supplemental services have trouble taking root. States do not even gather good data on how many students are being served by choice and supplemental services or how well their districts are complying with these features of NCLB. And they're doing little to encourage districts to develop more options for children. All this despite the fact that decades of federal education law make clear that Washington's proper relationship is with states, and it's the states that are supposed to work with districts to ensure that nationwide programs are successfully implemented.

Finally, the clash between the rules dictated by NCLB and preexisting account-ability systems in states like California and Florida is yielding immense confusion. This problem goes beyond the choice programs, to be sure, but has a palpable effect on them. Neither parents nor educators are entirely clear as to which schools and children are eligible for what or what dual school ratings under the state and federal systems actually mean. The confusion deepens in states (e.g., Michigan) where the penalties associated with failing to make AYP have led to an easing of academic standards or a softening of accountability systems.

NCLB's calendar is also unrealistic. Educationally, it makes sense to conduct student assessments near the end of a school year, so as to measure what pupils learned that year. Yet states that test in late spring are experiencing huge difficulty identifying "improvement schools" before Labor Day, which causes havoc for arranging time transfers and getting children into tutorial programs. Though it's surely possible to score and report test results faster, it may also be that a year's lag time needs to be built into the imposition of sanctions on schools.

Why NCLB-Style Competition Doesn't Sting Much

NCLB competition doesn't take a lot of money out of schools that lose students and has scant effect on the jobs of individual teachers or principals. Keep in mind that many schools that fail to make AYP, especially in urban districts, were already coping with high levels of student turnover, often more than 30 percent a year. Partly to address such tumult and partly out of convention, districts tend to allocate money to schools with little regard to marginal enrollment changes. Faculty positions are allotted based on expected enrollments but schools that lose students do not suddenly find themselves without resources to pay teachers or procure textbooks. Given the natural instability of student populations in troubled schools and the way that schools are buffered from enrollment changes, it is not surprising that losing a dozen students to intradistrict choice does not have a major effect.

Administrators at troubled schools, already coping with an array of challenges and feeling pressed to boost achievement, may well view public choice as little more than a nuisance. They may even see it as beneficial, especially if their school is crowded and teachers feel that classes are too large. As for district officials, public school choice *within* the district costs them no state or federal dollars, it merely creates headaches, can undermine policies aimed at promoting ethnic diversity, and can boost expenditures for pupil transportation. From their perspective, the less of it the better. And in districts that were already engaged energetically in choice programs as a result of their own decisions or state policies, NCLB-style choice is just a minor add-on that is apt to have little palpable effect on either schools or children.

Providing tutorial services may create different incentives. Here, the dollars that flow from a school to an independent supplemental services provider are Title I dollars, over which the principal usually enjoys a good bit of discretion. The prospect of losing such money may get the principal's attention. Districts, too, engage in obstructive, self-interested efforts to keep the Title I dollars within the system, charging rent to external providers, steering students into district-run tutorial programs, delaying in getting information to parents, and sluggishly turning the bureaucratic wheels that yield contracts with outside supplemental services providers. At the same time, some principals and district officials appear to regard after-school tutoring as a potentially useful tool with which to spur student achievement and help underperforming schools make adequate yearly progress, all of which serve to make it somewhat less threatening a stick.

Note, though, that the effects of someone else taking a bite from your slice of the pie are easily mitigated if the pie itself is growing. When it comes to the fiscal consequences of public school choice and supplemental services, NCLB has been accompanied by an infusion of significant new federal dollars into Title I schools and districts (though not as much as some desired). Between 2001 and 2004, federal Title I grants to local education agencies increased by 41 percent, from $8.7 billion to $12.3 billion. This new spending has further buffered schools and districts from the effects of students utilizing choice or supplemental services. It is simply inaccurate to term NCLB an "unfunded mandate."

Why Few Kids are Being Served

An inherent difficulty in the design of NCLB's choice provisions (and perhaps also its accountability provisions) is that it depends on state and district educators to police themselves. In places blessed with gifted leadership and the courage to take tough steps, such federal stimuli can provide a useful spur to ongoing reform efforts. (They can, for example, help a dynamic superintendent overcome bureaucratic and political resistance.) However, these aren't typically the states and districts that America is most worried about. In troubled districts, we're still relying on the existing leaders and old balky bureaucracies to create the NCLB mechanisms and ensure that these new programs work. The reason for this dismal participation rate is not that the schools are fine but that the system is stoutly resisting these changes—and parents have no other sources of information or assistance with regard to their options. Congress opted—it would now seem unwisely—to task districts with this new responsibility, notwithstanding that the programs bring headaches, demand expertise that districts may lack, and can require districts to overturn long-established procedures in order to implement them successfully.

Districts that are unenthusiastic about the NCLB remedies can and do drag their feet in myriad ways, sending parents indecipherable letters, making a "needs improvement" label on a school sound like a badge of honor, providing unclear direction (and plenty of red tape) for parents regarding their options, moving reluctantly to contract with tutorial providers, making little effort to find new space for transfer students, and erecting logistical roadblocks to outside providers of tutoring services. Meanwhile, many states are failing to identify eligible schools quickly, providing scant guidance for districts on how to fulfill the supplemental services and public school choice mandates, moving slowly to approve supplemental services providers, and doing nothing to encourage the creation of new options.

It's hard to believe, therefore, that NCLB's choice provisions are on track to make a big difference in many troubled districts. Indeed, they may well turn out to be the law's features that are most stoutly resisted by precisely those whom the law entrusted with implementation. Yet one ought not be too critical of the implementers. They are behaving in normal and predictable ways, and a free society gives them much leeway to continue doing precisely that.

Organizations simply do not do things that they perceive as inimical to their own self-interest unless they are forced to—and the choice provisions of NCLB contain little by way of compulsion, coercion, or punishment (or, for that matter, inducement or reward) from a school system standpoint. In that sense, it is a law defined more by its aspiration than its muscle. Moreover, thoughtful superintendents have raised two concerns that strike us as legitimate. First, no matter what Washington may say about not letting space constraints impede school choice, the fact is that buildings can comfortably accommodate only so many kids. If a school is full, inviting more students to enroll is not going to yield a happy situation for anyone. This is particularly true at a time when many believe that schools should be smaller and more intimate places and that classrooms should have fewer pupils. Moreover, it's a stark reality that in many districts with schools from which NCLB gives students the right to exit, there just aren't many high-performing schools with empty seats in their classrooms.

Second, with regard to supplemental services, a district may legitimately ask whether a tutorial provider's education program is reasonably aligned with the district's (or state's) course of study. Considering that the district schools attended by these students are still obliged to demonstrate AYP on state tests, if the provider is teaching something different from what is taught in the district, it may do neither the district nor the students much good. (Which is not to say that the district itself will do a good job of providing supplemental services to its students. After all, those luckless children are enrolled in faltering schools for which that same district is responsible.)

Remember, too, that, prior to NCLB, choice was already part of the educational fabric in many places. From intra- and interdistrict choice to magnet programs to charter schools to private schooling, roughly ten million U.S. students—about one in five—were already exercising some kind of school choice option. These programs were serving far more kids—and often far more flexibly—than the new NCLB mechanisms. Many school systems had already accommodated themselves to life with choice. This makes it unlikely that a modest increase in such options would have a profound impact on them. It's no great exaggeration to say that, in many communities, the families that most wanted out of troubled schools have already done so. As one participant noted at the conference where this research was presented, "Two years in, states with a culture of choice are experiencing very little change as a result of NCLB's choice provisions." Florida, Michigan, and Colorado all appear, in their way, to be examples of this.

The same is true locally, where the smoothest adaptation to NCLB's choice provisions appears to be in communities such as San Diego that had already embraced choice as a dynamic education-reform strategy and are able to blend the NCLB provisions into their own.

Going forward, no doubt there will be some places where NCLB pushes on-the-fence districts over the edge into using choice as an education reform strategy. But a choice-averse district, or one that's so dysfunctional that it simply cannot implement much of anything by way of bold policy change, will find ways of resisting these (and other) provisions of federal law. NCLB is pointed directly at districts that are doing poorly and not providing their students with other options, yet it depends on those very districts to react with alacrity and goodwill by finding new ways to provide options to their pupils. If the district wasn't doing so before, however, we cannot see why it will suddenly opt to do so now.

Recommendations

What to do? Though experience will likely yield some improvement in the current functioning of NCLB-mandated choice and supplemental services programs, we don't expect that time alone will bring significant gains. This is not due to any grand conspiracy of resistance across the land, nor to ill intentions on the part of the law's authors. It's simply a consequence of the awkward compromises that shaped the statute's convoluted provisions. In short: if NCLB's authors are serious about allowing children access to more effective educational opportunities, they will need to modify this part of the law. We make no attempt here to spell out a detailed blueprint for revising it. Instead, we suggest ten principles for lawmakers, addressing three major areas of concern: providing an effective system of options; making choice work in concert with NCLB-style accountability; and ensuring that parents, educators, and public officials have the information they need to make sensible decisions.

Structuring the Choice System

First, as much attention needs to be paid to the supply of potential alternatives (i.e., effective schools and viable tutorial providers) as to the demand-related rules by which children gain access to them. Confining a youngster's options to existing public and charter schools within the same district means that millions of girls and boys, especially poor kids living in urban America, will have no true options. Hence the supply needs to be expanded, whether by encouraging districts to open more charter schools or putting greater emphasis on interdistrict transfers and non-district options such as cyber schools, home schools, even private schools. In particular, this means offering incentives and support to entrepreneurs—within or beyond existing district borders—who wish to provide new classrooms and tutoring programs. In rural areas, this calls for heavier reliance on inventive options such as virtual schools, distance learning, schools-within-schools, and other learning modes that can mitigate the constraints imposed by geography. Today, however, whether urban or rural, schools are given no incentive or recognition for procuring space or otherwise being proactive. Schools should not merely be jawboned about finding new places for children. For instance, schools that attract low-performing students might be given a state "bonus" on a per-pupil basis. Or extra federal or state money might be set aside to fund the expansion of AYP-qualifying schools that are willing to grow. Given concerns about school size, there is also a case to be made for resources to help break such schools into smaller units, perhaps multiple schools sharing buildings on a single site.

Second, where a state or district is eager to use choice as a vehicle for school reform, and can demonstrate that by pointing convincingly to its own policies and programs, it should be given the flexibility to blend NCLB's provisions into its own. States like Colorado and Florida and districts like San Diego have made school choice a central tenet of their improvement efforts for years. Rather than being asked to alter these arrangements in deference to NCLB, these places should be treated as beta sites and allowed to demonstrate new and effective approaches. Enthusiastic districts should be rewarded and provided with assistance to support the expansion of existing options. States have the ability to pursue such waivers from the Department of Education, and state superintendents should not be shy about pursuing them. Federal officials say that "EdFlex" states already have the authority to grant districts such waivers. A useful tack would be for the Department of Education to encourage states to promote an "earn your freedom" approach, whereby states offer regulatory freedom to districts that attain certain benchmarks in terms of choice provision or use. This might, for example, mean installing a districtwide choice system that favors students in troubled schools, cultivating a portfolio of charter schools, focusing on interdistrict mobility, relying upon a state voucher program, or any number of other creative approaches.

Third, school districts need *either* to function as tutorial providers *or* as regulators of other providers, not both. It's never a good idea to allow the fox to guard the henhouse, however noble the fox's intentions. In districts that wish to provide supplemental services themselves, the state ought to be responsible for identifying another entity to screen, negotiate with, and oversee all local tutorial providers, including the school system. The likely result, which could be encouraged by federal seed funding, would be the emergence of organizations that can fill this referee and broker role. Some of these tutorial coordinators will likely operate in dozens or hundreds of districts, permitting them to build expertise in managing and evaluating providers, negotiating contracts with them, and ensuring that they deliver the promised services.

Harmonizing the Accountability Apparatus

Fourth, it may make sense to reverse the order in which supplemental services and public school choice are provided. For one thing, districts seem more comfortable with the tutoring provision than with facilitating school transfers. For another, it would seem to make sense to help children improve their performance within a school prior to exiting that school. We see a case for providing tutoring before offering transfers, meaning that (for example) a school's students would become eligible for supplemental services if it misses AYP two years in a row and for transferring out of the school if it misses AYP for the third consecutive year.

Fifth, the manner in which schools' adequate yearly progress is calculated today works to punish principals who might otherwise embrace the choice mandate. Schools that succeed in attracting a lot of transfer students will, by definition, receive an influx of pupils from low-performing schools. Typically, this is likely to pull down the performance of the receiving school, perhaps causing it to miss AYP. In other words, the law discourages rational principals from wanting to attract many students from weak schools via NCLB-mandated public choice. It would make sense to amend the evaluation system so that schools are not penalized for enrolling these students. One possibility: test all students in the school but base its AYP calculation only on the performance of pupils who have been there for at least two years. Another approach: focus on the academic improvement ("value added") of new arrivals, ensuring that students are adequately served by their receiving school without penalizing the school for having attracted low-performing students. In fact, this illustrates why it would be desirable more generally to modify NCLB's AYP calculations so as to attend to the rate at which students are gaining as well as the absolute level of their performance.

Sixth, the failure to distinguish truly horrendous schools from those that barely miss AYP cutoffs in one or two of the dozens of scrutinized categories creates too many "failing" schools and too few "successful" schools while making adequately performing schools nervous about small fluctuations at particular grade levels or among specific pupil groups. One result is that schools have done little to make new seats available for transferring students. Refining the law so that supplemental services and choice are mandated only for pupils in schools that are clearly inadequate would help districts focus resources, ensure that fewer students seek transfers and that more schools can receive them, and reduce the management problems. Admittedly, this suggestion conflicts with the goals of some of NCLB's shapers. If one believes that all children are entitled to additional school options and that the point of putting such provisions into NCLB is for federal law to supply a major boost to the school-choice cause—rather than to focus on failing schools—then such a change would be unwelcome. We expect it also to be resisted by those who don't want to let a single less-than-stellar school "off the hook" from NCLB's cascade of remedies, no matter how near it may be to performing adequately.

Seventh, states should revamp their testing and reporting cycles to identify targeted schools at least three months in advance of the opening of the following school year. Only in that way can districts prepare their transfer and tutorial programs and families make intelligent choices. No doubt this will mean reworking testing systems (and perhaps information technology systems) so that student performance can be analyzed and reported in more timely fashion. Such revision should not entail moving assessments up into January or February, but retooling operations and investing in information technology so as to dramatically shorten the turnaround time for reporting. Alternatively, NCLB might be amended so that the sanctions lag a year behind the test results: a school's performance in 2003–2004 would thus determine its students' options in 2005–2006. A third approach is to determine a school's status by a three-year aggregate or average performance, thus smoothing the year-to-year fluctuations that can be triggered by a wide array of phenomena, some of them purely statistical.

Informing and Parents and Policymakers

Eighth, most parents of children in schools that fail to make AYP are unaware of their school's true status. Survey data from Massachusetts make this devastatingly clear, and nothing that we have seen suggests that the situation is different elsewhere. This widespread public ignorance can be attributed partly to confusion about accountability systems, partly to the fact that parents have other matters on their minds, and partly to the unenthusiastic efforts by many districts to inform parents of their school's status and their options. States should prod districts to notify parents of their options early, often, and in plain terms. The state could provide, for example, all districts with the opening paragraphs of letters to be used in notifying parents, thus ensuring that the language of such letters is clear and to the point. It would be a mistake to assume that troubled districts will aggressively encourage parents to transfer among schools or use non-district tutoring services. Hence we must look to states to provide clear models, ensure that districts take the requisite steps, and monitor their implementation of these sometimes painful provisions.

Ninth, there is an acute need for better federal data on how the NCLB options are being used and how they are working. Today, nobody is responsible for compiling data on how many students are being tutored or which providers are serving how many students. Absent such data, it is impossible to assess the performance of various providers. Nor are there any systematic data on how many districts are notifying families of their alternatives in a timely fashion, how many schools are being offered as options to eligible students, or how many students are taking advantage of the opportunity to transfer. Such information is essential if we are to gauge what it takes to make choice effective and to fulfill the spirit of this law. This strikes us as a worthy assignment for the National Center for Education Statistics.

Finally, if families are to make informed choices, it is imperative that they actually be provided with information and options *whether or not the district wishes to cooperate.* If a district wants no part of school choice or supplemental services, families must have a viable "bypass" mechanism whereby choice can be exercised notwithstanding district recalcitrance or incapacity. In such places, states should identify a private organization to ensure that appropriate steps are taken to comply with the law of the land. One possible model: the long-standing arrangement in several states (Missouri, for example) whereby a private organization provides Title I services to private-school students that (under the state's own constitution) cannot be served directly by the state or local school system.

A Final Word

We close with this advice for school reformers as well as state officials: seize the opportunities before you. Notably absent from efforts to provide supplemental services and public school choice have been the advocates, funders, and thinkers who have spent a decade or more championing increased parental choice in American education. To be sure, NCLB's choice provisions were conceived more pragmatically and on a smaller scale than many choice advocates wished. Yet their potential is considerable. The tutorial provision alone could provide millions of families with the functional equivalent of a small voucher (about $1,000) with which to purchase tutoring services. As much as $2 billion could one day be devoted to this program. Is it not politically advisable and strategically savvy for voucher proponents to help ensure that this program works as intended? Yet they seem to have spent far more time and energy (and money) over the past two years promoting programs designed to serve a few thousand children than on this program already poised to serve millions.

State officials, too, seem not to have noticed that NCLB's choice provisions are tools they can use perhaps because federal lawmakers did not assign states much of a role in implementing these provisions or ensuring that they work. This argues for amending the law. But even under NCLB's current wording, energetic state education leaders could take more proactive steps. Though this provision has seldom been invoked, Title I has for years authorized state officials to withhold funding from a district that does not comply with the law, money that the state could reallocate to other districts or hold until the errant district comes into compliance. Because this provision has been used so infrequently—and because the state would need to justify before an independent hearing officer that the amount it is withholding is appropriate—its full potential remains unknown. It may, however, be possible for the state to redirect some of the money to enhance school options (e.g., create more charter schools) or directly provide parent information in communities that are failing to adequately notify families of their options. Though some further federal guidance on all this would help, it already seems that imaginative state officials have opportunities to redefine the permissible. Even without withholding money, for example, they could craft simple notification letters, then require districts to use those templates when apprising parents of their options.

No Child Left Behind is one of the defining pieces of domestic legislation of our time. It commits the nation to finally ensuring that all of its children are given an opportunity to pursue the American dream. Aiming to make the law more than a noble aspiration, lawmakers sought to sanction schools, districts, and states that fail to meet their obligations and to provide recourse for students trapped in ineffective schools. This was a laudable and courageous effort that policymakers and public officials at every level are now wrestling, for the most part in good faith, to put into practice.

Yet good intentions are never enough. The Elementary and Secondary Education Act of 1965 was landmark legislation in its day, yet in the four decades since its passage we have seen little evidence that it has made a significant difference in the schooling of disadvantaged youngsters or the performance of schools in poor communities. For NCLB to do better, it will not be enough to offer rousing speeches and calls to action. It is also necessary to reflect soberly on how the law is working.

The provisions for transfers out of failing schools and for free tutoring are but a limited part of NCLB. Yet they play a crucial role in it. They are the life rafts that Congress is throwing to children in our most troubled schools, and they are also hammers intended to pound districts into taking the hard steps essential to improving those schools. Making these provisions work as intended will not ensure that NCLB succeeds across the board, but it will be a promising and important step.

Congress was wise to craft NCLB in a manner that sought to harness the power of choice, enterprise, and market forces. Parents can be an energetic source of education reform, and competition can be a powerful spur to educational improvement. But as we have seen in a variety of locales, and as the National Working Commission on Choice in K-12 Education explained in late 2003, choice-based school reform is no simple thing. Especially in legislation as complex as NCLB, the choice provisions, like the rest, will have a steep learning curve. Now Congress and the White House face a choice of their own: whether to learn the emerging lessons quickly and capitalize upon them at an early stage, or to close their eyes and insist that things will somehow work out. To us that seems like an easier decision than picking between two schools.

Contributors

JULIAN BETTS, a professor of economics at the University of California—San Diego, is also a senior fellow at the Public Policy Institute of California. Examples of his recent work include a theoretical analysis of the impact of educational standards published in the *American Economic Review* and the coauthored books *Determinants of Student Achievement: New Evidence from San Diego* and *Equal Resources, Equal Outcomes? The Distribution of School Resources and Student Achievement in California.* From 2001 to 2003, Mr. Betts served on the National Working Commission on Choice in K-12 Education. From 2004 to 2005, Mr. Betts will serve on the Technical Review Panel for the Longitudinal Study of No Child Left Behind. ANNE DANENBERG is a research associate at the Public Policy Institute of California.

MICHAEL CASSERLY has served as executive director of the Council of the Great City Schools, the nation's primary coalition of large urban public school systems, since January 1992. Before assuming this position, Mr. Casserly served as the organization's director of legislation and research for fifteen years. Mr. Casserly has written numerous studies, reports, and op-ed pieces on urban schools, including *Beating the Odds*—the nation's first look at urban school performance on state tests. He has also appeared on numerous television and radio shows, including the *Julian Bond Show, All Things Considered, Larry King Live*, and many others.

RICHARD LEE COLVIN has been director of the Hechinger Institute on Education and the Media since May 2003. Before joining the institute, he was a reporter for the *Los Angeles Times*, where he wrote about education for seven years. For most of that time, he covered national education issues. He previously wrote about education for two other newspapers, as well as a number of education publications. In 2000, he was a Michigan Journalism Fellow at the University of Michigan.

CHESTER E. FINN, JR. is president of the Thomas B. Fordham Foundation and the Thomas B. Fordham Institute. Mr. Finn is also a senior fellow at Stanford's Hoover Institution and senior editor of *Education Next*. An author of thirteen books, Mr. Finn's most recent is *Rethinking Special Education For a New Century*. He has authored more than 300 articles; his work has appeared in numerous publications, including the *Weekly Standard*, the *Wall Street Journal*, and *Education Week*. Mr. Finn was a professor of education and public policy at Vanderbilt University from 1981 until 2002.

SIOBHAN GORMAN covers justice and homeland security for *National Journal*, where she has focused on the Department of Homeland Security and the Justice Department's war on terror initiatives. She previously covered education, politics, and agriculture. Ms. Gorman often writes on education policy for the *Washington Monthly*. She has appeared on NPR, C-SPAN's *Washington Journal*, and MSNBC's webcast. A reporter for *National Journal* since April 1998, she has also edited the magazine's "People" column, which covers the employment comings and goings of Washington players.

JANE HANNAWAY is an organizational sociologist whose work focuses on the study of educational organizations. She is the director of the Education Policy Center at the Urban Institute. She has also been a senior researcher with the Consortium for Policy Research in Education. Ms. Hannaway previously served on the faculty of Columbia, Princeton, and Stanford Universities. She has authored or coauthored four books and numerous papers in education and management journals. She served twice as vice president of the American Educational Research Association and also on its Executive Board. KENDRA BISCHOFF is a research assistant at the Urban Institute.

FREDERICK M. HESS is director of education policy studies at the American Enterprise Institute and executive editor of *Education Next*. He is the author of books including *Common Sense School Reform*, *Revolution at the Margins*, and *Spinning Wheels* and the editor of volumes including *School Choice in the Real World* and *A Qualified Teacher in Every Classroom*. His work has appeared in scholarly and popular publications including *Education Week*, *Social Science Quarterly*, *Phi Delta Kappan*, *American Politics Quarterly*, *Teachers College Record*, and *Urban Affairs Review*. Mr. Hess currently serves on the Review Board for the Broad Prize in Urban Education.

WILLIAM HOWELL is an assistant professor of government at Harvard University. He is the author of *Power without Persuasion: The Politics of Direct Presidential Action* and coauthor of *The Education Gap: Vouchers and Urban Schools*. He is currently editing a book on the politics of school boards. Mr. Howell's work has been published in scholarly journals, including the *Journal of Politics*, *Journal of Policy Analysis and Management*, and *Presidential Studies Quarterly*. He is the recipient of the 2001 E. E. Schattschneider Award for the best dissertation in American politics from the American Political Science Association.

ROBERT MARANTO teaches political science and public administration at Villanova University, and previously he taught at Penn, James Madison, and Southern Mississippi Universities. Mr. Maranto has done extensive research on political appointees in government, civil service reform, and school reform, producing more than forty scholarly publications. His op-eds have appeared in the *Washington Post*, *Washington Times*, *Baltimore Sun*, and *Hartford Courant*. Mr. Maranto and his wife,

APRIL GRESHAM MARANTO, coedited *School Choice in the Real World: Lessons from Arizona Charter Schools*. April Gresham Maranto is an education researcher.

ALEX MEDLER is an independent education consultant who specializes in education policy, school choice, and charter schools. Mr. Medler worked for the U.S. Department of Education's Public Charter Schools Program from 1997 to 2001. Before joining the Department of Education, Mr. Medler worked as a policy analyst for the Education Commission of the States, where he directed research and assistance to state-level policymakers regarding charter schools, public school choice, and deregulation.

DAVID N. PLANK is codirector of the Education Policy Center at Michigan State University and a professor in the College of Education. He is a specialist in the areas of educational policy and education finance. He has worked as a consultant in education policy development for the World Bank, USAID, the United Nations Development Program, the Ford Foundation, and Ministries of Education in Africa and Latin America. He has published four books and numerous articles and chapters in a variety of fields, including the history and the economics of education. CHRISTOPHER DUNBAR, JR. is an assistant professor of educational administration at Michigan State University.

DOUGLAS S. REED is an associate professor of government at Georgetown University and the author of *On Equal Terms: The Constitutional Politics of Educational Opportunity*. For the 2003–2004 academic year, he has received an advanced studies fellowship through the Education Department at Brown University and is currently a guest scholar at the Brookings Institution, where he is conducting research on the local politics of implementation of No Child Left Behind. His teaching and research fields include educational policy, federalism, constitutional law, and judicial politics.

Index

Italics indicate table.